MEN WHO RAPE
The Psychology of the Offender

MEN WHO RAPE
The Psychology of the Offender

A. NICHOLAS GROTH, PH.D.

Director, Sex Offender Program
State of Connecticut, Department of Corrections
Connecticut Correctional Institution at Somers

WITH
H. JEAN BIRNBAUM, B.A.

PLENUM PRESS · NEW YORK AND LONDON

Library of Congress Cataloging in Publication Data

Groth, A Nicholas.
 Men who rape.

 Includes index.
 1. Rape. 2. Criminal psychology. I. Birnbaum, H. Jean, joint author. II. Title.
HV6558.G76   364.1'53   79-18624
ISBN 0-306-40268-8

First Printing — November 1979
Second Printing — May 1980
Third Printing — January 1981

© 1979 Plenum Press, New York
A Division of Plenum Publishing Corporation
227 West 17th Street, New York, N.Y. 10011

Printed in the United States of America

To
ANN WOLBERT BURGESS

Friend, colleague, and teacher
With affection, admiration, and respect

Foreword

During the past decade or less, the impact of rape upon the victim and the circumstances under which rape occurs have been the subject of numerous studies. But the rapist himself still remains a mystery. What manner of man is he? Why does he rape?

Popular views on this issue are derived from at least three sources: the imaginings of fiction writers, including the authors of film scripts, television scripts, and pornographic works; the perceptions of the rape victim during her or his often brief encounter with the rapist; and newspaper accounts of a few sensational and in many respects atypical rapists. The purpose of this book is to focus a bright new light on the rapist himself as a person, a complex and troubled human being. It is based on Dr. Nicholas Groth's objective observations of and clinical experience with more than 500 offenders over a period of more than a decade.

Currently, Dr. Groth is the director of a sex offender program for the State of Connecticut's Department of Corrections. However, I first met him when he was chief psychologist at the Massachusetts Center for the Diagnosis and Treatment of Sexually Dangerous Persons. At this facility, Mrs. Birnbaum worked closely with him as a member of the psychology staff. As is the case with most such programs, their time was spent providing direct services to the patient population. Their clinical research was conducted on their own time and at their own expense, without any subsidy or grant support, and is a tribute to their dedication both to science and to human welfare. I congratulate them both, and I am pleased that Dr. Groth is now engaged in launching a sex offender program in Connecticut that will not only provide direct clinical services to offenders but also will incorporate research, training, and public education components to further his study of this facet of sexual psychopathy.

What interests us all most, of course, is the *prevention* of rape and the creation of a society in which no one will want to rape. This is particularly important in the United States, which has a far higher incidence of rape than many other civilized countries. This book is not a rape prevention handbook, but it is enormously useful in pointing out some of the erroneous ways to prevent rape which are currently being touted. The notion that curtailing sexually explicit material or legalizing prostitution will serve to lower the rape rate, for example, is based on the misconception of the rapist as an oversexed male seeking a sexual outlet. Belief in that myth can hardly survive a reading of this book. Many readers, I am confident, will find their own views on rape prevention changing and maturing as they peruse the data that are here presented.

The close study of any phenomenon almost always reveals that it is far more complex than was assumed while we remained uninformed. This is particularly true of the study of rapists. They are not all alike— indeed, no two of them are exactly alike. Yet one theme, it seems to me, runs through the early years of many, perhaps most, rapists. Somehow or other, they remained outsiders in their neighborhoods, their communities, their culture. Some rapists, as will be shown in this book, were themselves the victims of sexual abuse as children, and others were abused in quasi-sexual or nonsexual ways. All outsiders and abused children do not become rapists; but many rapists grew up under circumstances which deprived them of the civilizing influences and the rewards that mold the lives of nonrapists.

I do not ask readers to accept this hypothesis—but rather to keep it in the back of their heads as they read the chapters that follow. It suggests that the prevention of rape must begin in the kindergarten or earlier.

Preventing children from growing up to be rapists is one important aspect of prevention. Another is preventing convicted rapists from raping again. There is little evidence that long-term imprisonment by itself will accomplish this goal. Can treatment programs be devised that will minimize recidivism? Many new treatment programs, including Dr. Groth's program at the Connecticut Correctional Institution in Somers, are currently offering innovative approaches toward this goal.[1] Dr.

---

[1] Edward M. Brecher, *Treatment Programs for Sex Offenders* (Washington: U.S. Law Enforcement Assistance Administration, 1978). For sale by the Superintendent of Documents, U.S. Government Printing Office, Washington, D.C. Stock Number 027-000-00591-8.

Groth's and Mrs. Birnbaum's study of what rapists are like is basic reading for anyone whose work brings him into contact with the offender and/or his victim.

EDWARD M. BRECHER

Preface

Rape is a crime that requires the complex interaction of many community services and demands the development of professional competence on the part of these service providers. It is an interpersonal offense, and, therefore, to deal effectively with this issue, the needs of both parties involved—the offender and the victim—must be addressed.

As a result of the reemergence of the women's movement, increased awareness of and attention to the victims of sexual assault have become evident during the past decade in this country. Rape crisis centers have been formed to provide support and counsel for rape victims. Hospitals have improved their protocols for treating victims of sexual assault. Law enforcement agencies—local, state, and federal—have upgraded their training in regard to victimology. Improvements have been made in the prosecution of rape cases to reduce the risk of further traumatizing the victim–witness. Legislative reforms have been enacted in regard to the statutes pertaining to sexual assault. And public education programs have been instituted to raise community awareness and develop rape-prevention strategies.

This concern for the rape victim has led directly to an interest in the offender and in determining what can be done with men who rape to deter them from committing further assaults. Unfortunately, relatively little research has been conducted in regard to the study of rapists, and personnel in the mental health and criminal justice systems whose work brings them into contact with men who rape have been caught off guard and unprepared to deal effectively with such offenders. They have not been educated in regard to the dynamics of forcible sexual assault nor trained to deal with such clients.

This book is intended for agency personnel who are involved in some capacity with men who rape and/or with victims of sexual assault.

In the mental health professions, these would include psychiatrists, psychologists, social workers, psychiatric nurses, counselors, and other clinicians. In the criminal justice system, they would include police, lawyers, district attorneys, judges, probation officers, prison administrators, correctional officers, members of the parole board, and parole officers. This book is also written with other audiences in mind, those who for a variety of reasons have an interest in the offender and/or his victim: personnel in rape crisis centers; clergy; physicians, nurses, and other hospital staff; sociologists; criminologists; legislators; researchers; and educators.

The purpose of this book is to examine the psychological and emotional factors that predispose a person to react to situational and life events with sexual violence. The book is written from a clinical perspective in which the act of rape is understood to be a reaction to a psychological crisis and thus, in a dynamic sense, a symptom equivalent.

The book is based on extensive clinical study of identified offenders and their crimes. The patterns of the assault and the psychology of the rapist are presented both descriptively, as derived from data collected on over 500 offenders who were seen in evaluation, and conceptually, as derived from the clinical examination and treatment of these men. The clinical observations are organized in such a way as to differentiate patterns among the offenders and to highlight their psychological characteristics.

From our work in both institutional and community-based programs, we have had access to six different samples of identified sexual aggressors:

1. *Offenders who were not apprehended.* Information about such individuals was retrieved from their victims, who reported the incident and gave an account of the offense, and from consultation with state and federal law enforcement agencies in their investigations of particular unsolved cases.

2. *Offenders who were identified or detected but who, for a variety of reasons, were not prosecuted.* Information about such individuals was obtained through private referrals and through requests to the Forensic Mental Health Program of Harrington Memorial Hospital in Southbridge, Massachusetts, for court diversion evaluations.

3. *Offenders who were apprehended but adjudicated either incompetent to stand trial or not criminally responsible for their offense.* Information regarding these individuals was acquired through research and clinical work by the senior author at the Whiting Forensic Institute in Middletown,

Connecticut, a maximum-security mental hospital whose patient population included such subjects.

4. *Offenders who were apprehended and tried but not convicted.* Information about such individuals was derived in some cases from referrals for pretrial evaluations of accused offenders and, in other cases, through functioning as victim advocates or expert witnesses in trials that resulted in acquittal for the accused.

5. *Offenders who were convicted of sexual assaults or other sex-related offenses and sentenced to prison.* Information about these individuals was obtained through clinical work and research with inmates in the Connecticut Correctional Institution in Somers, Connecticut, a maximum-security prison.

6. *Convicted offenders who were adjudicated dangerous and committed to a special security treatment center.* Information about these individuals was drawn from clinical work and research performed at the Center for the Diagnosis and Treatment of Sexually Dangerous Persons at the Massachusetts Correctional Institution in Bridgewater, Massachusetts. Convicted sexual offenders who were adjudicated as "dangerous" (that is, likely to repeat their offenses and, in doing so, to jeopardize the safety of a potential victim) and civilly committed for an indeterminate period of one day to life (in lieu of or in addition to a fixed prison sentence) composed this population sample.

These offenders, then, constituted the principal sources of our clinical data. There is no way of determining whether the subjects we have worked with and studied constitute a random sample of all men who rape. They are representative, however, of those offenders who directly or indirectly come to the attention of criminal justice and mental health agencies and with whom law enforcement officials and providers of social services are expected to deal in some effective manner.

One of the objectives of this book is to help the reader more fully appreciate how the offender himself experiences his offense by permitting the offender to speak for himself and express his thoughts, feelings, experiences, and attitudes in his own words. To this end, we have made extensive use of direct quotes to illustrate particular issues or points of discussion. Although, in a few cases, these quotes were edited to maintain grammatical consistency with the text, they have not been expurgated. The language, therefore, is often explicit and sometimes crude, but it retains and reflects the style and character of the speaker. It may at times be offensive to the reader, but never more so than the offense itself.

Also, for literary ease, and in order to simplify what otherwise would be an awkward and cumbersome grammatical structure, we have elected to use the pronoun "he" to refer to the offender and the pronoun "she" to refer to the victim in most sections of this text with the full awareness that it is not always the case that the offender is a male or that the victim is a female.

Finally, and most importantly, we are clinicians and have therefore approached the topic of rape in this book from a clinical perspective. But rape is much broader than simply a clinical issue. It is a cultural, social, political, legal, and economic issue and must be understood from all these perspectives if we hope ever to find a solution to this serious problem.

In writing this book we have been repeatedly confronted with the gaps in our knowledge, the many questions we still cannot answer, the numerous impressions that await verification. The major aim of this book, then, is not to provide anything approaching a definitive work on sexual violence but to provide, instead, a framework for the developmental histories, the lifestyles, and the motivations of men who rape, in order to draw attention to the difficult issues of early detection, identification, treatment, and rehabilitation, and to the impact of their behavior on the victim. It is our hope that sharing the observations and thoughts we have derived from our clinical experience with men who rape, and offering some guidelines for dealing with such offenders, will serve to encourage thought and discussion, to generate new ideas, and to stimulate further research that will refine our knowledge about this serious social problem.

We wish to express our appreciation to the various individuals and agencies who have contributed to our understanding of this serious social issue and to the many persons who were of support and assistance to us during the writing of this book.

Although they are identified by pseudonyms in the text, we are indebted to the many offenders and victims whose life experiences appear in this book and who have helped to advance our knowledge and understanding of this subject.

Most of all, we are deeply grateful to Dr. Ann Wolbert Burgess, to whom this book is dedicated, for her direct contribution to the theoretical and research base for this work and for her ongoing advice, support, and encouragement of our professional development and advancement.

Special thanks are due to Edward M. Brecher for writing a foreword to this book and to Dr. Lynda Lytle Holmstrom of Boston College; Dr. David Finkelhor of the University of New Hampshire; Maureen P.

McCausland of the Department of Health and Hospitals for the City of Boston; Anna T. Laszlo, Director of Criminal Victimology Consultants, Inc.; First Lieutenant Robert H. Robertson of the Michigan State Police and his staff; and Susan B. Rosenbaum for their contribution to our study.

We also wish to express our appreciation to Allen G. Burgess for his help in programming and computer processing our data, to Deborah K. Blum and Thomas S. Gary for their research assistance, and to Vivian R. Stewart, Lana M. Koneski, and Peter B. Daigneau for their secretarial help. We are grateful to Leonard R. Pace and Harvey Graveline of the Plenum Publishing Corporation who directed the editorial production of this book.

Special mention must be made of a very special person who has been of continual help and assistance to us in our work: Aaron J. Birnbaum.

We also wish to acknowledge the support given us by Bernard R. Milton, Director of Police Training for the Massachusetts Criminal Justice Training Council, and to express our appreciation especially to William F. Hobson and Michael J. Feingold, of the Mental Hygiene Unit at the Connecticut Correctional Institution in Somers, and to Fred W. Hosea for their invaluable help and assistance.

Finally, the senior author of this book would like to take this opportunity to express publicly his deep appreciation to his mother, Sophie M. Groth, for her unceasing love and devotion. Her inspiration, encouragement, and support throughout his life has been responsible to a large extent for whatever success he has achieved. He is grateful also to his cousin, Dorothy H. Molis, and to his special friend, Rebeca F. Alvarez, for their love and support, which have been of help not only during the preparation of this book but at all times in his life.

To all these people we wish to acknowledge our deep appreciation.

Webster, Massachusetts   A. NICHOLAS GROTH

                                                                   JEAN BIRNBAUM

Newton Center
Massachusetts

Contents

1

Rape: Myths and Realities

Rape is a topic that abounds with myths and misconceptions. It is a complicated, emotionally charged, and highly misunderstood subject. Fortunately, as a direct result of the reemergence of the women's movement, increasing attention is being given to this major social problem. National consciousness has been raised, especially in regard to the victim of this offense. The public media—television, radio, motion pictures, books, newspapers, and magazines—continue to focus interest on this important subject. Rape crisis centers function throughout the country. Laws have been changed and rewritten, and special rape-investigation training programs have been established for law enforcement officers to deal more effectively and efficiently with this serious offense.

Interestingly, however, relatively little attention has been focused on the perpetrator of this offense, and our understanding of the offender—who he is, what he does, why he does it, and what can be done to prevent such behavior—remains incomplete.

Although there have been some data available from statistical surveys on the offender, and a descriptive profile can be drawn of the rapist, he nevertheless continues to remain pretty much of an enigma, and we are left with stereotypes and misconceptions about men who rape. Part of the reason for this state of affairs is that behavioral scientists have not studied such individuals. Rapists do not characteristically self-refer to clinics, hospitals, or private practitioners. And those who are identified through conviction and imprisonment either do not appreciate that their behavior is inappropriate or symptomatic or fear that revealing their concerns to someone will result in their being locked up in a prison or a mental hospital. In many cases, treatment facilities themselves are not available. Services are not provided for such individuals through their local community mental-health agencies. Without an opportunity to work with and to study a sizable number of such persons, a body of knowledge has been slow to develop regarding this form of sexual psychopathy. In the absence of such knowledge, the exact nature of such behavior is misconstrued and misinterpreted, with the result that victimization is perpetuated rather than prevented. Without an understanding of the offender, one cannot fully appreciate what the victim is a victim of.

RAPE: A PSEUDOSEXUAL ACT

A number of popular notions and stereotyped images persist in regard to the offender, his victim, and the offense. With regard to the offender, he is frequently regarded as a lusty male who is the victim of a provocative and vindictive woman, or he is seen as a sexually frustrated man reacting under the pressure of his pent-up needs, or he is thought to be a demented sex-fiend harboring insatiable and perverted desires. All these views share a common misconception: they all assume that the offender's behavior is *primarily* motivated by *sexual* desire and that rape is directed toward gratifying only this sexual need. Quite to the contrary, careful clinical study of offenders reveals that rape is in fact serving primarily nonsexual needs. It is the sexual expression of power and anger. Forcible sexual assault is motivated more by retaliatory and compensatory motives than by sexual ones. Rape is a pseudosexual act, complex and multidetermined, but addressing issues of hostility (anger) and control (power) more than passion (sexuality). To regard rape as an expression of sexual desire is not only an inaccurate notion but also an insidious assumption, for it results in the shifting of the responsibility for the offense in large part from the offender onto the victim: if the assailant is sexually aroused and is directing these impulses toward the victim, then it must be that she has deliberately or inadvertently stimulated or aroused this desire in him through her actions, style of dress, or some such feature. This erroneous but popular belief that rape is the result of sexual arousal and frustration creates the foundation for a whole superstructure of related misconceptions pertaining to the offender, the offense, and the victim.

DEFINITION OF RAPE

There are three basic ways in which a person gains sexual access to another individual: through consent (negotiation), through pressure (exploitation), or through force (intimidation).

A consenting sexual encounter is one in which both parties freely participate as the result of mutual interest and negotiation.

A nonconsenting sexual encounter is one in which an unwilling individual is either pressured or forced into sexual activity by a person in a position of power or dominance. In pressured situations, advantage is taken of a person's vulnerable status, so that refusal to engage in sexual activity may have serious social, economic, or vocational consequences for her.

The defining characteristic in forced assault is the risk of injury or bodily harm to the victim should she refuse to participate in sexual activity. Her physical safety is placed in jeopardy.

All nonconsenting sexual encounters are assaults. In the pressured assault, the victim is sexually harrassed or exploited. In forced assaults, she is a victim of rape.

Although the statutes differ among states in regard to the legal definition of rape, it usually refers to some form of sexual intercourse against the will of the victim. Massachusetts, for example, redefined the elements constituting the crime of rape as "sexual intercourse or un-natural sexual intercourse by a person with another person who is compelled to submit to force and against his will or by threat of bodily injury, or sexual intercourse or unnatural sexual intercourse with a child under sixteen (16) years of age."[1] Actually, from a clinical rather than a legal point of view, it makes more sense to regard rape as *any* form of forcible sexual assault, whether the assailant intends to effect intercourse or some other type of sexual act. There is sufficient similarity in the factors underlying all types of forcible sexual assault—and in the impact such behavior has on the victim—so that they may be discussed meaningfully under the single term of *rape*. The defining element in rape is lack of consent. Although, typically, physical force or the threat of physical injury is envisioned in such assaults, the concept of rape can be expanded—and has been in the criminal codes of some states—to en-compass those situations in which the position of authority can be used to exploit a person sexually. In New Mexico, for example, although the legal age of consent is fourteen for sexual conduct in general, this does not apply in relationships where the adult participant occupies a posi-tion of authority in regard to the youngster, such as parent, relative, household member, teacher, employer, or the like. Likewise, *force* or *coercion* can refer to taking advantage of a person who is "unconscious, asleep, or otherwise physically helpless, or suffers from a mental disease

---

[1]Massachusetts General Laws, Chapter 474, Section 7.

which renders the victim incapable of understanding the nature or consequences of the act."[2] Therefore, the concept of rape may properly encompass all nonconsenting sexual encounters, whether the victim is pressured or forced.

The particular emphasis of this book is given to those sexual assaults that involve physical contact and pose a risk of harm or injury—whether intentional or inadvertent—to the victim.

RAPE: A SYMPTOM AND A CRIME

Clinicians have been very slow to recognize rape as a symptom of psychological dysfunction. The American Psychiatric Association's *Diagnostic and Statistical Manual of Mental Disorders (DMH-II)* does not list rape as a sexual deviation, nor will it be found in the World Health Organization's *International Classification of Diseases (ICD-8)*. Although both manuals label unconventional but innocuous sexual interests, such as transvestism or fetishism, as disordered behavior, they fail to recognize rape in this fashion. Rather than being understood to result from psychological determinants within the offender, rape is more often viewed as the outcome of situational factors. It is ironic that there is an abundance of psychological literature pertaining to what is essentially unconventional but consenting sexual activity and a paucity of information about those forms of sexual behavior that jeopardize the safety of others. One reason for this state of affairs has been the inaccessibility of rapists as subjects of clinical study. For the most part, dangerous behavior of all types has been dealt with almost exclusively through criminal justice agencies. Rapists, then, do not come to the attention of mental health professionals. As a result, such professionals are not trained and do not have the opportunity to develop an expertise in this area and, in turn, are content to relinquish all responsibility for dealing with such offenders to the criminal justice system. The result is that little is known about the psychology of rape, its diagnosis, and its treatment, and much confusion continues to surround this form of sexual psychopathy.

Fortunately, this state of affairs is beginning to change somewhat. In Massachusetts, for example, a law, known as the Sexually Dangerous Persons Act, was passed in 1958 that provides for the diagnostic observation of anyone convicted of a sexual assault.[3] This same law created a

[2]Legislature of State of New Mexico, Law 1975, Chapter 109, Section 2, B1.
[3]Massachusetts General Laws, Chapter 123A.

security treatment center to which sexual assailants could be sent for diagnostic study and psychosocial rehabilitation. Mental health professionals were mandated to evaluate the risk a convicted offender posed to the community, that is, the likelihood that he would repeat his sexual offense and, in so doing, jeopardize the safety of a victim. Today, some 20 programs, both institutional and community-based, are in existence across the United States, but, without exception, the primary, if not the exclusive, focus of these programs has been on direct services more than research. However, out of such clinical experience, observations are derived and information is accumulated that contribute to knowledge about the offender and an understanding of his offense.

Myths about the Offender[4]

To describe the rapist as oversexed is not only an oversimplification but not at all accurate. Rape is, in fact, not an expression of sexual desire as much as it is an expression of other, nonsexual needs. Rape is never the result simply of sexual arousal that has no other opportunity for gratification. In fact, one-third of the offenders that we worked with were married and sexually active with their wives at the time of their assaults:

> The only way my wife and I could relate was in bed. We had good sex together, but that's all we had. We couldn't talk; we couldn't discuss things, how we felt—there was no communication.

Of those offenders who were not married (that is, single, separated, or divorced), the majority were actively involved in a variety of consenting sexual relations with other persons at the time of their offenses.

Rape is always a symptom of some psychological dysfunction, either temporary and transient or chronic and repetitive. It is usually a desperate act which results from an emotionally weak and insecure individual's inability to handle the stresses and demands of his life:

> (How were you feeling at the time of the incident?) I was very depressed at the time. Empty, lonely, out-of-it feeling. I was trying like a bastard to get someone to stop me. No one listened. I wanted

---

[4]The remainder of this chapter is adapted from A. Nicholas Groth and H. Jean Birnbaum, "Portrait of a Rapist: Is He Someone You Know?" *Pageant* 31, no. 11 (May 1976): 122–130. Copyright 1976, Good Earth Corporation. Reprinted by permission.

to kill the woman; I didn't intend to rape her. In the struggle her clothes were ripped, so I got charged with attempted rape. They showed her dress in court; it was a mess. (How did you find your victim?) How do you find a glass of beer? You go look. I was looking, but mostly I was running. (Did you try to get help?) I went to two different churches. I told everybody my history, that I had been in trouble before. I got in touch with suicide prevention and told them I didn't know whether I would act out against myself or someone else. I went to a mental hospital and got kicked out because I wasn't a resident of the state. I went to the police and was told, "Fuck off." Half an hour after I left the police station I jumped this woman. There was nothing she could have done. She tried to stop me; she tried to talk to me. She talked a lot, but I don't remember one word she said. I wanted to kill her, and when I was strangling her, I thought I heard a child cry in the next room. I stopped and apologized and left. I bought a package of razor blades and went into a theater to kill myself, and the police picked me up there.

Although rape may cut across all diagnostic categories of psychiatric disorders, the majority of such offenders are not insane—nor are they simply healthy and aggressive young men "sowing some wild oats." The rapist is, in fact, a person who has serious psychological difficulties which handicap him in his relationships to other people and which he discharges, when he is under stress, through sexual acting-out. His most prominent defect is the absence of any close, emotionally intimate relationship with other persons, male or female. He shows little capacity for warmth, trust, compassion, or empathy, and his relationships with others are devoid of mutuality, reciprocity, and a genuine sense of sharing.

Although when he is under stress his judgment is poor, there is no problem with his intellect. He is not retarded. Why, then, does he commit such an irrational act? Out of desperation and emotional turmoil. He resorts to rape as a last desperate attempt to deal with stresses which he feels will otherwise destroy him; he often fears that he is losing control and may go insane. The consequences of his behavior, what may happen to him or to others, have no meaning at the time. Therefore, he is not deterred by such logical considerations as punishment, disgrace to his family, injury to his victim, etc.:

> I felt I had to go out and do it. I realized that sooner or later I'd get caught. I realized this would jeopardize my marriage, my job, my freedom, yet I just had to go out and do it, as if some force deep inside me was controlling me.

Some men who ordinarily would never commit a sexual assault commit rape under very extraordinary circumstances, such as in wartime, but the likelihood of such a person's being a repetitive offender is very low. There are other men, however, who find it very difficult to meet the ordinary or usual demands of life, and the stresses that we all learn to tolerate are unendurable and overwhelming to these individuals. The extent to which they find most life demands frustrating, coupled with their inability to tolerate frustration and their reliance on sex as the way of overcoming their distress, make the likelihood of their being a repetitive offender very high. Furthermore, they constitute an immediate and ongoing threat to the safety of the community. It is they about whom we are most concerned and on whom this book is primarily focused.

Myths about the Victim

One of the most persistent myths about rape is that the victim in some way was party to the offense: she was seductive or provocative and "only got what she asked for." Even if it were so—that is, if the victim did in fact act seductively or provocatively—she still retains the right to change her mind. There is no law against saying no, but it is against the law not to accept her refusal.

At times there are instances that give the impression of active participation on the part of the victim. Nevertheless, careful study of the offender in these cases will usually reveal evidence of his pathology and his responsibility for the offense: flaws in regard to self-control, respect for others, perceptual interpretation, frustration tolerance, social skills, and the like which, in fact, activate the assault. Yet old ideas die slowly, especially the notion of sexual provocation and false accusation, and in the prosecution of a rape case, the defense attorney typically attempts to impeach the victim's credibility by addressing rape as a crime of passion, implying that the victim has aroused such desire.

Issues of provocation really are ridiculous when one realizes that the victims of rapists include males as well as females and occupy all age categories from infancy to old age. Places of assault have ranged from the victim's own home to public parks, cemeteries, beaches, shopping malls, public rest rooms, churches, side streets, and alleyways. There is no place, season, or time of day in which a rape has never occurred, nor any specific type of person to whom it has never happened.

It is also frequently believed that, if she really wanted to, a woman could always prevent the assault. The fact is that rape occurs through intimidation with a weapon, threat of harm or injury, and/or brute force. Different motives operate in different offenders, and, therefore, what might be successful in dissuading one type of assailant might, in fact, only aggravate the situation with a different type of offender. Physical resistance will discourage one type of rapist but excite another type. If his victim screams, one assailant will flee, but another will cut her throat:

> (What was going on in your mind at the time of the incident? What were you feeling?) Intense rage. I was blind to everything else around, didn't care about myself or anyone else. (When did you know you were going to rape someone?) When I grabbed her, not before. (Why did you have a weapon?) Because I work in construction and I carry the tools. The knife was just a tool; unfortunately, it turned out to be a weapon. But I didn't plan it. (Could your victim have stopped you in any way?) Maybe if she'd put a bullet through my head, no other way.

Myths about the Remedy

Again, since rape is commonly thought to be aimed at satisfying a sexual urge, the remedies often proposed likewise address themselves to sexual needs. For example, it is sometimes suggested that one way to stop rape is to legalize prostitution. However, the fact of the matter is that prostitution does exist and it offers no solution since, again, the offender is not seeking primarily sexual gratification. In fact, prostitutes themselves are sometimes the victims of rape, since they may represent everything the rapist finds threatening and resents in women:

> I was extremely lonely. It had been eighteen months since I got out of prison, and I couldn't communicate with females. I only had sex with prostitutes. I couldn't seem to meet anybody. It wasn't just for sex. I started going around picking up women hitchhikers and just talking to them because I was lonely. But that didn't satisfy me. My fantasies started again—girls that I would have control over, grabbing someone and forcing them to like me. Prior to this incident, I had another incident, and I was frightened. One particular night I felt it was going to happen again. So I got a prostitute for the whole night and stayed with her. For a week after that I was not bothered, but then it started up again, the fantasies. The night it did happen, I didn't start out to do it. I was drinking and got very drunk and got in

my car to go home, only I went past my apartment and kept going and knew I was going to do it. (Is there anything your victim could have done to have stopped you?) No doubt if they had struggled, nothing would have happened. I had a penknife, and I opened it and showed it to them. A few hours after I was arrested, I tried to commit suicide. You know you are going to get caught. I just didn't care anymore. I thought I would keep going till I got caught and then commit suicide. When I got to the police station, they took everything but my wristwatch, and I used that to dig a hole in my wrist.

Rape is sometimes attributed to the increasing availability of pornography and sexual explicitness in the public media. Although a rapist, like anyone else, might find some pornography stimulating, it is not sexual arousal but the arousal of anger or fear that leads to rape. Pornography does not cause rape; banning it will not stop rape. In fact, some studies have shown that rapists are generally exposed to less pornography than normal males.[5] This is not to suggest that pornography should be encouraged, however, or allowed at all, because from a cultural rather than a clinical perspective, it is not only an insult to women (and to men), but it appears to validate sexist attitudes and support the position that women are legitimate targets for sexual abuse and humiliation. The difficulty is in determining what is pornographic as opposed to what is merely sexually explicit. Pornography is difficult to define, but we regard something as pornographic when it represents some type of sexual encounter in which the participants do not occupy the same status or position of consent, power, or control. In this respect, pornography is a medium equivalent to the crime of rape. It is the sexual expression of power and anger. From a cultural perspective, pornography is one of the dimensions that must be addressed in efforts to resolve the complex problems of rape, but, from a clinical point of view, it is no excuse for an offender's accountability for his behavior.

What these misconceptions tend to do is shift the responsibility from the offender to something outside of him. This is what the offender himself does. He projects the responsibility for his own behavior onto external objects like liquor, drugs, the dress and behavior of his victim, and the like—anywhere but where it really belongs. What he cannot face is that he himself has serious psychological handicaps which lead him,

---

[5]See, for example, Royer F. Cook, Robert H. Fosen, and Asher Pacht, "Pornography and the Sex Offender: Patterns of Previous Exposure and Arousal Effects of Pornography Stimuli," *Journal of Applied Psychology* 55, no. 6 (1971): 503–511; or Harold S. Kant and Michael J. Goldstein, "Pornography," *Psychology Today* (December 1970).

under certain circumstances, to behave in this inappropriate, antisocial fashion.

Another of the common misconceptions regarding the treatment of rapists is that castration is the solution. Even if castration always rendered the individual sexually impotent—which it does not—it certainly would not solve the underlying conflicts and problems in the individual that prompted the assault. His anger and rage will continue to find behavioral outlets, if not in rape then in other forms of physical violence, such as assault and battery, homicide, and suicide.

Nor is putting the rapist in prison effective in rehabilitating him psychologically. Since prison terms have a maximum limit—and rapists are seldom given a life sentence unless they kill their victims—there will come a time when the offender will be returned to society without any assurance that he no longer constitutes a danger to the community. As an alternative to traditional imprisonment, a number of states[6] have developed special mental-health facilities to which a convicted sex offender may be committed indefinitely in lieu of or in addition to a prison sentence. In such programs, any individual who is likely to repeat his sexual assault is quarantined, and while he is hospitalized—in what must be a humanistic environment—a very serious effort is constantly made to bring to bear everything the mental health professions have learned about human behavior to remedy personality defects that operate in the offender to jeopardize the safety of others. In this way, society is afforded an extra degree of protection. The offender will not be released to the community while he continues to be a risk to others. At the same time, once he has been rehabilitated, he may hopefully then return to society without having to fulfill a specified but meaningless period of institutionalization. Unfortunately, few such forensic mental-health institutions exist, and even more importantly, the majority of offenders are dealt with either only through the criminal justice system or not at all.

Why Do Myths about Rape Persist?

The appeal of these myths about the offender, the offense, and the victim is that they reduce a very complex behavior to a very simple,

---

[6]California, Colorado, Florida, Indiana, Maryland, Massachusetts, Minnesota, Missouri, New Jersey, New Mexico, Pennsylvania, Washington, and Wisconsin.

single motive. It is frustrating to conceptualize and grasp the many complex, interrelated factors operating in rape and then to find a clear, practical and effective solution to this problem. The myth is simpler to understand and easier to accept and, therefore, more satisfying than the reality.

Rape is a serious social problem about which, fortunately, we are at last becoming increasingly concerned. With psychology entering into a new frontier of criminology, a body of knowledge is beginning to be developed about these types of sexual offenders.[7] It is important to discover and dispell the persistent misconceptions and fallacies about rape which, although they prove comforting in their simplicity, ultimately serve only to perpetuate the jeopardy and danger that this form of sexual psychopathy poses to us all by leading us to adopt preventatives which, in truth, are ineffective.

To combat rape demands multidisciplinary and interagency efforts. It is a problem that needs to be dealt with at all levels—individual, social, cultural, legal, economic, and political.

[7]Two highly recommended texts are Richard T. Rada, *Clinical Aspects of the Rapist* (New York: Grune & Stratton), 1978; and D. J. West, Chunilial Roy, and Florence L. Nichols, *Understanding Sexual Attacks* (London: Heinemann), 1978.

2

Psychodynamics of Rape*

One of the most basic observations one can make regarding men who rape is that not all such offenders are alike. They do not do the very same thing in the very same way or for the very same reasons. In some cases, similar acts occur for different reasons, and in other cases, different acts serve similar purposes. From our clinical experience with convicted offenders and with victims of reported sexual assault, we find that in *all* cases of forcible rape, three components are present: power, anger, and sexuality. The hierarchy and interrelationships among these three factors, together with the relative intensity with which each is experienced and the variety of ways in which each is expressed, vary from one offender to another. Nevertheless, there seems to be sufficient clustering within the broad spectrum of sexual assault so that distinguishable patterns of rape can be differentiated based on the descriptive characteristics of the assault and the dynamic characteristics of the offender.

Rape is always and foremost an aggressive act. In some offenses, the assault appears to constitute a discharge of anger; it becomes evident that the rape is the way the offender expresses and discharges a mood state of intense anger, frustration, resentment, and rage. In other offenses, the aggression seems to be reactive; that is, when the victim resists the advances of her assailant, he retaliates by striking, hitting, or hurting her in some way. Hostility appears to be quickly triggered or released, sometimes in a clear, consciously experienced state of anger or,

*This chapter contains excerpts from A. Nicholas Groth, Ann Wolbert Burgess, and Lynda Lytle Holmstrom, "Rape: Power, Anger, and Sexuality," *American Journal of Psychiatry* 134, no. 11 (November 1977): 1239–1243. Copyright 1977, American Psychiatric Association. Reprinted by permission.

in other cases, in what appears to be a panic state. In still other offenses, the aggression becomes expressed less as an anger motive and more as a means of dominating, controlling, and being in charge of the situation—an expression of mastery and conquest. And in a fourth viscissitude, the aggression itself becomes eroticized so that the offender derives pleasure from both controlling his victim and hurting her/him—an intense sense of excitement and pleasure being experienced in this context whether or not actual sexual contact is made. These variations on the theme of aggression are not mutually exclusive, and, in any given instance of rape, multiple meanings may be expressed in regard to both the sexual and the aggressive behaviors.

In every act of rape, both aggression and sexuality are involved, but it is clear that sexuality becomes the means of expressing the aggressive needs and feelings that operate in the offender and underlie his assault. Three basic patterns of rape can be distinguished in this regard: (1) the *anger rape*, in which sexuality becomes a hostile act; (2) the *power rape*, in which sexuality becomes an expression of conquest; and (3) the *sadistic rape*, in which anger and power become eroticized.

Rape is complex and multidetermined. It serves a number of psychological aims and purposes. Whatever other needs and factors operate in the commission of such an offense, however, we have found the components of anger, power, and sexuality always present and prominent. Moreover, in our experience, we find that either anger or power is the dominant component and that rape, rather than being primarily an expression of sexual desire, is, in fact, the use of sexuality to express these issues of power and anger. Rape, then, is a pseudosexual act, a pattern of sexual behavior that is concerned much more with status, hostility, control, and dominance than with sensual pleasure or sexual satisfaction. It is sexual behavior in the primary service of non-sexual needs.

ANGER RAPE

In some cases of sexual assault, it is very apparent that sexuality becomes a means of expressing and discharging feelings of pent-up anger and rage. The assault is characterized by physical brutality. Far more actual force is used in the commission of the offense than would be necessary if the intent were simply to overpower the victim and achieve sexual penetration. Instead, this type of offender *attacks* his victim, grabbing her, striking her, knocking her to the ground, beating her, tearing her clothes, and raping her. He may use a blitz style of attack, a violent surprise offensive, in which the victim is caught completely off guard. Or he may use a confidence-style approach to gain access to the victim and then launch a sudden, overpowering attack. In the former situation, the offender approaches the victim directly by hitting her. In the latter situation, victims often relate that at first the assailant seemed pleasant enough, but that at some point he changed. Suddenly and without warning he became mean and angry. His later behavior was in sharp contrast to the initial impression:

> Listening to how the victims described me in court, the impression that I got was almost a Jekyll and Hyde. I approached all of my victims in a very acceptable manner, but then I seemed to change suddenly. When I went into these bars, I was looking for someone that would be comfortable. I was looking for people to talk to, and these women were willing to talk to me. But during the course of sitting and talking, something would happen inside of me, the anger would erupt. The assault with intent to rape wasn't it—I was trying to kill them!

The rape experience for this type of offender is one of conscious anger and rage, and he expresses his fury both physically and verbally. His aim is to hurt and debase his victim, and he expresses his contempt for her through abusive and profane language. If his primary motive is one of anger, and if he is not sexually motivated, why doesn't this offender confine his assault to a battering of the victim? Why does he also rape her? The answer seems to be that such a man considers rape the ultimate offense he can commit against another person. Sex becomes his weapon, and rape constitutes the ultimate expression of his anger:

> I wanted to knock the woman off her pedestal, and I felt rape was the worst thing I could do to her.

Often this type of offender forces the victim to submit to or to perform additional sexual acts that he may regard as particularly degrading, such as sodomy or fellatio. In some cases, contempt for the victim is expressed by urinating or by masturbating and ejaculating onto her.

Characteristically, this type of offender does not report being in a state of sexual excitement or arousal. In fact, he may be initially impotent during the assault and able to achieve an erection only by masturbating himself or having the victim perform oral sex on him. Sexuality itself is typically regarded by this type of offender as something basically "dirty" and offensive at some level of his subjective experience, and, therefore, it becomes a weapon, a means by which he can defile, degrade, and humiliate his victim. The anger rapist typically finds little or no sexual gratification in the rape—in fact, his subjective reaction to the sexual act itself is frequently one of revulsion and disgust. Satisfaction and relief result from the discharge of anger rather than from sexual gratification:

> I was enraged when I started out. I lost control and struck out with violence. After the assault I felt relieved. I felt I had gotten even. There was no sexual satisfaction; in fact, I felt a little disgusted. I felt relieved of the tension and anger for a while, but then it would start to build up again, little things, but I couldn't shake them off.

Typically, such an offender reports that he did not anticipate committing a rape. It was not something he fantasized or thought about before-hand—it was, instead, something that happened on the spur of the moment. Sometimes he will say that he felt "something was going to happen" but could not identify or anticipate what course of action his feelings would lead to. Even during the offense itself the offender may psychologically dissociate himself from the assault as if he were in a trance or were more an observer than a participant; the event is experi-enced as unreal, and the offender may not fully appreciate the extent of his aggression:

> It wasn't until afterwards, it wasn't until after I had been able to get rid of all the anger and all the feelings that I had inside of me that I could in some ways come back to the real situation and to what I had done. And, in that way, I did in a sense sort of feel like I became an animal, and it was only then that I felt very upset by what I had done.

Relatively speaking, such attacks tend to be of short duration. The offender strikes, assaults, and flees. Such assaults appear to be more impulsive or spontaneous than premeditated, and the offender finds it difficult to account for his assault, when he cannot deny it, except to rationalize that he was intoxicated or on drugs, or that he just "flipped out":

> My offense was pretty bad. I believe I was flipped out at the time. I have no defense at all. I was drunk. I was standing on the corner and—I don't know. I don't know what the hell happened. I just was

standing around, and I saw this girl pull up in her car, and I didn't
see her face or anything. I just saw her pull up to the stoplight, and I
walked up to the car, opened the door, pushed her over to the
passenger side, and I took off with her in the car. And I can't be sure
why I did it, but, anyway, I took off with her and got her to an area
that I thought was a good place, and I got out of the car and hit her. I
hit her right in the eye, and I still don't know why I raped her.

In describing the evolution of the assault, the offender typically
reports being in an upset and distressed frame of mind at the time of the
offense. His predominant mood state appears to be a combination of
anger, distress, frustration, and depression, and the offense itself is typically preceded by some upsetting event, often, but not invariably, involving some significant woman in the assailant's life. The assault is in
response to some identifiable precipitating stress. For example, some
offenders reported a serious dispute with their wives prior to the offense. These arguments revolved around a number of marital issues,
such as the wife's threatening to or, in fact, leaving him, arguments over
his drinking, complaints about her housekeeping skills, suspicions of
infidelity, and the like. Others felt aggravated with their parents for
imposing unfair restrictions on their activities or unjust punishments for
their misbehavior. Some offenders cited conflicts with their girlfriends,
such as being stood up, rejected, taunted, or sexually frustrated. Others
reported feeling upset over such things as being rejected from military
service, being fired, being burdened by financial debts, or being harassed
in some fashion by other people. The common theme appeared to be
one in which the offender felt that he had been wronged, hurt, put
down, or treated unjustly in some fashion by some individual, situation,
or event. Rape served to discharge the resulting anger, resentment, and
frustration. In this fashion, the anger rapist revenges himself for what he
perceives to be wrongs done him by others, especially women.

The anger rapist's relationships to important persons in his life are
frequently fraught with conflict, irritation, and aggravation. The anger,
resentment, hostility, and frustration engendered in these relationships
is often displaced onto other individuals, and, therefore, the victim may
be a complete stranger to the offender, someone who has been unfortunate enough to be in his presence at the point at which his controls begin
to fail and his rage erupts. Although she has done nothing to warrant it,
she becomes the target of his revenge—not revenge in a calculated,
planned fashion but, instead, the recipient of an impulsive reaction precipitated by a situation she has had no part in.

In some cases, the victim of the anger rapist is the actual person toward whom the offender harbors such anger, but in other cases, she is simply a substitute person, a symbolic and available "object" against whom the assailant discharges his wrath and fury. In a few cases, the victim may have no actual or symbolic significance for the offender, but she is targeted because of her relationship to the individual against whom the offender is seeking revenge. It is through a female victim that the offender retaliates against a male or through a child victim that the offender retaliates against an adult.

As an example, Terry, a 24-year-old, white, married male, is serving a 15- to 20-year sentence for rape and attempted murder whose masturbatory fantasies focus on sexual violence:

> Right now I wouldn't put anything past me. Some of the stuff that goes through my head—I could do anything. I've always been one that never let anyone fuck me over and get a second try. In fantasy I take it out on anybody: cops, judges, prosecutors. Usually I think of a cop or prosecutor, and I think of his wife, daughter, or sister. I rape her in front of him, and then I kill her, and maybe I hurt him, but I always leave him alive so he'll remember.

The anger rapist strikes sporadically and infrequently, because his assault does serve to discharge his anger, and it then takes time for his frustrations and aggravation to reach a volatile point again. His intent, then, is to hurt and degrade his victim. His weapon is sex, and his motive is revenge.

Derek is an example of this type of rapist. He is 26 years old, six feet tall, and weighs 190 pounds. He is the youngest of three boys. When he was one year old, his mother abandoned the family. The impression Derek's father instilled in him about his mother was that

> she was the perfect Catholic virgin girl. After I was born—what happened—all of a sudden she turned out to be like a whore. That's what he claims. There was no controlling her—like an animal turned loose. He got the attitude not to trust a woman, and that was the thought I was brought up with: never trust a woman; they are no good. And that's how I carry it. Almost all my life so far is "never trust."

Derek's father never remarried, and, initially, Derek and his brothers were placed in a foster home for about four years:

> Then I went to Boys' Retreat, a parochial boarding school, where I was taught by brothers. When I was in the seventh grade, I went to the School of the Blessed Virgin, where I was taught by sisters.

Derek remained at the residential school until age 12, when his father brought him back home. In reflecting back on these formative years, he described them as "rotten":

> I don't know how to explain it. There was something missing to me all my life. Like my mother—I kept pretending that I didn't have a mother and I didn't need a mother. I refused to believe any idea that I had a mother or that someone had to give birth to me. And the fact of being with men all the time, and then with my father and his attitude toward women. I felt sorry for myself then.

It was when Derek reached the age of 14 that he

> started knowing I actually had a mother. She contacted me. Before that I never knew where she was. She tells me she had visited me at my foster placement, but I don't remember that. Anyway, she got in touch with us, out of loneliness, I guess. I didn't know, I just thought this was a passing fancy of hers. She had remarried several times, and she's with us now because she doesn't have anyone else. Now that we're grown up, she wants us. My father's attitude didn't help. He'd say, "She wants you to love her now, now that there's no more responsibility for her." And my father threw us onto her actually: "Go and see her and get everything you can financially from her, she owes you this." We didn't have much, and that's what we used to go over there for. Yet, it was like a new life. My mother was very good-looking, whatever else you want to say, but I didn't respect her for being my mother. And then one time—I don't remember exactly when—I think I was about 15—the age doesn't matter so much—she seduced me, and it has always left a weird impression on my mind, a kind of revulsion. I can look back and say she had a problem. She had been drinking, and she held me against her breasts, and she took them out and wanted me to fondle them. It frightened the hell out of me. The desire for women had been building up in me, I knew that, but here was someone who was supposed to be my mother, even though I couldn't appreciate her as my mother. Mothers just don't do this. I didn't know what to do. She didn't have anything on. I really don't know what the hell she wanted. I don't know if she really knew what she wanted. I'm saying this now. At the time, I didn't know.

Derek fled the situation, terrified. His first experience with intercourse occurred at age 17 with

> a girl my own age, someone who was known to be loose. At that point, I wasn't scared. It was like I had been scared out of my wits

with my mother and I couldn't be scared of anything else. I knew I had certain desires, but I didn't know what the experience would be like. Afterwards I felt awful about it—very guilty, dirty and guilty. It went against all I had been taught, my Catholic upbringing.

Derek later had a number of casual experiences while in the service, usually with prostitutes. Derek denies any sexual encounters with men but reports being propositioned a number of times while stationed in California:

Out there, there are a lot of queer, odd people—whatever you want to call them—that are attracted to the opposite sex—I mean the same sex. Once I was waiting at a bus station and a guy tried to pick me up. We always joked about it on base. I tried to be polite to the guy, "You don't want me and I don't want you; please leave." I was in uniform, and that was it.

Derek was not a behavioral problem as a youngster, and his medical history was unremarkable. Although above average in intelligence, his grades were only fair "because I didn't care about school. I never studied." Derek was proficient in athletics, however, and he played contact sports "like a savage."

Following graduation, Derek enlisted in the Marine Corps

because it was my illusion of being a man: physical strength; rough, tough type of guy; he's a *man*, period! My father used to talk about my uncle all the time because he was in the Marines, and my oldest brother went into the Marine Corps, and I just had to become a Marine I thought to be accepted by my father.

Derek's father, a truck driver, put a premium on toughness and emotional control:

He didn't show nothing. I'm striving to find something and "You gotta be tough; you gotta be a man; you gotta be tough to be a man"—you know—so I figured this would show him that I am a man by becoming a Marine.

Derek did exceptionally well in the service:

That's one thing I took pride in. That was my idea of being a man. That is where I was able to let out everything I had, all the hate and everything inside me. I could function here very well, learning guerrilla warfare training: how to move, how to sneak up on people, and you don't let people get too close to you, which I never did in my life—even before the Marines that was how I was brought up. I could never get close to my father—I always wanted to know why—so I couldn't let anyone get close to me in return.

Whatever Derek did to win his father's recognition and approval,

it never seemed to satisfy him, and I couldn't confide in him ever, because I couldn't get close to him or let him get close to me. Although I loved him deeply, it was just I had to do things to always impress him, but still it never got to that point. I got some kind of recognition but never verbally. He could talk to other people, brag to his friends, but he could never tell me he was proud of me. That's the way it always was. Even today I know how he is. I love him as my father, but he has problems. I'm not trying to bring out his problems like he's a bad man or something, I'm just trying to bring them out so he can look and judge for himself. He keeps coming back and saying to me, "You can't teach an old dog new tricks." I keep saying, "That's just a saying. I'm not trying to teach you anything. I'm just trying to talk to you as a son to a father, and I was hoping you'd want to talk to me as such." Still there is something lacking there. Now I can understand why my mother left—that it wasn't all her fault. Now that I'm better in touch with myself I can start looking at other things. Before I couldn't. I'd always take his word. It's not that way anymore. Even though my crime is serious and I might have to do time in prison for it, I can't say I wished it had never happened. In some respects I do wish it never happened— true. But there's no getting away from the fact it did happen, and it has really come about that I'm happy in some sense of finding myself. It's not like I'm a completely changed person. It's just a controlled person where there was no controls before.

Derek reports two incidents during which he felt completely out of control. One occurred while he was boxing in boot camp:

I got knocked out on my feet in the ring, and I began screaming and climbing trees—this lasted through the night until the next morning, and I didn't remember any of it.

The other happened after his release from the service. He was at a beach one day and got into a fight with some motorcyclists:

One of the bikies threw a firecracker at me, and I beat the hell out of all four of them in a blackout.

After four years in the Marine Corps, Derek received an honorable discharge: "I got wounded in the leg in Vietnam, So I couldn't stay in the Marines any longer anyway." For a short time immediately after leaving the Marines, Derek drank heavily; then, six months following his discharge, Derek married:

> I had known my wife before I went into the service. I met her in high school. She was just another girl, but I liked her better than the beauties that were around. She loved me, and I was actually scared of this because this is the thing my father warned me to be careful of—not to let women get close to you. So when I went into the service I said, "Forget me and I'll forget you, and when I come out, if you still feel the same way, then maybe something will happen." In the meantime I was lonely for her—that's why I was in confusion. Here is something that I wanted and feared—wow, that was really messy! Then finally when I got out of the service she came to me, and I thought it was beautiful that she came to me. I wanted to see her as badly as she did. We got married six months later. No big wedding or anything. As a matter of fact, my father was against it—totally against it. He wouldn't give us his blessing and didn't attend.

Derek and his wife have been married five years and have two children. There have been no separations or serious problems in their marriage:

> We wouldn't get into arguments because that is one thing I lack: I lack control in arguments. When my wife got mad at me, because of the influence of my father, I couldn't take criticism from any woman in my life. At these times, I would get out of the house. This used to upset her. She would want me to sit down and talk to her instead.

In time Derek came to question his wife's faithfulness:

> Just that idea from my father: all women will ultimately be unfaithful—but I had no reason to believe this of my wife; none at all.

Following his discharge from the service, Derek worked in construction for four years:

> I worked all kinds of hours and made pretty good money. Then I began going to school nights to prepare me for college. I realized I needed more education. All I knew were the four-letter words when I was in the Marines. I buckled down when I entered college and

found I could do it. I majored in economics with a strong sociology background, and I made the dean's list last year. I don't know about right now . . . .

Derek's schooling was interrupted by his arrest:

I had gone to school that day, and it was the last day of the semester, and I had been celebrating. I do not in any way, form, or manner say that it was the drinking. It was more the irritation I had gone through in school that day. My last class was U.S. history, and the teacher was a woman, the only woman teacher I ever had—well, besides the nuns. You kind of get away from the idea that they are women. But this history teacher was a very radical person, and whether she was against me and everything I upheld—I don't know. There was some conflict between us. She would dispute everything I was for. In other words, she was against the war in Vietnam, and she was against this and that, and against our whole system of government and all the laws pertaining to it. And I was the only one in class who was a Vietnam veteran, and I felt it wasn't right of her to speak about something she really didn't know. And she would cut off my comments in class, and I didn't go for that. I felt—not like the father of the flock or anything—but I felt I had a certain kind of justice not to let her persuade . . . I know the kids were only 18, and I was the oldest in the class; I was 25, and I was the only one who had been at Vietnam. That day, she was talking about Vietnam, you know, and I got into a discussion with her, and the next thing, she kind of incited the class against me. The questions that were thrown at me were not questions, they were "facts" just thrown at me. They didn't want any answers from me, just throw out these things; this messes up your whole line of thought and this and that, and I was trying to defend why we were in Vietnam. I became very, very, *very* angry, and I couldn't talk anymore. I slammed my books down and walked out of the class. I was just very angry, very angry because here was . . . I know *now*, the control was no longer there. I was infuriated, and everything was there: "Women, my father told me they were rotten, dirty bastards and you can't trust them." And there was no control there. I was just infuriated enough that, you know, POW! I went and had some more drinks—I guess in drink I was looking to relax—and then I went on the subway. I don't re- member the actual ride itself, just I got to the station where my car was parked, and when I got to the parking lot, I saw this woman putting bundles into her car. She was somewhere between 30 and 40, and I'd never seen her before. In fact, I really don't know what she looked like. It wasn't the idea of what she looked like. She looked like an older lady. I came up to her, grabbed her by the throat, punched her in the mouth, knocked her to the ground, I ripped off her clothes, and I proceeded to rape her.

Derek, however, cannot retrieve many of the details of this assault—"everything isn't completely clear in my mind as to exactly what I did"—for example, he doesn't remember saying anything to his victim. His victim reports that after striking her, Derek asked, "You've heard of blowing a guy?" and that she was frightened from his manner that he might kill her. She told him she understood what he was talking about and tried to stall for time in the hope that another subway train would come into the station and people would come by. Derek pulled her jersey up around her neck and twisted it tight around her throat. He was having trouble getting an erection and told her, "You'll be released a lot sooner if you suck me off. I need you to help me get it up." Although terrified, the victim refused, and Derek forced his penis into her mouth, saying he "hadn't had a blow job in a long time." He then masturbated himself until he became erect and performed intercourse.

His victim did not know if Derek ejaculated, but when he stopped moving, she asked several times, "Are you finished, are you finished?" and he finally answered, "Yes." As to his sexual response, Derek reported "not knowing whether or not I came off—I don't really have any awareness of it. When I got back to my car, I realized my wallet was gone." He attempted to retrieve his wallet, but his victim struggled into her car, locked the door, and began sounding the horn, and Derek took off.

The victim then drove home, fighting hysteria all the way. She did not go directly to a police station because she doubted, in her condition, that she would be able to tell them what had happened. As she drove home she actually considered "forgetting the whole thing" and not reporting it to anyone, but then she told her married daughter of the attack and decided to inform the police. At the police station, the victim was very distraught and upset. She was examined by a physician, who noted a laceration on the side of her face and blood inside her nose. Her lips were bruised and swollen, and there were welts and abrasions on her throat. There were bruises at the entrance of her vagina, and the vagina itself was red and inflamed. Derek was identified from papers in his wallet.

Following the attack, Derek drove home:

> I don't remember the exact ride home, but when I got home I told my wife what I had done. After it was done was when it really dawned on me what had happened. I mean it wasn't like I was someone else. It was me. But it finally dawned on me that I had done this, and it was kind of horrifying in a way. So many things I've

thought about since it's happened, trying to figure it out. There are a
lot of things about it now that are beginning to make sense: for
example, her car was the same as my mother's car. . . .

Although Derek had no previous criminal history whatsoever, one
month subsequent to his arrest, while out on bail awaiting trial, Derek
was accused of approaching a woman as she walked from the subway to
her car, exposing himself, and masturbating in front of her. He completely denies this incident.

Victim Impact

Although all rapes involve anger, power, and sexuality and impact
on the victim to disrupt her physical, behavioral, social, and sexual
lifestyle, depending upon the type of rape the victim is a victim of,
certain issues may be more prominent or take on an added significance
in the recovery process.

Medical examination of the victims of an anger rape generally reveal
considerable physical trauma to all areas of the body, often requiring
X rays and consultation of other medical specialists. Victims report experiencing the rape as a life-threatening situation. Although the anger
rape is a physically brutal and violent assault, the victim may have less
long-lasting traumatic effects from the attack, relatively speaking, for a
number of reasons. First, she is visibly injured, and there is much concrete evidence (as bruises and torn clothing) to support the fact that she
is a victim of rape. There is less suspicion of either false accusation or
victim participation. She may receive much more comforting and support from those who subsequently come into contact with her (police,
hospital personnel, family, and friends), and there may be less of an
accusatory undertone to their questions and comments. Also, psychologically the aim of this victim is to survive the assault, since she has
suddenly and without warning become the target of an excessively brutal and uncontrolled rage on the part of the assailant which has placed
her life in jeopardy. She hopes to live through the attack and she does.
So her primary aim or objective is accomplished. Perhaps the most salient issue, then, is one of her vulnerability and her increased awareness
of being at risk. The awareness of life-threatening dangers, the realistic
assessment of high-risk situations, and the devising of strategies that
will serve to protect her better and make her less accessible and vulnerable are key issues for this type of victim. Safety becomes a principal

issue. The aggression is far more blatant that the sexuality, and if the victim has been a significantly older or even elderly woman, this may serve to help reduce the sexual overtones of such offenses. However, since the physical effects of such an assault are highly visible, the victim has less choice in keeping her victimization secret.

Another key issue in working with the victim of an anger rape may be to help her appreciate the dynamics of such an assault. The victim will want some understanding of why this has happened to her and what has prompted the offender to behave in such an apparently irrational manner. When something is understood, it is less threatening and disturbing than something which appears mysterious, or bizarre, or unexplainable. The victim's sense of intimidation may be partly relieved by being able to make some sense out of what initially appears incomprehensible. The victim may also fear that she continues to be at risk of further assaults from her offender. In fact, this is not at all likely. Frequently, anger rapists report that they had no idea of who their victim was or what she looked like. Many have said that even when they saw the victim again in court, they were unable to recognize her. It appears that at the time of the assault they were "blind with rage," so to speak. Even if not apprehended, the offender is unlikely to assault the same victim again simply because women are objects to him, and objects are interchangeable. They are symbols but have no meaning in and of themselves to him. Therefore, when the offender again reaches that point where his anger is erupting and his controls are failing, he does not seek out a specific victim but, instead, discharges his anger onto someone who is immediately available.

POWER RAPE

In another pattern of rape, power appears to be the dominant factor motivating the offender. In these assaults, it is not the offender's desire to harm his victim but to possess her sexually. Sexuality becomes a means of compensating for underlying feelings of inadequacy and serves to express issues of mastery, strength, control, authority, identity, and capability. His goal is sexual conquest, and he uses only the amount of force necessary to accomplish this objective. His aim is to capture and control his victim. He may accomplish this through verbal threat ("Do what I say and you won't get hurt!"), intimidation with a weapon ("I came up behind her and put a knife to her throat and told her to come with me"), and/or physical force ("I told her to undress, and when she refused I struck her across the face to show her I meant business"). Physical aggression is used to overpower and subdue the victim, and its use is directed toward achieving sexual submission. The intent of the offender usually is to achieve sexual intercourse with his victim as evidence of conquest, and to accomplish this, he resorts to whatever force he finds necessary to overcome his victim's resistance and to render her helpless. Very often, the victim is kidnapped or held captive in some fashion, and she may be subjected to repeated assaults over an extended period of time.

Such offenders entertain obsessional thoughts and masturbatory fantasies about sexual conquest and rape. The characteristic scenario is one in which the victim initially resists the sexual advances of her assailant; he overpowers her and achieves sexual penetration; in spite of herself, the victim cannot resist her assailant's sexual prowess and becomes sexually aroused and receptive to his embrace:

> The fantasies began with going out to a nightclub or bar and picking up a girl, and these changed to increasingly more drastic attempts. I'd think about either going to big parking lots or to a quiet area where there might be girls walking and confronting them. I began to have the thought that perhaps sometime if I did this, that the woman would agree or perhaps almost attack me—perhaps just my appearance or whatever would just turn her on and she would almost literally attack me in a complete state of sexual excitement, that she would rape me as if I were just what she had been waiting for. I would fantasize about confronting a girl with a weapon, a knife or a gun, and that she would tell me that I didn't need it and that she wanted me, and that she wanted me sexually. She would say, "No, you don't need it, you don't need a gun, you don't need any of this, you're enough."

Since it constitutes a test of his competency, the rape experience for this type of offender is a mixture of excitement, anxiety, anticipated pleasure, and fear:

> I don't know how to explain the feeling I got. My heart just started to pound, and I got sort of a funny feeling in the pit of my stomach, sort of like the feeling I had the first time I ever had sexual intercourse, and I felt that I had to go out and get her. I didn't have an erection at all; I just had the feeling and desire to have a woman.

In reality, the offender tends to find little sexual satisfaction in the rape. The assault is disappointing, for it never lives up to his fantasy:

It never came down the way I imagined it would. In the fantasy, after the initial shock of the attack, I thought the victim would be more accepting and responsive, but, in reality, that was not the case. I did not have the good feelings I fantasized about. I felt let down. I didn't experience the same feelings in the actual assault that I had expected to feel. Everything was pleasurable in the fantasy, and there was acceptance, whereas in the reality of the situation, it wasn't pleasurable, and the girl was scared, not turned on to me.

Whatever he may tell himself to explain the situation, at some level of experience he senses that he has not found what he is looking for in the offense—something he cannot clearly identify or define is missing or lacking. He does not feel reassured by either his own performance or his victim's response to the assault, and, therefore, he must go out and find another victim, this time "the right one." His offenses become repetitive and compulsive, and he may commit a whole series of rapes over a relatively short period of time:

I felt I needed something more. I just felt that there was something more, and that I had to have it. I really felt a compulsion, I mean a strong... something. It's funny. Even when these assaults happened, my life, my wife, my responsibilities, my parents, and so forth would flash in front of my mind, but it seemed to be of no consequence. I mean, I just had to no matter what. The crime itself just frustrated me more. I wasn't sexually aroused. I had to force myself. I felt some relief coming off because there was some tension release, but very shortly afterwards the feelings were worse. I blamed the victim and felt it was her fault and that a different girl would give me the satisfaction I craved, so I went out looking for another victim.

The amount of force used in the assaults may vary depending in part on situational factors, but there may be an increase in aggression over time as the offender becomes more desperate to achieve that indefinable experience that continues to elude him:

Somehow I felt I had not accomplished what I wanted to. The first three victims I approached resisted in some way or other—they just sort of laughed in my face—so the next time I went out, I took a knife with me. And even when I succeeded in committing a rape, the fantasies didn't go away; they just intensified, and I got more and more aggressive.

The offenses themselves are either premeditated (the offender goes out in search of a victim with the clear intent of sexual assault) or opportunistic (a situation presents itself in which the offender unexpectedly finds that he has access to a victim and this access activates his propensity for sexual assault).

The victim of the power rapist may be of any age but generally tends to be within the same age range as the offender or younger. The choice of a victim is predominantly determined by availability, accessibility, and vulnerability. As one offender put it, "I always looked for a victim who was smaller than me."

Although the power rapist may report that his offense was prompted by a desire for sexual gratification, careful examination of his behavior typically reveals that efforts to negotiate the sexual encounter or to determine the woman's receptiveness to a sexual approach are noticeably absent, as are any attempts at lovemaking or foreplay. Instead, the aim of the offender is to capture, conquer, and control his victim. Sexual desire, in and of itself, is not the primary or paramount issue operating in this assailant. If it were, there are a number of opportunities available in our society for consensual sex. In fact, sexual assaults always coexist with consenting sexual relations in the life of the offender. In no case have we ever found that rape was the first or only sexual experience in the offender's sexual history, or that he had no other alternatives or outlets for his sexual desires. To the question, "If what you wanted was sex, why didn't you just go to a prostitute?" the power rapist is likely to reply, "A real man never pays for it," revealing that one of the dynamics in the assault is reaffirmation of his manhood. Such offenders feel insecure about their masculinity or conflicted about their identity. For this reason, they find homosexual activity particularly disturbing or frightening and often adopt antagonistic attitudes in this regard:

> I didn't understand homosexuality. I thought it was the lowest, degrading thing there was. After my crimes, I'd be thinking and trying to figure out why I did what I did and then saying to myself, you know, "I wonder if I'm homosexual and if a guy would satisfy my needs." That was *then*. I don't see myself like that today. I'm certain I'm not a homosexual. When I first went to prison and I was exposed to people who were homosexual, I despised them. I really hated them, but what they were showing was love and affection and caring, and they could sit and talk with one another and be very sociable and very lovable in some ways, and that I could not handle at that point. So I really hated them and called them all kinds of names.

Rape, then becomes a way of putting such fears to rest, of asserting one's heterosexuality, and of preserving one's sense of manhood. The power rapist frequently reports becoming preoccupied with and troubled by homosexual thoughts at some point in the evolution of his offense. One offender remembered first becoming curious about homosexuality while he was in the service, but

> it wasn't until just before I was arrested that I began to give it any serious thought in relationship to myself—the fact that I was married and so forth, and it sort of scared the hell out of me. I'd try all the harder to get the satisfaction I wanted from a woman because, you know, I can't go to men. You don't do these sort of things. It's all right for them but not for me. I became very dissatisfied with women and thought well maybe men are my "bag"—the fact that women weren't working out and maybe men would—but any thoughts I ever had or any fantasies I ever had of a homosexual relationship were always one way: me sodomize the guy or have the guy blow me. I never thought of reciprocating. After I was arrested and in jail a while, I got involved in some homosexual activities, and at first I began to wonder—because it was very satisfying and was very gratifying—that maybe it was true, but after a while I started to realize it was no different.

Sometimes clinicians tend to misinterpret such thoughts as latent wishes or unadmitted desires on the part of the offender, but, in fact, they seem to be more a reflection of his insecurity and personal discomfort in regard to human sexuality in general. Even heterosexual acts other than genital intercourse may be regarded as "perverted," and masturbation, likewise, may be thought of as abnormal. Although such rapists may engage in homosexual activities with the same frequency as normal males, they are not comfortable with such encounters. In fact, they experience all types of sexuality as threatening, and their heterosexual pursuits have a driven, compulsive, counterphobic quality. Their anxieties may be converted into a tough, assertive, macho stance, or they may be reflected in a rather curious demand for validation and reassurance in regard to their victims.

This offender tends to engage in conversation of a sexual nature with his victim that is both assertive (giving the victim instructions, orders, or commands) and inquisitive (questioning her about her sexual interests or asking her to evaluate his sexual skills), reflecting both the power issues and the reassurance needs:

> I undressed her and told her to undress me. I began fondling her and asked her if she enjoyed sex. Then I told her to go down on me and when I got hard I entered her. I noticed she was wearing a wedding ring, and I asked her if I was as good as her husband.

The quest for power, mastery, and control appears to be an unresolved life issue operating in this offender that he acts out in his sexual assaults:

> All my life I felt I was being controlled, particularly by my parents, that people used me without any regard for my feelings, for my needs, and in my rapes the important part was not the sexual part, but putting someone else in the position in which they were totally helpless. I bound and gagged and tied up my victims and made them do something they didn't want to do, which was exactly the way I felt in my life. I felt helpless, very helpless in that I couldn't do anything about the satisfaction I wanted. Well, I decided, I'm going to put them in a position where they can't do anything about what I want to do. They can't refuse me. They can't reject me. They're going to have no say in the matter. I'm in charge now.

Not only may the victim symbolize everything the offender dislikes about himself (being weak, powerless, effeminate, and the like), but his desperate need to reassure himself of his virility and sexual competency often results in his attributing his own wishes to his victim, distorting his perception of her and misinterpreting her behavior:

> She wanted it, she was asking for it. She just said "no" so I wouldn't think she was easy. The only reason she yelled rape was she got home late and her husband knew she hadn't been out with her girlfriend.

Frequently, the power rapist denies that the sexual encounter was forcible. He *needs* to believe the victim wanted and enjoyed it. Following the assault, he may insist on buying the victim a drink or dinner and express a wish to see her again. In some cases, this may be understood as a way of "cooling the mark," that is, a gesture of friendliness and "no hard feelings," or a way of discrediting any subsequent report of rape by her; but in other cases, it reflects his fantasy expectation that sexual conquest has created a desire for him on the part of the victim. Even when entrapped and apprehended in this fashion (that is, the victim may agree to a "rendezvous" at an appointed time and place which the police stake out), the offender cannot accept that the victim was not attracted to him but rationalizes that she had to allege rape to protect her reputation.

The assault may be triggered by what the offender experiences to be a challenge by a female or a threat from a male, something which undermines his sense of competency and self-esteem and activates unresolved underlying feelings of inadequacy, insecurity, and vulnerability. He attempts to restore his sense of power, control, identity, and worth through his sexual offense. When one feels there are no other avenues of expression left, there are always the physical resources: strength and sexuality. The relative importance of power needs over sexual needs for this type of offender is reflected in some cases by the offender's keeping his victim captive, that is, in his control, for an extended period of time beyond the sexual activity. In other cases, the offender may be deterred from an intended offense when his victim addresses the power need in some fashion. For example, one offender who had raped six women reported being deterred on one occasion: he spotted his potential victim while riding on a subway and decided that if she got off alone at her stop, he would rape her. She did exit alone in a rather remote area of town, but as the offender followed her, she turned to him and explained that because it was so late at night she didn't feel safe walking home alone and asked him if he would be kind enough to accompany her until she reached her house. He did so and never touched her, puzzled that his wish to rape her had suddenly disappeared.

Power rapists often experience a sense of omnipotence through their assaults and may express this by identifying themselves to their victims, by offering to drive them to the police station, or by some other such defiant act. Unfortunately, such offenders can and do frequently get away with their crimes, which only further increases their sense of power and control.

The intent of the power rapist, then, is to assert his competency and validate his masculinity. Sexuality is the test and his motive is conquest.

Warren is an example of this type of rapist. He is 23 years old, six feet tall, and weighs 180 pounds. He is the fourth of five children and has one older brother, two older sisters, and one younger sister. His father is a construction worker and his mother a sales clerk. Although Warren was a physically healthy child, he became enuretic and developed a slight stutter in his speech. The large family lived together in a cramped, two-bedroom house in a small seashore community:

> At this time in my life I was sharing a bedroom with two of my sisters. There might not have been as many family squabbles if there'd been more room. I guess the problems I had with my family took effect from the beginning of school. My grades were never very good, and I seemed to have a hard time concentrating on my schoolwork. During my grammar school days, I participated in the Boy Scouts and church events, but only because it was the thing to

do. My brother had been a Scout and was part of the church fellowship, so although I could care less, I went through the motions. Even
with all the kids around me my age in school or in these other
activities, I never had a real friend or buddy to chum around with.
I'd try to get interested in things that most guys my age liked to do,
but I felt so insecure that I just wanted to go home, and when I got
there, my mother wondered why I didn't have any friends, and my
dad would order me to get outside and make friends. He'd yell at me
and tell me I was a sissy, a cream puff, that I wasn't normal. I felt like
I was trapped. I hated to go home and face him even though I could
be alone there, and I hated to stay away from home because I just
couldn't make it with people.

Although Warren was of average intelligence, his grades ranged
from fair to poor, and his school, identifying him as immature and
inhibited, referred him to a child guidance clinic. Although his mother
attended counseling at the clinic, his father refused to have anything to
do with it. The clinic recommended a residential school to give Warren
some respite from the problems at home, but his family could not afford
this placement.

When Warren was 10 years old his mother suffered an emotional
breakdown and was hospitalized with a serious depression. Following
her release she was maintained on antidepressant medication and supportive counseling for a number of years, and she slowly improved.
Warren did get along well with his sisters, who felt sorry for the way
their father treated him:

My curiosity about the sexes started when I was about 11. My
sister, who was two years older than me, was also curious, and we
would talk about the changes happening in our bodies, and on a
couple of occasions, we'd undress and explore each other, which I
guess is common among kids. I never did talk about sex or girls
with any of the guys in school or from the neighborhood. My high
school years were as lousy as my grammar school days. I'd look
around me and see kids my age doing things together: going to
dances, sports events, parties, social gatherings, and the like. At the
time I didn't care about being a part of this, but now I realize that this
was what life was all about and that I was on the outside. I was still
having problems with my schoolwork. The teachers used to tell me I
had the intelligence but was too lazy. They just didn't realize I had
too many worries on my mind. When a teacher would ask a question
and I'd know the answer, I still wouldn't raise my hand. I know I
could have done better if I was living a better life. If you're living a
real shitty life, how can you do well in school? I couldn't keep my

mind on schoolwork. I had other problems on my mind—no specific problem, just unhappiness in general, not being able to fit in with friends and all—being kind of a loner—not really wanting to be but not being able to get the tools to make friends, what it takes to be able to be friendly to somebody. I found the most popular kids in school had the best grades too. The loners usually flunked out—not just me but everybody. At age 14, an older male cousin showed me what to do with my penis when it got hard. I remember us wrestling and his groping me and me not thinking anything wrong with that, and I went along with him. After that, I would masturbate a lot. It felt good, and it seemed to relax me. I guess I wanted to show what I had just learned to someone, and one day I masturbated in front of a 6-year-old niece and fondled my 9-year-old nephew.

This incident was dealt with within the family. Warren's mother attempted to explain the "facts of life" to him, but he found this embarrassing and remained confused as to the nature of human sexuality and reproduction. At age 15, Warren began to develop breasts and underwent surgery (bilateral gynecomastia) at age 16. He felt self-conscious about the resulting scars and slight distortion in the shape of his nipples, although, in fact, this is hardly noticeable. After his release from the hospital, his parents divorced and his father moved out of the home. Warren became interested in sports, but these too were all solitary activities: swimming, hiking, and body building. He developed a fine physique and matured into an exceptionally handsome young man. His first experience with intercourse occurred at age 17, the summer he graduated from high school:

I used to go down to this beach. It was known as "Snatch Alley." You didn't need any charm or anything. They were after your body and you were after theirs. That was it. That was the first time. Then I went into the navy. It seemed like a good way to get away. I thought about the Marines in the beginning. They were gung-ho and everyone looked up to a Marine. If you could be a Marine, you could do anything, handle anything, and people looked up to you. But I backed out at the last minute and settled for the navy because I wanted to travel. I was in the service for three years, and that didn't even turn out like I wanted it to. I did the traveling, but I didn't make the most of it—just like in school. I turn everything to dirt.

Warren had no difficulties adjusting to military life:

I did what I was told. I took orders and didn't mind it. People would tell me what to do, and I was glad to show them I could do it. I'd want to do it so they'd be proud of me and say, "This kid takes good orders," you know?

However, Warren did not take advantage of the opportunities the navy offered him to learn a vocation. He could not bring himself to care about advancing himself or bettering his station.

Shortly after entering the service, Warren became sexually involved with a 27-year-old man named Brian:

> Living with this guy was probably as easy as I ever had it in my life. I didn't have to eat the navy chow. I had a place to go, a car to drive, sharp clothes to wear, and I always had money in my pocket. I was living pretty good. Brian worked and was gone most of the time. He said I could come and go as I wanted and could do my own thing, but if I was going to live there, he was going to have what he wanted. I wanted him to think I cared about him, but I really didn't. I didn't know the meaning of the word *homosexual* before I met him. I probably heard it before, but it never really crossed my mind—I never really thought about it. I was very naive. This guy Brian, I didn't know what was going on even when he had me in his bedroom and tried to kiss me. Maybe I didn't have enough respect for myself to say, "No, I don't want any part of this." Instead, I figured, "Well, he's treating me good, so I'll give him what he wants." When we'd lie in bed and he lay near me I wouldn't feel turned on, but if I was lying near a girl, I'd get an erection, so I'd fantasize about having sex with a girl to get an erection. Then we'd have sex together. Although Brian didn't approve of pot, sometimes I would get stoned before having sex with him. I enjoyed it more then—maybe I didn't feel as guilty.

Warren's relationship with Brian terminated when he left the navy. Although Warren was being kept by Brian, he found he had not managed to save any of his navy pay:

> That's another thing I kick myself for. I could have saved up so much. I could have had $10,000 when I got out. But I went through several cars and motorcycles. Just foolish things: dope, clothes now and then. Overseas I'd go out and blow the money. I had nothing to show for it.

During the time he was living with Brian, Warren's heterosexual encounters were mostly confined to prostitutes:

> The only kind of romance I ever had was with a girl named Susan that I began dating, and I never had sex with her. I often tried, but

she told me she was a virgin and she was saving it for the guy she married. I really liked her, but I also had an interest in being the first one to get in her—you know, this was something to me, to pop her cherry. Her being a virgin, it would feel like she's all mine and nobody else has touched her before—it's brand-new, not second-hand.

After receiving an honorable discharge from the navy, Warren planned to marry Susan:

The summer I got out, I went to spend it with her, and I blew the relationship because I couldn't handle it. She never gave up on me. I gave up on myself, because I felt I didn't know how to express my feelings with her—probably from lack of experience. I returned home that summer where my family was and where I knew I had a place to stay until I got my thoughts together. Everything was there that I needed, but still there was something missing. I wasn't satisfied living like I was. I tried attracting girls. I'd go to the beach in my sports car, tight jeans, and really fine tan and have everybody looking, but I'd say to myself, "They are probably thinking he thinks he's too good for us," and here am I feeling not good enough. At least, this way I could believe I had what it took and didn't have to put it on the line and risk being turned down by some girl after she found out what I was really like: even with a fine cover, what a dull book!

Warren began to depend more and more on marijuana and alcohol to feel comfortable with himself:

When I was high, I thought I was as good a sex partner as anyone ever had. I still have this tightness about jumping into the sack, even though I've been there. It's easier when you have a few drinks and smoke some dope. It really wasn't all that good when I was stoned. I was just pretending to enjoy sex a lot more than I really was. Pot didn't help me any. Thank God I never got into hard drugs—Brian helped me to keep away from them. Most of the time, the girls I'd get lucky with wanted it as much as I did, and then it was a letdown. As far as sex goes, I feel I have to be the aggressor: if the girl wants it as much as I do, I can't enjoy it. It's pop-pop, and that's it. I can get as much out of masturbating. When I've had sex with a girl who's been eager to have it, I didn't really enjoy it too much. I enjoyed it some, but I thought if I was in charge, like the master—she's going to do what I say—I thought I'd probably enjoy it a whole lot more.

Warren's mother had now remarried, and he was asked to find a place of his own by the end of the summer:

I started traveling again and went back to South Carolina, where I was stationed in the navy, to stay with Brian. I still wasn't sure of what I wanted in life. I knew I wasn't gay, and Brian knew that too. He kept bugging me about what I was going to do with my life. I didn't know myself. He said why not go out and find a girl and get married—it did bother me, him saying that, because he was letting me go. I tried to think ahead and it kind of scared me. I'd be out on my own and I didn't know what I was going to do, how I was going to live. I wanted to go to California, but I didn't know what I was going to do when I got there. I hoped I could get into the movies. I was kind of scared. I wanted to have some kind of plan—what to do with my life for the next couple of years. Heading west was the only one I could come up with, but it didn't work out. I just crawled into a shell. I tried. I started out but only made it as far as Kansas. I came home. I didn't have a job or any ambition to find one. I was thinking about the past, not having any friends, not going anywhere in my life. I was drinking more than I ever had and smoking grass. My family would ask me how come I wasn't dating anyone. I felt I didn't have anything to offer a girl. I'd give up before I even tried. It seemed so much easier just to be by myself and not have to keep someone interested in you. But really deep down I wanted someone, to be able to say she was mine and have what other guys had and not appear to be an oddball.

Warren scraped along day by day, working some for his father, collecting welfare, and living in the basement of his sister's home:

I dreaded living there, and I had the feeling they really didn't want me, but I couldn't seem to find myself. I'd get very depressed sometimes and just feel like giving up. I'd get these crying jags. I'd go down into the cellar, and it would be so cold there at night. I was living this kind of life, and I didn't want to. I just didn't care what happened to me. I didn't care about living, but I didn't want to die either. I just wanted to take time out for a while and get myself together. I got so depressed. Much of the time I'd cry. I'd go down the cellar in my sister's house and just break up and bawl my eyes out. Then I'd get a grip on myself and I'd go about living my dull life again.

During this period, Warren's sexual activity was predominantly masturbation:

I felt it was a waste. Why masturbate when I could go out and put it to use and not just me enjoy it but someone else too? But I'd take the easy way out and masturbate. When I wasn't horny, a chick didn't mean all that much. The way I've handled sex, it's just been to relieve myself. I can get as much out of a hand job as I can having sex with someone, because there's not any feeling with it as there should be.

While masturbating himself, Warren would fantasize

having a girl tied up, spread-eagle, to the bed. She was helpless, and I was the master. I'd satisfy myself, get what I wanted, and she would enjoy it—even though I had her tied up, she would enjoy it and have an orgasm. She wouldn't try to fight me or break loose from the ropes.

Warren then became sexually involved with a neighborhood girl named Betty:

She lived next door, so it was convenient. Betty told me I was a great-looking guy. She wasn't ugly, but she wasn't all that pretty. She didn't have much of a figure. She'd come over and pick me up, because I no longer had a car. I felt she was nothing special— nothing great-looking—but I knew I would never lose her; no one else would want her. I never took her out to clubs or anything like that. If you have a really pretty girl, you want to show her off. I didn't really care to show Betty off. I'd think others would think I couldn't get anything better. I've seen guys with ugly-looking girls, and I've thought that myself. I never introduced her to my family. They knew I had trouble making it with girls and would figure I was with Betty because no one else would have me. She was my last resort, but she was more serious about me than I was about her. It was probably wrong not letting her know I did not have as strong a feeling toward her as I pretended to. Having sex with her was just to relieve myself. It's very easy for me to be selfish. Nothing was work- ing out for me. I didn't have the ingredients it takes to make it in life. I didn't have any confidence in myself, and I couldn't handle any responsibilities. I didn't have a job. I just lost my driver's license. I had no place to live. I felt like I was just existing—you don't know what you are going to do next, and sometimes you don't really even care. I had problems, not just making it with girls but having friends in general. I didn't understand myself, and I couldn't relate to others. If you don't understand people, it's going to get you into trouble.

One day, Warren was hitchhiking and a woman stopped and of- fered him a ride:

She asked me where I was headed, and I told her I was going into town, and she said she had some time to kill while her clothes were drying in a laundromat so she could give me a lift. As she drove down the highway, we got into some small talk about the beaches and beautiful scenery. I had some marijuana on me and asked her if she'd like some. She said "Yes," so we smoked a joint along the way, and I was thinking in the back of my mind, "She told me she had some time to kill," so naturally I thought we'd make the best of it. It sounded like a come-on. I slid over, put my foot on the brake, and stopped the car. I put my arm around her neck—not choking her or anything—and said, "You know what I want." She said "No," and I held the joint up to her face and said, "You don't want to get hurt, baby, you want to get laid. You want it as much as I do." I just thought she needed a little extra encouragement. I figured she was the type who would say no up until the last minute. I really wasn't horny or anything, but I told her to drive into a clearing among the sand dunes. We got out of the car, and I told her to take off her clothes and then to undress me. She said, "You want it, okay, you're going to get it, the best screwing of your life." I began balling her and came off really fast. She wouldn't stop, and this turned me off. After I had come, she kept on going. I said, "Okay, that's enough." It was a letdown. It wasn't like I wanted it to be. After it was over, we got back into her car, but it got stuck in the sand, so we walked about a mile or so to a gas station. On the way I said to her, "I'll tell you what, why don't I take you out to dinner and then we'll go back to your place?" and she, "Okay." When we reached the garage, she told the attendant about the car, and I told her I was going into the men's room to roll another joint. When I came out, she was going across the street to a police cruiser. I figured she was going to ask for help with her car. It was the last thing on my mind that she was going to yell rape—she had just broken off with her boyfriend, so I guess that's why she said it.

Warren was arrested and released on personal recognizance to await trial:

It was Saturday night, a week later, and I had had a few drinks. I don't know what I was going to do. I wanted to see her and talk her out of pressing charges. It was just a misunderstanding, and I remembered where she said she lived. I found the street, but I couldn't remember the number of her house. I was wandering around and saw a house all lit up. I knocked on the door, and a girl opened it and asked me if I was looking for Bill. I said, "Yes," and she let me in. She stood there in her nightgown, and you could see right through it—you could see her nipples and breasts and, you know, they were just waiting for me, and it was just too much of a temptation to pass up. Here I was—there was nobody else there, and I got the feeling,

"Wow, I've got her body and I can maybe enjoy this if I want to. She probably figures, 'Well, heck, I don't have to go out tonight, he's going to come to me and I don't have to go out looking for a cock.'" I could have tried to make it with her as far as rapping and trying to seduce her, but I didn't want any of that because maybe if she agreed, I wouldn't have enjoyed it. As it was, I picked her up, laid her on the floor, spread her legs, and balled her. I don't even remember getting off, but I guess I did. It was the way I wanted it. I wanted to be the aggressor, but I really didn't enjoy it. In my fantasies, in my mind I had, but when it really came down to the actual getting it on, it was worthless. I stood up and asked her for a drink. She said she didn't have anything in the house. I offered to go to the package store, but when I got there, it was closed, so I went back to her house. It was 20 minutes later, and I guess she figured I pulled a fast one on her—that I had just come in for the sex and wasn't going to stick around—so she'd fix me. She left to get a friend, and I came back and didn't find anybody there. I waited for her, and if she had come back alone, I would have stayed there and we would have talked, and because she had had sex with me, I figured I can say pretty much what I want because maybe she liked me, to let me in to have sex with her—maybe I just had enough going for myself with her that she would sit down and listen to me, and I could probably talk to her. But, as it turned out, I heard more than one voice—I heard a guy coming back with her, so I took off.

Warren was arrested, let out on bail, and within a few days committed a third offense. It involved a girl he had met at the beach the past summer and with whom he had occasionally had consenting sexual relations:

I'd call her up when I wanted to see her, and usually she'd be home or be around, and I'd get ahold of her and she'd come by and pick me up. We'd go out and not do a whole lot: ride around, talk, smoke some reefers, go bowling sometimes, go down to the beach and park—not do a whole lot of anything. I figured it was going to be another one of these days, you know. I was up around her neighborhood that day, and it was starting to rain, and I needed a ride home anyways, so I called her up. She told me she was waiting for someone and she couldn't come by. I talked her into it, so she did give me a ride. I figured we'd go someplace and do something, you know. She didn't want to; she didn't want any part of me that day. She has before, you know, she'd say no and say she was afraid of getting pregnant, but she'd end up doing it anyways. I figured it was just her way of holding out, you know, pretending that she wasn't easy. She had never turned me down yet. But this day, I had been drinking a little bit and she just told me I had to get out and leave. I said, "I'm not getting out here, it's raining." I unzipped my jeans and tried to make out with her there. I didn't have to force myself on her because I never had to. I didn't know she was married, and she didn't get home until after her husband had come home from work, and I guess he talked her into pressing charges.

Warren was ultimately persuaded to plead guilty to all three offenses. The district attorney acknowledged that had he not pleaded guilty, he most likely would not have been convicted. The first victim's local reputation, the second victim's psychiatric history, and the third victim's previous sexual involvement with the defendant would in turn have served to impeach the credibility of each woman's testimony. Warren himself decided to plead guilty in exchange for a commitment to a treatment center rather than risk going to prison. However, he did not think of himself as a rapist:

I don't feel I have a sex hang-up. I can make it with a girl if I wanted to. I can make it into her arms without attacking her. I never had the urge to go out and rape anyone. I never even thought about it. I never even really knew that many dirty jokes about sex or anything like that. When you're standing around with a bunch of guys, usually there's some stories going around about sex, dirty stories. I don't even care to listen to them. I don't know why they listen to them; maybe it turns them on or they get a few laughs or something. I never really cared to hear them, and sex really didn't mean all that much to me. The reason I probably got into trouble was that I don't know when a girl wants it or not. How can you tell? Like, she's not going to say, "I want it" or "I don't want it." You're supposed to be able to tell by the way she reacts to you, what she says, or what goes on between you, and if you don't have that much experience with a girl—like I said, I was never the aggressor, I was always the aggressee—so I didn't know. It was kind of hard to be able to tell when a girl wants it. Usually a girl won't say no—she'll come up with an excuse of why she doesn't want to, like she's afraid she'll get pregnant or we don't know each other that well, or we shouldn't do it here in the back seat of the car, or something like that—but it just turns out usually to be an excuse. I figure a no wasn't really meaning it—I heard it before. Up to now, I've had a clean record. I'll admit I've picked up girls before and we've gone out and had sex and they've said no before, but they haven't meant it. They enjoyed it. In these three cases, I probably could have gotten in their pants without them yelling rape or anything like that. I know I could have, 'cause, like the second girl, she wouldn't have stood in the doorway like that or let me in. In a way, I feel like I showed her a good time, and there was no reason for her to yell rape other than I didn't come back when I said I would. I guess when a girl did say no I was glad. I probably wanted her to say no—this is what I wanted to hear, maybe it's more stimulating—in the end it would never have to be rape; she'd say no until—even after I did have sex with her, even if she said no up to then, she never would yell rape, because there would be no need for it, because I never would make a threat or anything like that. I'd talk nice, like "Oh, yeah, you really want it; you can keep saying no, but I know you really want it." In the end, she would have enjoyed it as much as I had, and I would have felt like the dominant person, the one in charge. Once I got inside her, she wouldn't try to fight me off or anything like that. She would stay with the rhythm, and when I kissed her, she would suck my tongue, and it was like she wanted to be taken advantage of, but she didn't want to be made out to be easy, so she would say no. And I think really this is the way most girls are—the ones I've been mixed up with.

Later in treatment, Warren became more accurate in recognizing the dynamics underlying his sexual offenses:

I have a hang-up showing my feelings, expressing love. I never really loved anybody that I can think of. I don't know what love really is. I felt all I had to offer anyone was sex. If I had something else to offer, I wouldn't be in prison now. Something's screwed up. I'm not a bad-looking guy. Like if a guy has one eye and is weird-looking, maybe he has to go out and rape because he can't get it any other way. In my case people would say I could get anyone I wanted, so there must be something screwed up with me to do it. A lot of the guys here are real good-looking. They could have gone out and picked up a girl. That's probably not the real reason guys go out and rape—because they can't get anybody—a lot of them are married anyways. Me, I could have had it any time I wanted it. I could have turned on the charm and picked up a girl at a bar, but I thought I would enjoy it more by taking advantage of the situation—but I sure as hell didn't. It was far from enjoyable. I had a few drinks both times, and I didn't even realize I had gotten off—I just went limp and said, "Well, I guess that's about it." I thought it would be better if I took advantage of the situation, like I would have the power over her and she was going to do what I wanted her to do. I just though I'd enjoy this power over somebody's body. I thought I'd like to be like an animal, to take her body without her say-so. I thought by having the power, I'd enjoy it a whole lot more. There were some other incidents that happened prior to the ones I was arrested for. I got into some trouble with some kids who were younger than me. I don't know what it is—maybe it's that I feel more masculine with somebody younger than me. With someone more my age I feel she's equal or better than me or I have to ask pretty please if we can have sex. These happened at the end of last summer. All of my offenses took place within six months. A couple of girls about 14 years old were hitchhiking. I picked them up. I was pretty drunk—it's not an excuse, they looked young. All of a sudden, I thought, "They're going to do what I want them to do—I'm in command," like I'm in charge. I drove my van off the road. They knew what I wanted, and one of the girls tried to get out of the van. I grabbed the other one and said to the first one that she'd better come back in or I would hurt her friend. She came back in. I felt so powerful—it was weird—here were two girls, and I was in command, and it was going to be a threesome. I exposed myself and started to slowly masturbate. One girl said, "We're too young; we're only 14," but I made them both undress. Then I balled one of them, but it wasn't easy. It hurt, and I just did enough to get off. And the other girl sat right beside us and watched, and I didn't do anything to her. Then, I told them to get dressed and let them go. Later, I kicked myself for not getting more out of it. I could have had them stay with me longer, an hour or so; as it was, the whole thing was over in 10 minutes. After I had gotten my rocks off, I did feel dirty and guilty—I mean, like a bad person. I used to refer to my van as my whore wagon. I'd just pick up a girl hitchhiking. It was just an inner urge I couldn't control. I just wanted to have sex with her and that was all. It was like something I had to do even though I wasn't enjoying it—I was scared the whole time. I'd read about it in the newspaper, but I never thought of myself as a rapist. Sometimes, after we'd have sex, I'd give the girl my telephone number, but none ever called. I guess they figured I didn't give them the right number. Of all these girls—maybe four or five—only one ever fought me off. She said she had a knife in her pocketbook and said, "I'd rather you murder me than rape me." I got scared and stopped trying to get into her pants. I asked her to jack me off, and she was willing to do that. I didn't really need the sex. I wanted to have a relationship with a girl, but I thought it was something I had to do, to have sex with her was just to prove to myself that I was halfway normal. I've done things with girls just to please them, and I wasn't getting any satisfaction, so maybe doing something that would please me and wasn't pleasing them would give me more satisfaction. I don't know. I wish the guy didn't have to be the aggressor. I wish there were more aggressive girls around—there probably would be a lot less rapes.

Victim Impact

The victim of the power rapist is typically within the same age group as her offender, or she may be younger. Hospital examination may show minimal or inconclusive evidence of physical trauma. Although she may have come out of the assault relatively uninjured physically, the response of others to her plight may be less supportive. Hospital personnel, police, family, friends, and the like may be more accusatory in their questioning. They are dubious about her efforts to resist assault and may tend to feel that she deliberately or inadvertently invited or encouraged the assault—participation is misinterpreted as provocation and cooperation as consent.

As noted above, in power assaults the language of the offender is typically instructional and sexually inquisitive. He may ask his victim if she enjoyed the sexual encounter, if she'd like to see him again, if before they part she will give him a kiss, etc. Many times, the victim plays along with the offender, reassures him that he is sexually impressive, tells him that she really did enjoy the sexual encounter, kisses him—in other words, cooperates in the service of survival. However, should she go to court, these coping strategies may be used to impeach her credibility about her resistance and lack of consent.

Following the assault, the power rapist may not immediately release his victim. He may, for example, drive around town with her in his car. He may stop for gas or go into a fast-food stand to get himself and his victim something to eat. People find it difficult to understand why the victim does not call out for help to the gas station attendant or make good her escape when her offender goes into the fast-food shop. To understand this, one must realize that the victim feels powerless. She hopes that, if she cooperates, her assailant will ultimately release her. She does not want to chance doing anything that might antagonize him. She is fearful that, if she attempts to escape, he will hurt her. And where can she run to? Her home? Her job? At some point prior to, during, or after the assault, the offender usually questions the victim and learns where she lives and where she works. He may also have gone through her purse and found some identification. He knows where to find her if he wants to. This knowledge extends his sense of power and control, and the victim cooperates in the hope of not alienating him and of reducing the risk of further victimization.

In the course of such assaults, when the offender does learn the victim's identity, she becomes fearful that he will return. Typically, the offender may make such threats as a continuation of his power and control over the victim. In fact, however, the likelihood of his actually carrying out such threats appears minimal. In our professional experience with over 250 rape offenders, we have yet to find a single instance where this actually did occur, although it is a very common threat.

Whereas for the victim of an anger rape, her vulnerability becomes a prominent issue, for the victim of the power rape, it is her helplessness. It is important, therefore, to respond to such victims in ways that serve to undo their feelings of powerlessness and reestablish a sense of personal control and self-determination. Their cooperation and permission should be requested in regard to examination and investigative procedures. Consent, choice, and decision making on their part must be respected—they should not be pressured into agreeing to something they are undecided about or opposed to.

One of the key issues in working with victims of power rapes is their anger at themselves and self-blame for being victimized and not being able to escape the assault. It is important to help them realize that no strategy would necessarily have been more effective than the one they tried. What deters one assailant only encourages another, but frequently the victim feels that if she had said or done something different, she could have discouraged the assault. And it is this feeling of not having achieved her primary goal—that of escaping the offender—that affects the victim and retards her recovery from the trauma of sexual assault.

Sadistic Rape

In a third pattern of rape, both sexuality and aggression become fused into a single psychological experience known as *sadism*. There is a sexual transformation of anger and power so that aggression itself becomes eroticized. This offender finds the intentional maltreatment of his victim intensely gratifying and takes pleasure in her torment, anguish, distress, helplessness, and suffering. The assault usually involves bondage and torture and frequently has a bizarre or ritualistic quality to it. The offender may subject his victim to curious actions, such as clipping her hair, washing or cleansing her body, or forcing her to dress in some specific fashion or behave in some specified way. Such indignities are accompanied by explicitly abusive acts, such as biting, burning the victim with cigarettes, and flagellation. Sexual areas of the victim's body (her breasts, genitals, and buttocks) become a specific focus of injury and abuse. In some cases, the rape may not involve the offender's sexual organs. Instead, he may use some type of instrument or foreign object, such as a stick or bottle, with which to penetrate his victim sexually:

> My intention from the outset was to give my victims an enema and
> follow it with anal sex, but in most cases I "came off" during the

enema without requiring anal entry. I have found as much pleasure, if not more, reaching a climax with masturbation during the administration of the enema—sodomy or coitus being unnecessary.

In extreme cases—those involving sexual homicide—there may be grotesque acts, such as the sexual mutilation of the victim's body or sexual intercourse with her corpse. Eric, an infamous sex killer, committed four grisly murders in the span of one summer. As described in the pathologist's report, each victim had been dismembered into five parts. The skin was peeled off the breasts and vagina. On the legs and buttocks, there were multiple stab wounds and punctures. Stab wounds were also present in the anterior chest wall. Sperm were found in both the vagina and the rectum of the body, and findings were consistent with its having been deposited postmortem.

Prostitutes, or women whom the offender regards as promiscuous, may be particular targets of the sadistic rapist. Usually, his victims are strangers who share some common characteristic, such as age, appearance, or occupation. They are symbols of something he wants to punish or destroy. The assault is deliberate, calculated, and preplanned. The offender takes precautions against discovery, such as wearing a disguise or blindfolding his victim. The victim is stalked, abducted, abused, and sometimes murdered.

In contrast to the anger rapist, the sexual sadist's offenses are fully premeditated. He is not suddenly exploding in a rage:

> At no point during the incident was I aware of any anger towards the victim, although I now recognize a resentment or jealousy of girls.

Usually, he captures his victim and then works himself into a frenzy as he assaults her. The rape experience for the sexual sadist is one of intense and mounting excitement. Excitement is associated with the inflicting of pain upon his victim. Such abuse is usually a combination of the physical and the psychological. Hatred and control are eroticized, so that he finds satisfaction in abusing, degrading, humiliating, and, in some cases, destroying his captive:

> As my victim's attitude of submission increased, my sexual excitement proportionately increased. I was aware that this excitement derived from the prospect of having a young, pure, upperclass girl and bringing her down to my level—a feeling like "Well, there's one fine, fancy bitch who not only got an enema in front of a man but

was given it by a man and fucked in the ass besides. And from a freak like me to top it all off! Bet she don't feel so uppity now, contaminated by a crud like me." I had long identified enemas with humiliation, probably because that was my reaction to the enemas I received—from my guardian aunt and hospital nurses.

For some sadistic rapists, the infliction of pain itself provides gratification; for others, it is a necessary preliminary to other forms of sexual activity. Their arousal is a function of aggression. The more aggressive they are, the more powerful they feel; and, in turn, the more powerful they feel, the more excited they become. This self-perpetuating and self-increasing cycle results, in extreme cases, in the offender's working himself into a frenzy in which he commits a lust murder. The sadistic rapist may report feeling aroused by his victim's futile resistance. He may find her struggling with him an exciting and erotic experience. He may initially be impotent until his victim physically resists him, or he may experience a spontaneous ejaculation during his assault without intromission.

Because of the ritualistic and potentially lethal nature of his offenses, the sadistic rapist is often believed to be blatantly psychotic, but, in fact, he is usually able to conceal these darker impulses from others. There is a hidden side to his personality which harbors these forbidden wishes. One of the disconcerting features of such offenders is that they are often quite personable, an impression in sharp contrast to the expected stereotype of the vicious "sex fiend" and a quality they capitalize on to gain access to unsuspecting victims.

After over eight hours of interviews with the multiple murderer, Eric, we noted the following impressions in our diagnostic report:

At his best, Eric impressed us as personable, likeable, and friendly. He was able to express affect which ranged from warm humor to painful hurt freely, openly, and appropriately. He demonstrated an ability to describe people and situations clearly and to articulate his feelings well. Although rapport was established, Eric appeared guarded and careful in the material he related. In part, this appeared to be a conscious suppression of material which was available to him, and, in part, a repression of material which was no longer retrievable because of its disturbing nature. He related in a rather passive—submissive manner; he responded to our questions but asked few of his own and made very few demands while here at the center.

In fact, one of the strongest impressions Eric made in interview was his reluctance to express any negative or angry feelings whatsoever. It seemed very important to deny or negate any negative features of people or events in his life and, except for the addiction to drugs, he typically described people or life situations as "beautiful" when clearly they were not always so. He seemed to have difficulty in acknowledging the faults and flaws in others—especially those close to him. He is not a person who is comfortable with anger; he appears unable to express it and denies aggressive impulses through a reaction-formation type of defense. Another strong impression was the obvious distress he experienced whenever our discussions touched upon the current offenses, or "the nightmare," as he would refer to it. At these times Eric would become noticeably depressed. His eyes would become moist; his voice, choked up; his hands would tremble slightly; his facial expression would become somber; and his voice would falter slightly when he spoke.

One consistent observation noted by previous examiners, and apparent in the current interviews, was Eric's tendency to ramble on when asked an open-ended question. Although his quality of verbalization was good, his long, rambling replies to questions seemed in part to suggest that he had some difficulty in comprehending the point of the questions and in sorting out what was trivial from what was pertinent in his answer. Although talking a lot, he actually said very little, but we did not get the impression that this was an intentional device to evade the issues. Typically, when he wanted to evade something, he would simply not bring up the material even when we set the opportunity for him to do so. For example, when we asked him about his reading interests, he avoided mentioning his books on the occult until we revealed that we knew of them. He then tended to explain this away as representing more of a philosophical interest.

Finally, there was a subtle quality of omnipotence in his response to the examination: it was not an attitude of open defiance, condescension, or disdain; it was more of a sense of comfort in realizing that no one knew in fact exactly what had happened in regard to the current offense, except himself, and that he had the ability or skill to explain away the incriminating but circumstantial evidence. Except for the times when Eric spoke of the deaths of those close to him (a theme that consistently appeared through his life) and his sense of loss, we had the distinct impression of our never quite touching, never quite making exact and direct contact in our relating. It was very much like our talking *to* him and his talking *to* us, but only on a few rare occasions did we talk *with* each other. It should be pointed out that all the above were very subtle qualities in Eric's relating. There were no evidences of gross pathology obvious in these interviews, and, if one met him casually, he would impress one as a fairly ordinary, bright, and pleasant individual; at worst, he would appear somewhat remote and private. He is a person who lives within himself and keeps parts of himself permanently concealed from others. There is more to him than what he is willing to reveal to anyone.

The sadistic offender thrives on a feeling of omnipotence. Eric stated that he gave up his Catholicism when he was 12 because he could not believe in the literalness of the Bible, especially the story of the Garden of Eden and Christ as God. He continued to believe in Christ the man. After his 12th birthday, he learned stone masonry and carpentry from his stepfather. He calls himself a carpenter and described some of the buildings he had built as monuments that his children might look up to. When he was 23 years old, he began to accumulate a group of teenage drug users around him, and he was called by them "Sire" and "Lord Eric." He called these followers his disciples.

The morbid, the occult, the violent, and the bizarre may preoccupy the sadistic rapist, and sadistic themes are the focus of his masturbatory fantasies. He is interested in sadomasochistic pornography and may have a collection of souvenirs or mementos of his victims, such as photographs, and articles of clothing. His sadistic attacks are repetitive and interspersed with other less dramatic offenses as well as consenting sexual encounters. However, there may be a progression over time in regard to his offenses, with each new assault showing an increase in aggression over the prior one. As one offender observed:

> I found myself having sexual fantasies that would put women in precarious positions. I was thinking about this more and more, like devising a rack, perhaps, that would spread her legs as wide open as they could possibly be spread—something of this nature. I acted tough with them. The first one and the last one pleaded for their virginity [sic]. I told them to do what they were told and they wouldn't get hurt. I said that if they didn't do what they were told, they would be sorry. I don't know if I actually threatened to kill them or not, but I very strongly feel that I never would have. The only thing is, perhaps if I continued on and hadn't been caught this time, seeing what happened from the first three times to the second three times—I just wonder—maybe in the next set of three somebody would have gotten hurt, you know, somebody would have really gotten hurt.

His sadistic impulses may also be apparent both in the context of his consenting sexual encounters, as, for example, in his marital relationships, and in activities that are not explicitly sexual, such as cruelty to animals and fighting.

Shortly after his marriage, Eric's wife found him moody, often preferring to be alone. He states that there was much pressure at work and that he found the responsibilities of father and husband too difficult to bear. During the first year of marriage, his wife reports that he would smother her with a plastic bag or a pillowcase until she passed out, and then he would have intercourse with her. He would also suspend her head downward from a hook in the ceiling and have her perform oral sex and masturbate him. He would at times beat her with belts and burn her with cigarettes until she finally refused to have sex with him. Eric denied this, explaining that he would

> just fool around, like boxing and wrestling and tossing her around which sometimes got rough because she was so fragile. She did not like this and would become frightened and angry even though I was just teasing.

The intent of the sadistic rapist, then, is to abuse and torture his victim. His instrument is sex, and his motive is punishment and destruction.

Oliver is an example of the sadistic rapist. He is of short stature, only 5'3" in height, but he is stocky, weighing 175 pounds. He is the youngest of nine children. His father was self-employed as an appliance dealer. Oliver describes him as an honest and hardworking man who provided adequately for his family and was always very proud of the many successes of his older children:

> I was continually wanting to prove myself to my father, but he had too many geniuses by the time I came along.

This instilled in Oliver a feeling of futility and insignificance. Although he felt closer to his father than to his mother, as his father grew older he seemed to grow tired and become increasingly impatient with Oliver. Then, following a heart attack, he died. Oliver, who was 18 at the time, was home when his father was fatally stricken. He tried to revive him through mouth-to-mouth resuscitation, but this effort failed.

It had been Oliver's mother who actually ran the family business. She ordered the parts, made cost estimates, and billed the accounts. Oliver felt that his mother's major concern was his father. She was cold in the way that she dealt with her children in order to keep some order in such a large family. Oliver's mother felt that her husband had little commercial sense and that the family business was very close to failing. It required her efforts in order to make it a financial success. Although the family income fluctuated, her children were always well dressed and carefully groomed when they went off to school.

Oliver was brought up in the charge of his older sisters: "My siblings ran the house and my parents ran the business." He describes his relationship to his parents as "distant":

> I don't think my parents had time with the number of kids they had plus the worries of the business. So there was strong competition among us kids for whatever affection we could get.

Oliver attended a parochial school from grades 1 through 8:

> The school was over a mile from home, and I had to walk through a pretty rough neighborhood. A bunch of tough kids used to pick on me because of my short stature and mismatched ears, plus I couldn't fight well.

All my teachers were nuns, and the discipline was strict, although favorites were common. When I was in the third grade, I had a bad day: an older brother had just won a full scholarship to Harvard, and I found I couldn't concentrate; I feared that I would never be a credit to the family, and I still have nightmares about not finishing high school or college.

I was the shortest kid in school, and between the fourth and fifth grade I was found to be nearsighted.

When Oliver entered high school, he was administered an intelligence test and found to have an IQ of 135, which put him in the very superior range. All his grades in school were A's and B's, with a single exception: he got a C in Russian. He graduated in the top 10% of his class and scored above 700 in his college entrance exams. Oliver was described as being very bright and academically superior. He was regarded as having well-rounded abilities, with a special interest in the area of research physics. His high school file indicated that he had been accepted at a major engineering school in the East. It also noted that he had missed the school year of 1960–1961. He had been arrested and charged with assault with a deadly weapon. He was 16 years old, and, although no one suspected it then, he was already a murderer.

The incident that interrupted his schooling was an intended kidnap and rape. Oliver had taken his father's van and had decided to go out in search of a girl to have sex with. He had with him what he referred to as his "rape kit," which contained a sawed-off shotgun, two pairs of handcuffs, some sections of rope, gags, and a .32 caliber revolver:

> It was set up as an off-the-street kidnapping. I selected a number of victims. I believe it was the fifth or sixth one that chose to walk down a somewhat less than brightly lit street, more deserted than the others had been, better timing—little variables. When she came within five feet of the van, I stepped out in front of her, pointed my gun at her and told her to get into the van. She panicked and started screaming and tried to claw at me. I fired a number of times, completely wild, and one bullet went through her neck. She fell. I scrambled into the truck, peeled out, sideswiped a car, got a goodly distance away, and disposed of my "kit." At that point, I realized that since my father's name was all over the van, it wasn't going to be too much of a problem for the police to track me down, so I returned to the scene.

The police immediately apprehended him, and Oliver pulled his coat over his head and said, "I did it." His victim, a 30-year-old woman, had been rushed to a nearby hospital. Oliver was brought to the emergency room, where she identified him:

> Then I was taken to the police station. My mother and father were notified and came to the station with their attorney, a friend of the family. I was released into their custody with some thought that I would continue with school, which was a farce, because I wasn't ready for it. After three or four weeks, it was arranged that I be committed to a local state hospital.

Court action against Oliver was postponed so that he could receive psychiatric treatment. His hospital records indicate that he talked about his feelings of inferiority and inadequacy. It was also noted that he did not show any remorse for his criminal act. However, when he would talk about his father, he would become emotional and burst into tears. After six months, Oliver's condition was considered improved, and he was discharged with the recommendation that he continue to receive outpatient psychotherapy. After another six months, his charges were nolled:

> I knew before I left the hospital that I was not straight, that despite all that was available there, nobody was sharp enough to pick up my secret. And I didn't want anyone to learn my secret.

Oliver grew up in a home where any mention of sex was forbidden. Although bright in other respects, he remained sexually naive and uninformed. His parochial schooling instilled in him the attitude that sex was sinful and that girls were good and boys were bad:

> I was a very good boy until about 12. Then the change started. I caught a reflection of one of my sisters exercising in the nude. I was fascinated. Later, I bored a peephole through an adjacent closet to spy on her. Desire for information led me to search my mother's bureau and commit housebreaks looking for women's apparel— shoes, girdles, bras, panties—and I would wear them, trying to discover some secret. I would cut out ads for women's underwear from newspapers and magazines. I went from feeling unworthy to feeling evil, and I started shoplifting about this time.

What had been an interest in guns starting from about age 7, now, at adolescence, became an obsession with Oliver, and he began to collect guns and to learn how to use them:

I became good with a gun and used to practice by shooting at my image in the mirror with wax bullets.

My guilt about sex was followed by a sense of persecution, leading to thoughts of revenge, and by the age of 14, I began to fantasize about committing a rape. I would read crime magazines and save the somewhat obscene covers, pictures of bound female victims who were exposed and in no position to fight back. The stories were pretty graphic, and they got very descriptive about the way the offender would wipe out his victim.

I really didn't know anything about sex, and I didn't dare ask, so somewhere the thought came to me that one way of finding out would be to grab a kid. I spotted a girl and a boy about the age of 8 or 9 walking together, so I put on a disguise (airplane goggles, a cap, and a pair of gloves), and I jumped them and tried to drag them into the woods. They struggled, broke free, and got away, and I got rid of the disguise. As I left the area, a police car passed me with the two kids in the back seat, but they didn't recognize me. I was never caught, and there was no suspicion.

I felt that bringing up sex-related matters at home, in school, or with friends would result in instant retribution, whereas committing a crime was something you might get away with. To further my fantasies, I stole a revolver, got some handcuffs, and bought a tear-gas pen. A month and a half before my 16th birthday, I pulled the gun on a woman who was parked in a picnic rest area. I had been bicycling and saw her and decided this was it. She was about 21 or 22 years old. I engaged her in conversation, pretending to be lost. Then I pulled the gun and froze. I was in fact terrified of what I was doing. She made a mistake, thinking I wanted her out of the car, and she swung the car door open. It struck me, and I just started shooting. The situation was out of my control. I shot her four times—the final shot was an act of mercy, because there was no doubt that she was going to die. I fired the last shot into her temple. She started to fall out of the car, and I had to make sure she stayed in the car, because I was interested in giving myself getaway time. I got on my bike and rode to a reservoir, where I got rid of the gun and washed my shirt, which was covered with blood. The panic subsided, and I was able to lead an overcontrolled life that was essentially espionage, being in an enemy camp. I kept good track of the case in the newspapers. I was very much interested in knowing what the media had to say so that I could be in a position to counteract being caught. I was anxious about being discovered and angry with myself for having fouled up the situation.

The next one, the one I got caught for, took place six months later. In all my offenses, I think there was a definite challenge to the authorities to catch me. Certainly, I was able to evaluate the risk of using my father's van, but, then again, it wasn't the sort of risk that was sufficient to prevent me from doing it. So whether it was a direct challenge, or a subconscious wish to get caught, or some other possible explanation, I can't be sure at this time—I know I felt more confident with each successive offense. My first arrest did offer the prospect of some psychiatric help, but any desire to get well ended when it became obvious how easy it would be to get out of the hospital—so I left without disclosing anything about the murder I had committed or the fact that I still was having rape fantasies. I knew I wasn't straight, but I managed to con myself to some degree, believing that I would check back into the hospital before I would let anything like this happen again. When it did in fact get serious again, I did not at all consciously consider readmitting myself, no way. This just did not occur—the thought just wasn't there. Basically, I don't think I ever was really serious about turning myself in to mental health or law enforcement authorities because I didn't really believe there was such a thing as help—I'm not sure that I really believe there's help now.

I left the hospital and went back and finished school, saw a shrink regularly, and lived without much terror or hostility until a civil suit came up during my first year at college, resulting from the incident where I shot the woman in the neck; that's when I went back into my "bag." The lawsuit upset me so much I wasn't able to study, so I dropped out of college and went back to the family business for a while. The sadistic fantasies and urges became much stronger than they had been for a long time. I returned to school on a part-time basis and kept telling myself, "I'll get through school, find a girl, get married, and the problem will disappear." That was a cop-out. It didn't work. I found a girl, a girl I loved and still love, and I intended to be open with her in regard to my past history, but I kept putting it off, waiting for the right moment. We married, and I stopped putting it off—I just decided not to open up. My wife was basically a very loving person but with a kick-ass exterior. She had no idea of how horrible I thought I was. My sadistic fantasies were extremely revolting to some of my sensibilities, and yet, in other respects, they were extremely pleasurable and satisfying.

I had a few opportunities for legitimate sex prior to marriage, but I was always scared to proceed. My wife had to coax me beyond heavy petting. I wanted it, but I was goddamn scared for myself and of hurting her. I didn't really trust women in the first place—women are particularly powerful in regard to sex, and they can turn on and turn off at a whim. They can use sex to take advantage and manipulate by granting or withholding or first granting and then withholding.

Marriage was no solution. Our sexual relations were satisfactory when we had them, but there were a lot of times when sex didn't interest her at all, and I never got to the point where I was able to admit my need for affection. Perhaps my wife was semifrigid, but I suspect a great deal of it was the way I was handling the situation. The only way any sadomasochistic urges entered into the sexual relationship with my wife was my occasional wish to wrestle. How-ever, she objected to that kind of nonsense, and if she got angry, it was a matter of holding her until she calmed down. I was scared she'd flip out. I have never struck my wife, not even a slap. In fact, as far as being angry, aside from slamming a door or pouting, I've never expressed my anger.

It was about 14 months after my marriage that the next murder went down. What precipitated it? In a short-term sense, nothing. In a long-term sense, getting to the point where it was either suicide or do it. My wife was working and loved her job. I was unemployed and couldn't find work. I was trying to scramble through college, but I screwed up because of some language credits. My car broke down, and I had to spend time I should have used for studying to fix it. I'm reasonably good at feeling sorry for myself and blaming my troubles on others. It started to pile up, and suddenly I was on overload and crashed to a certain extent.

I went out looking for a victim. Sometimes I couldn't find one. Other times, I did but managed to avoid doing it. Then, the right time, the right place, the kit, and the right person, a hitchhiker. I picked her up and then pointed the gun at her and told her not to do anything stupid. I drove off the highway onto a dirt road and pulled over. She tried to talk me out of doing anything. I was going to tell her, "Do as you're told and you won't get hurt," but I knew that was a lie. So instead I said, "Shut up and do as you're told." I told her to put her hands out in front of her for the handcuffs, but she wasn't about to buy that. She was pleading and trying to bargain and made a move for the door. I sprayed her in the face with some tear gas, whereupon she turned around and came at me to defend herself. She was doing a lousy job of it—no way was she as strong as I was. There it was, the situation was out of control again, and I started shooting. I disposed of the body, washed the bloodstains out of the car, and tried to maintain a normal facade. I deliberately did not read the newspapers, which made it easier to pretend that nothing had really happened, although I knew it had.

I quickly became depressed, and my wife knew I was consider-ing suicide. She didn't know what else I was considering. The weapon I had used in the latest murder was still in my possession, and it was becoming very probable that I would go out again some-time very soon. I figured the only way to prevent this was to destroy the gun. I took me 10 days, but eventually I did do it. Nevertheless, a month or so later, I was again out looking for another victim, but armed only with a knife, and it never came down, mainly because I was not sure that a knife was sufficient. I'm a real coward. So I bought a .22 and put a silencer on it. I was living on welfare, which, because of my middle-class ethics, hurt, and I was on a two-week spring vacation from school. Every day of that two-week period, except when my wife was home, like on weekends, I went out looking. There were a number of times when it got close. I had worked out the time I needed to find a victim, carry out the fantasy, and return to the house before my wife came home from work. And I found my last victim. She was thumbing a ride, and when I stopped she got into the car. I had an attaché case, my rape kit, on the front seat, and I told her to get into the back seat and attach the seat belt. I sped away, looking for a place to turn off. I found a side road. She was awfully surprised, and before she could think to undo the seatbelt, I had the gun pointing at her head and said, "Don't!" I told her to clasp her hands together and to hold them out in front of her. I handcuffed her wrists. At that point, I blew it, because, according to my plan, the next move was to open the passenger side door, still pointing the gun at her, put handcuffs on her ankles, and then take a cord and draw her legs and arms closer together—by the way, as I recount this, I find I'm getting an erection—then I would have gagged her and found a place to assault her. Instead, I climbed into the back seat and attempted to do that just by physical force alone. She had been talking to me during this time, trying to talk me out of it. I told her to shut up, and we fought for a bit, all the time I'm attempting to complete binding her up. It didn't work, because she was struggling, resisting any attempts, but, importantly, she did not *ever* attempt to hurt *me*. During this time, I clearly knew that the way to get cooperation was to hurt her, to inflict pain on her, but I found that I could not do it, despite my fantasy, despite all my hostilities. She was hurting from the handcuffs and from struggling, and certainly she was scared, but I couldn't hurt her. Why not? Either within the few minutes we had been struggling she had become a nonstranger, or perhaps I never could have hurt any of them. I had my thumb pressing against her left eye. If I had pushed she would have been in pain. I couldn't do it. I had my hands around her throat, and I wanted to squeeze and choke her, but I could not do that. I realized the situation was hopeless. Although I knew at this point that I couldn't hurt her, I decided to kill her. I picked up the gun and I pushed it up smack against the front of her teeth, and she knew that she was either going to die or not die in the next few seconds. At that point, she was not struggling anymore. She had given in. She would have done anything at that point to save her life, and she didn't think struggling was going to work. Logic saved her life: "If I can't hurt her, how the hell am I going to kill her." She was a remarkably cool young lady—damn good control. She didn't get hysterical at any point. I sat down in the back seat, and I guess I was in kind of a stupor. She asked me to take the handcuffs off her, and I gave her the key. I was resigned. She told me that she couldn't remove the handcuffs herself in a kind of snotty way. I felt a twinge of anger, but I undid her cuffs. We talked, and I asked her if she wanted a ride to the police station. She bargained for all the gear from my kit, and she left. I drove home slowly. I was scared to death, because my failure might drive me in the direction of harming someone else, someone very close to me. I wanted to be locked up quickly. I called my wife and she came home. I had already contacted my psychiatrist. My wife drove me to the hospital, but when I got there I was arrested.

Oliver was charged with kidnapping and released on bail. A police detective noted the similarities between the latest offense and the prior unsolved homicide, and a murder warrant was issued. Oliver admitted to all his offenses and then attempted suicide. He was sent to a security treatment center to await trial. In discussing his crimes, Oliver stated that they were all premeditated:

> Without a plan, one is likely to botch the job. I managed to botch it quite consistently anyway, but cold-blooded murder was always a part of all these plans. Murder is sadistic, and there's no doubt that I planned to be sadistic. The very thought of murder was appealing, even though I don't consider murder as evil as rape.
>
> In the first killing, I had an erection up to the point I fired the gun. I have no memory of ever having a legitimate, consenting sexual fantasy. Originally, the fantasy associated with my offenses was that sexual intercourse itself would be painful to the victim. After my hospitalization, it was much more the humiliation of than the pain of sex. I never found the fantasy to be convincing in reality. It was always a future-type want.
>
> I suspect a good deal of it was finding a scapegoat for my anger—anger at everybody and everything. Yet, no one had ever seen me angry—a little bit flustered and upset at times, but never angry. Aside from slamming a door or pouting, I've never expressed my anger. It came out in the fantasy, the power to hurt, taking out an awful lot of hate that I am unable to show otherwise, a combination of hostility and sexual tension. The picture in my mind was one of torturing a victim with everything from matches and cigarette butts to a propane torch, electrical stimulation, needles, and so forth. I picked strangers for victims. A complete stranger is less human than someone you know. The first victims were female, because I had an impulse to rape and hurt. The last three were female for rape reasons, but with more emphasis on hurting and humiliation. They were all shorter and lighter than I am. And, on a few occasions, there have been concepts of taking a "dry run" or a practice run using a small child as victim, male or female. The offenses were conceived as a safety valve. If I didn't have the safety valve, what the hell was going to happen? It's reasonably obvious that I hated my mother. Perhaps I still do. Yet, I long to feel loved by her. Actually, I'm kind of ambivalent toward my mother. The safety valve also

kept me from losing my mind. I've often wondered about how close the line is between reality and insanity, and I don't know why I've managed to stay on my side of the barrier. Sometimes I wish I hadn't.

As to the question of remorse, I'd enjoy being able to say that there wasn't any, just because that would make me more despicable. The truth is another story. I literally cannot pass the scene of someone in real trouble without doing everything in my power to relieve suffering or a risk to life and limb. My car is equipped with a rescue kit and a first-aid disaster kit. If I had seen somebody trying to do what I was trying to do, I would have at the very least disabled the vehicle they were using for that purpose, even if it took ramming. I would have risked injury to prevent their victim from getting killed or raped. I am one of the world's lousiest first-aid people, because I really cannot handle dealing with someone else's pain. But in an emergency situation, I'll do the best I can. Every one of those damn tools in my car were there because I ran into a situation where I needed them to save a life, or at least prevent additional injury. Now fit that all together and tell me what you have. I'm not sure if in my mind I can separate feeling badly about what I've done from feeling badly about what I am. Now I curse my actions, but I curse my actions in two ways: one, for what I had actually done, and, two, for what I hadn't done: I hadn't achieved what I'd set out to achieve. I still have the fantasies, and I've got enough curiosity to make me think it might happen again. There are already plans on the drawing board for the next time out.

I suffered long before I committed my crime. I've suffered since. If society is willing to help me straighten out my head, fine and good. I don't care how much pain. But, given the personality I've had and, to some extent, do have, I'm not sure that I really believe I can be helped. If I'm anywhere near the same me that I am now when I am released, I might just decide to strike again. I'm dangerous.

Victim Impact

The victim of the sadistic rapist may not survive the assault. For some such offenders, the ultimate satisfaction is the murdering of their victim, not only to eliminate the witness to the crime and thus avoid detection, but also because such killing is intrinsically pleasurable to them—"better than an orgasm," as one offender put it. An autopsy will identify sexual homicides by evidence of rape in some cases, of bondage or mutilation in other instances, and by "overkill" in still others.

When the victim survives the assault, her treatment needs extend beyond crisis-intervention counseling and usually require protracted and expert psychiatric care. The terror and horror of the assault may have been so overwhelming that the victim wished to die rather than endure it any further. Frequently, such victims express the fear that they will "lose their mind" or never fully recover from the impact of such an assault. Sometimes, the victim experiences a severe depression as an aftermath to the assault, and there may be a risk of suicide. If the victim has sustained permanent injury from the assault, this will continue to remind her of her nightmare experience. Some victims may adopt ritualistic behavior patterns in an effort to undo the trauma. For example, one victim who was run off the road, abducted from her car, sadistically assaulted, and left for dead found that she felt compelled to retrace the route she had been driving at the time over and over again.

INCIDENCE

In examining the incidence of these three primary patterns of rape, we find that power rapes constitute the most prominent pattern. More than half (55%) of the cases referred to us were primarily power rapes. Approximately 40% were anger rapes, and about 5% were sadistic rapes. However, since we were seeing primarily convicted offenders, this may very well be an inflated estimate in regard to the anger rapist and an underestimate in regard to the power rapist. Since there is characteristically more physical abuse in anger rapes than in power rapes, there is, relatively speaking, more corroborating evidence of assault and a greater probability of conviction in cases of anger rapes. It is our opinion, then, that power rapes, in fact, far outnumber anger rapes in our culture. The relatively low incidence of sadistic rapes is in sharp contrast to the amount of attention paid to such assaults in the news media. From Jack the Ripper to the west coast Hillside Strangler, the sadistic rapist appears to capture the interest and fascination of the general public. Probably, the very fact that such cases are rare and atypical explains the inordinate amount of attention they receive. However, it may be that the projected figure in regard to the incidence of sadistic rapes is an underestimate, since the sexual components in some murders may go undetected and the crime is not identified as a sexual homicide. Another possibility, that such offenders may not be convicted because psychiatric examination did not find them to be either competent to stand trial or criminally responsible for their actions at the time of the offense, was ruled out by a study of the types of sexual offenders committed to a hospital for the criminally insane. The types of rapists found in this setting corresponded to the distribution among types found both in prison and in a security treatment center designed especially for dangerous sexual offenders.

Resistance and Deterrence

One of the most frequently asked questions is: What should a victim do to deter an offender? Should she scream? Should she fight? Should she try to talk her way out of it? Should she carry a whistle or a weapon? It is not a question that can be easily answered. First of all, in many cases the victim may have no opportunity to attempt a defense strategy or maneuver. She may be attacked without warning. She may be at home, in bed, asleep, or she may be knocked unconscious. And although many offenders do report having been deterred from some of their intended assaults, there is a wide variety of individual differences among men who rape, and what serves to deter one assailant may only encourage another. For example, one offender said, "When my victim screamed I ran like hell." But another stated, "When my victim screamed I cut her throat." In discussing the issue of deterrence with convicted offenders, three common qualities emerged in those cases in which the victim had an opportunity to confront her assailant and to resist the assault successfully. First, she managed to keep self-control and refused to be intimidated. Second, she did not counterattack; she was assertive without being aggressive. And third, she said or did something that registered with the offender and communicated to him that she was a real person and not just an object.

Most offenders advised trying to talk the assailant out of the assault on the premise that even if this strategy does not succeed it does not create further jeopardy for the victim. They suggested that the victim capitalize on the offender's underlying sense of ambivalence toward the assault—something to the effect that "You know what you are doing is wrong, and it's not too late to stop"—rather than humoring him or being condescending. Obviously, what options are available to the victim are in part determined by the offender she is faced with, the situation she finds herself in, and her own physical and mental resources. Most offenders advised against the victim's carrying a weapon unless she is capable of using it and intends to do so:

> The minute you show it, use it. Don't just point it at the guy, because he'll take it away from you. He's desperate, and he's not afraid of being hurt. And he might use it against you.

Confronting the assailant with the enormity of what he is doing (asking him how he would feel if someone attempted to sexually assault his mother, his sister, or his wife) and the futility of his efforts (rape is not going to provide a solution to his troubles, nor will it be a satisfying sexual experience), as well as encouraging him to verbalize his feelings, may help to lessen his tendency to attack.

However, not all offenders can be talked out of an assault. In the last analysis, there is no one defense strategy that will work successfully for all victims, against all offenders, in all situations, and the goal of survival is more important than the goal of escape. It is for this reason that submission may be an adaptive coping strategy in some cases. Unfortunately, just as the victim is often blamed for precipitating her assault, she is also frequently faulted for not successfully deterring her assailant. Every strategy that has been used to deter an offender has succeeded in some cases and has failed in others. It is important to recognize that the victim did the best she could in the situation, and she should not be faulted for not having successfully resisted. There is no guarantee that any other strategy would have been any more effective in averting the assault, and it could have proved even more disastrous for her.

MULTIPLE MOTIVES UNDERLYING RAPE

Regardless of the pattern of the assault, rape is a complex act that serves a number of retaliatory and compensatory aims in the psychological functioning of the offender. It is an effort to discharge his anger, contempt, and hostility toward women—to hurt, degrade, and humiliate. It is an effort to counteract feelings of vulnerability and inadequacy in himself and to assert his strength and power—to control and exploit. It is an effort to deny sexual anxieties and doubts and reaffirms his identity, competency and manhood. It is an effort to retain status (in gang rape) among male peers, and it is an efort to achieve sexual gratification. Rape is equivalent to symptom formation in that it serves to defend against anxiety, to express a conflict, and to gratify an impulse. It is symptomatic of personality dysfunction, associated more with conflict and stress than with pleasure and satisfaction. Sexuality is not the only—nor the primary—motive underlying rape. It is, however, the means through which conflicts surrounding issues of anger and power become discharged. Rape is always a combination of anger, power, and sexuality, and each of these components must be examined in evaluating the offender and assessing the impact of the assault on the victim and the nature of her trauma.

Sexual assault represents a crisis for both the offender and the victim. For the assailant, it may result from a sudden and unexpected inability to negotiate life demands adaptively or from a progressive and increasing sense of failure in this regard. It may be symptomatic of transient and extraordinary life stresses that temporarily overwhelm the individual's ability to manage his life, which, under ordinary circumstances, is usually adequate, or it may result from a more endogenous state of affairs in which the offender's psychological resources are developmentally insufficient to cope with the successive and increasing demands and stresses of life. A crisis is precipitated when that individual begins to experience the biological, psychological, and social impact of adolescence or when he is confronted with the responsibilities and life demands of adulthood. His sexual assault is symptomatic of an internal or developmental crisis in the offender which, in turn, precipitates an external crisis for the victim. The assault triggers an acute disruption of the victim's physiological, psychological, social, and sexual lifestyle as evidenced by somatic problems, disturbances in sleeping and eating patterns, and the development of minor mood swings and fears specific to the circumstances of the assault.[1] The sexual offense, from this standpoint, constitutes a situational crisis imposed on the victim, and the impact of the assault may disrupt the bio-psycho-social functioning of the victim for an indefinite period of time. Tragically, her victimization often does not end with the assault.

The Case of Linda

Linda is a 19-year-old college student whom we interviewed slightly more than a year following her rape experience. She is small (5' 1" tall) and slightly built, and she wears no makeup. At the time of the assault, she could easily have been mistaken for a 15-year-old. She was wearing a rain poncho of a drab, olive-green color, with a hood, over her usual garb of blue jeans and a very loose-fitting, smock-type top. She was also wearing knee socks and heavy hiking boots with ribbed soles,

---

[1]Ann Wolbert Burgess and Lynda Lytle Holmstrom, *Rape: Crisis and Recovery* (Maryland: Robert J. Brady Co., 1979).

and she was carrying a green canvas knapsack, which held her school-books. Linda states:

> There was nothing, absolutely nothing seductive-looking about my appearance on that morning, as there rarely is. I don't wear a bra, but only because I am small-busted and don't need it and not for any other reason.

Her assailant was a man close to 6 feet tall, of slightly heavier than average build. He was home on leave from the Marine Corps, and his blond hair was cut in the old-style military crew cut. Linda describes the clothes he was wearing at that time as being of "hunting-gear" type.

At the time of the offense, Linda was attending college in a small country town. She lived in a farmhouse, about three miles from the school, where the basement rooms were rented out to college students. The morning of the assault, Linda was preparing to leave for school but found that her car would not start. Her landlord was away, and all the other students who lived in the house had already left for school. As she was sitting in her car, trying off and on to start it, she noticed an unfamiliar silver-colored car in front of the house, in the driveway. She also saw an unfamiliar young man going back and forth a number of times from the car into the house:

> This didn't really seem particularly unusual to me, because my land-lord had a bunch of kids, some of them of high school age, and sometimes there were people around there that I didn't know.

Linda left her books in her car when she went back into the house to call a friend, Mark, to see whether he could drive her to school. However, because of a storm the previous night, the phone had no dial tone, and she could not complete the call. The young man had noticed her trying to start her car and offered to drive her to wherever she had to go. Before accepting his offer, Linda asked whether he was a friend of her landlord's family, and he identified himself as a son-in-law:

> I knew my landlord had an older daughter who was married, that her husband was a Marine, that they had a little baby, and that they were home on leave and were staying with his mother. I was pretty familiar with the family. So I said, "Are you sure I'm not keeping you from anything?"

The man was holding a hunting rifle, which he apparently had got from the storage room, explained that he was just going to go hunting, and insisted that it really wouldn't be much out of his way to drive her to school first. Linda left the house through the basement door, got her bag of books from her own car, and climbed into the silver-colored car. The man, in the meantime, left the house through the front door, reaching his car after Linda was seated in it:

He got in his car, and he started it, and it started up, and I said to him, "Boy, it's good to hear a car start." And then we backed out of the driveway and started heading towards school.

These were very rural, kind of isolated dirt roads that you take towards the campus. We were going down this dirt road, headed towards the school, and we passed kind of a main street where there's a sign that says, "Towards College." And as soon as I saw that sign, he pulled out a gun and simultaneously said: "We're not going to school," and he turned the car around. I was really scared. At this point, it didn't seem real. I had been a little nervous along the way, because he was not saying much. It is only about five-minute drive to school, but just nothing was being said, and I was a little nervous.

When he pulled out the gun I was really scared. I had never seen a gun; I had never had contact with that. My verbal reaction was: "Oh, my God!" He had turned the car around and seemed to be heading back towards the house. And he said, "Do you have any money?" And I said, "All I have is a dollar, a dollar and a couple of pennies," and I pulled it out of my pocket, and I wanted to give it to him. And I said, "Wait, I have my checkbook with me. Drive to my bank, it's just down this road here, and I'll take out all my money; I have about $150; I'll give it to you, I'll give it to you, just take me there, I'll give it to you." And he didn't say anything, and that's when he pulled off to the side of the road, and he told me to get out of the car. I got out of the car, and I took my books—they were in a knapsack—I took my books with me.

He still had the gun pointed at me, and he led me off the side of the road where there was a field bordering a forest with lots of trees. He had the gun at me and just told me to come with him. At this point, I just knew what was going to happen; I knew I was going to be raped; I just had that gut feeling. I thought that I was going to be raped and shot and left there, and I think my biggest fear was that I was going to be dead in these woods, and nobody was going to know, nobody was going to find me.

We walked through the woods for about three minutes, until he led me to this place. With the gun pointing at me, and with this real sick look on his face, he said, "Take off your clothes." I was crying, and I took off my raincoat, and I took off my shirt. I wasn't wearing a bra, and I was standing there with my back to him while I was getting undressed. And I just began to unbutton my pants when he approached me and started feeling my breasts. I was crying, and I was frightened. He still had the gun, and he told me to get down on my knees. I was just going, "Please, no," and I was crying, "No, please," pleading with him. He unzipped his pants, and with the gun at my head, right at my head, and with his other hand pulling my hair, he had me perform fellatio, and it just went on and on, and he would jerk my head back and forth. During this time he said things like "Oh, you know you like it, you know what you're doing." And I was just totally nauseated and very frightened. He said things like "Gum it; suck harder," and it went on for a really long time until finally he ejaculated into my mouth. I felt really sick. It was dripping out of my mouth, and I was dirty, I was in the mud up to my knees.

After this, he told me, "Rinse out your mouth," in a sarcastic tone of voice. There was a puddle next to me, and I started to scoop up this filthy water and put it in my mouth, and he just shoved my head down into the puddle, and he held it there, and I couldn't breathe. I thought he was going to drown me, and I tried to resist, I tried to push up, but his strength was too much. Then all of a sudden, he just let go, and I was all right; I shouldn't say all right; I could breathe again.

Immediately after that, he flipped me over, kind of sat on top of me and started to strangle me, and I couldn't breathe again, his hands were around my throat, choking me. Then he just backed off again. I was crying, and I told him, "Please, don't kill me; please, don't kill me." That's all I remember saying; that's all I said. He told me to get up and stand against this small tree that was there, so I did that. He still had the gun this whole time. He took out this piece of rope and wrapped it around my throat and then wrapped it around the tree, and he pulled on it, and it slipped and scraped my neck. My throat got scratched, and once it slipped and he put it back again, and he pulled very tight. Again I lost my breath, and then he just backed off. He told me to put my shirt back on, and I did that. I was still crying, and I said, "Please let me go, please let me go, don't kill me, don't kill me." I said, "I don't know you, just let me go, I'm not going to say anything." He said, "You know too much." I said, "No, no, I don't, I don't know anything." He said, "Well, you know that I'm your landlord's son-in-law." And I said, "Yeah, but I don't want to tell anybody, I'm not going to say anything, I don't want anybody to know."

And at this point, I knew that I was lying, I knew that I was saying these things, but this bastard wasn't going to get away with it; I'm not the kind of person that could let him. So I was acting. And during this whole horrible thing I really felt like I was acting; I felt like I was playing a poor, unconvincing role, the words that came out; it was a feeling like I had stepped aside and I was watching myself go through this whole thing. And I kept thinking, "The tears aren't convincing, your words aren't right, it's not working out, it doesn't sound like it's real." I probably went into some sort of shock, because I really didn't feel like I was there; I didn't feel like it was at all real. I felt totally humiliated when I had to take my clothes off and perform that act. I wanted it to be over, and I think my basic concern was that I really wanted to live; I didn't want to die. He had the gun at my head, and I didn't feel there was any way out. I kind of felt like a little dog who had to do whatever his master told him to do. I had never been put in such a situation before, and I found it very degrading.

Afterwards I told him I was really embarrassed by what had happened, that I didn't want anybody to know and wouldn't tell anybody. I felt he was really kind of "off," unstable, I don't know the word; it was just the way he would torture me a bit and then lay off, and then do it again and be pretty inconsistent with that type of thing. I think finally he became frightened himself, and I think that's why he let me off. He said some very humiliating things during the attack, but afterwards he tried to be real chummy, and then he'd be threatening again, real on and off.

Anyway, he told me that I knew too much, and I said, "I don't know anything." I told him that I didn't know what kind of car he was driving, and this was a lie, because once he pulled the gun, I started taking mental notes about the whole scene kind of. I did notice what kind of car he was driving; I looked at the glove compartment and saw the name of the car written on there. I was like collecting evidence or something.

After a few minutes of pleading, "Please don't kill me," he said: "Let's go." I put my coat back on, and he still had his gun, but for the first time, he turned his back on me, and I noticed that he was wearing this gold hunting vest, and he had a hunting license on it, and I noticed the colors, which were white and black and red, and I noticed the numbers, I can't remember them exactly now, there was an x and a couple of zeros and some eights, and I tried to memorize that real fast. And he had put the gun in his back pocket, and I saw the gun had a brown handle.

He started walking into the woods with me, and he started asking me questions, like "So, where are you from?" And I lied; I gave him some fake city in the state. And he said, "Oh, what are you doing way out here?" And I said, "I'm going to school here." We were walking, but we weren't walking in the same direction as the car; I knew that, but I didn't know where we were going. I told him before this that he could blindfold me and I wouldn't look at the car and he could just drop me off at home, but this time, I knew we weren't even going back to the car, and I was really scared again. I didn't know what he was going to do until we started walking out towards a clearing and I saw the house in the distance beyond a large field of crops that grew behind the house. So he had brought me back towards the back of the house. He obviously knew his way around and pointed out the house and told me that I was lucky that he was letting me go and stuff like that. The last thing he said was "You know, you shouldn't talk to strangers. Didn't anybody ever tell you you shouldn't talk to strangers?" He also said, "If you tell anybody I'll kill you; I don't care if I go to jail; first I will come back and kill you." That was the threat he left me with, and it terrified me, it really did.

I just walked away, straight towards the house, I was really scared. I didn't want to turn, and I thought he was going to shoot me; my back was to him. I thought he was going to kill me right there, in the field, in the dirt, and I didn't turn around; I assume that he took off. I walked through the field and finally got to the house. I was crying, and I was dirty and wet; my clothes were all soiled and muddy, and I walked into the kitchen and went straight back through the hallway into my room and locked the door. And I sat down on the floor, and I started spitting into a kleenex and into my towel, and I took off my clothes and got into a robe. I was so scared, I was so scared that he was going to come back to the house. I didn't think that there was anybody home, but I kept hearing noises up- stairs, and I thought he had come back, and I didn't know what to do. I couldn't be alone. That was my reaction: I could not be alone, somebody had to know; I was too afraid to be alone there, I wanted to get out of the house. I looked at my clock. It was about 10:40 A.M. This whole thing, from the time I first went into his car until the time I got back to my room hadn't taken more than 20 minutes. It had seemed much, much longer.

Linda sat on the floor of her room, crying awhile longer. However, her fear of being alone overcame her fear of coming out of her room and using the telephone in the open kitchen area to try to reach help:

> I picked up the phone, and then I started to hear some noises, so I hung it up and ran back into my room, and I sat there crying and scared for about another 10 minutes, when I got the nerve again and went back into the kitchen and picked up the phone again.

Although the telephone had been out of order earlier in the morn- ing, at this time it was working, and Linda was able to reach her friend Mark, who lived in the area and was actually the boyfriend of Ellen, another woman who rented a room in the same house in which Linda lived. He and Ellen and Linda were all very close friends. Mark realized at once that Linda was crying and asked, "What's wrong?" but Linda felt that she couldn't discuss the situation over the phone and asked him to come over:

> I remember I really wanted to take a shower, I felt really filthy. I started to make myself some tea; I had this horrible taste in my mouth, and I put on the water, and about the time it was ready, Mark came over. I had locked the door. I unlocked it and let him in, and I said, "Mark, I was raped," and I started crying on his shoulder.

Mark was both shocked and sympathetic. Linda told him very briefly what had happened and who the assailant had been and that she was terrified to stay in that house for fear that he would come back and assault her again. Mark asked whether she had called the police. Linda repeated the assailant's threat to kill her if she told anyone, and she emphasized that all she wanted to do was to get out of that house as quickly as possible. At that point, the telephone rang, and it was Ellen. She was calling because she and Linda had planned to meet at school at 11:00 A.M., and she was becoming concerned because it was now 11:30 and Linda had not yet showed up. Mark did not tell Ellen what had happened but asked her to come home at once. While waiting for Ellen to arrive, Linda dressed in clean clothes, and when Ellen came in, Linda cried and told her what had happened:

> And she hugged me and cried, and then we left and went to Mark's house in his car.

At his house, Mark convinced Linda that the police must be notified, but she felt unable to make the call herself. Mark made the call for her to the state police, relaying the information to them as Linda told it to him, including a description of the assailant and the type of car he was driving. A police officer arrived at Mark's house about 10 minutes later. By now, Linda was calm enough so the officer could interview her in person while Mark and Ellen waited in another room:

> This police officer was really good, he was very good to me. He didn't insist that I tell my story right there. He said, "If you're not up to telling it right now, just sit here and relax." He told me exactly what was going to happen: that we were going to go back and get my clothes from the house, that we were going to go back to the scene of the crime, and that we were going to go to the hospital to

make sure that I was all right. I asked him if Ellen could come along with me, and he said, "Sure."

Linda and Ellen got into the police cruiser, and Linda states:

> My moods were real on and off. I would be feeling all right, and then all of a sudden, it would hit me, and I would start crying. Ellen was a real big comfort to me at this time. It just didn't seem real, it seemed like it was a movie, and it was a strange feeling.

The cruiser arrived back at the farmhouse, and Linda and Ellen and the policeman went inside. Linda collected the clothing she had been wearing at the time of the assault and put them in a paper bag and gave them to the policeman. The address of the assailant's mother, with whom he and his wife and baby were staying while he was on leave, was sent out over the police radio, and the house was staked out. Then Linda was taken back to the scene of the crime. When they arrived there, a police photographer took pictures of the tracks that had been made by the hiking boots Linda had been wearing at the time of the assault, as well as pictures of the tire tracks made by the car. However, it was later learned that the camera had not worked properly, so this evidence was lost. The police cruiser then drove Linda to the hospital:

> ... and this is probably one of the worst contacts I had with the agencies we had to deal with.

The ride to the hospital took approximately 40 minutes, and Linda and Ellen waited in the emergency room while the policeman talked to the nurse on duty. The nurse apparently advised him that Linda could not be examined at the hospital but would have to be taken to a private clinic, which was another 10-minute drive. Here the waiting room was very crowded, and Linda states:

> I was just a mess, really feeling like I looked like a mess, and really feeling like everybody in that crowded waiting room knew what had happened.

Linda and Ellen and the police officer were led toward an examining room at the end of a hall. As they walked down the hallway, a nurse coming toward them commented in a most insensitive voice: "Oh, two of them?" Linda found the callousness of the nurse very upsetting. While she was alone in the examining room, she heard the nurses laughing outside the door, and her thoughts were:

> "How come they're doing this; don't they know what just happened to me? Are they laughing at me?" I started to have another relapse, being very upset, and I started to cry.

At this point, Linda heard a voice outside the room say in a derogatory tone of voice, "Oh, another one?" This was said by the doctor who was going to examine her. She heard the policeman reply emphatically, "No, no, no, this is the real thing." The doctor's sarcastic reply, as he opened the door to the room, was "Oh, yeah!" Linda described herself as being "paralyzed with fear" that she was being so judged, sight unseen, by this man who was supposed to take care of her. She states:

> I really needed someone with a little bit more compassion to take care of me at this point, but I didn't get that.

When Linda told the doctor, who was a fairly young man, that she did not require a pelvic examination, that she had been raped orally, the doctor's reply was "Are you sure?" When Linda replied that indeed she was sure, the doctor merely repeated:

> Are you sure? Are you sure you didn't take your pants off?

Linda describes his attitude and questioning as extremely humiliating. The doctor dispensed with the pelvic examination and just swabbed Linda's throat and prepared to leave the room. He didn't examine her any further until she showed him the bruises and scratches on her neck, so he looked at those. He then asked if she wanted "aspirin or anything" and again prepared to leave the room. Linda asked, "What about venereal disease? What if I contact venereal disease?" Incredibly, his reply was: "Oh, just wait for sores to form for that." Linda states:

> I couldn't believe what he was saying. Even now, when I think about it, I can't believe it. What a sick answer. This man is a doctor. How could he say something like that? I could understand that not everybody gives preventive medication, perhaps he didn't believe in giving preventive medicine, like doses of penicillin, but his answer was just really so crude.

After the examination, the throat swab had to be taken back to the hospital for analysis, and Linda and Ellen waited in the patrol car while the police officer took the material into the hospital. While waiting, two women walked by the car:

> And one of them shook her finger at us, like, "Shame, shame!, what are you girls doing in a police car?"

While Linda could appreciate the fact that these women could not have known what had happened, their reaction again added to her feelings of being humiliated and judged, again being victimized.

When the police officer returned to the car, he explained apologetically that again they would have to return to the clinic because of some technicality with the paperwork involved with the examination. When they made this return trip to the clinic, they were again sent back to the hospital, and this went on for several trips back and forth, which was very upsetting to Linda. It seemed to her at the time that the people involved, who should have been committed to helping her, didn't really care that their carelessness in following procedural matters relative to this paperwork added unnecessary trauma to her ordeal. When all this driving back and forth finally ended, it was three o'clock in the afternoon, and the police officer took Linda and Ellen to lunch. Linda remembers, perhaps surprisingly, that she was able to eat lunch: "I remember I didn't lose my appetite."

Linda describes her basic concerns at this time as being centered on her need to have the assailant apprehended rather than concern about her feelings regarding herself:

> My basic concern was to catch this man; that's all that was on my mind; my own feelings just escaped me. I wasn't thinking about what had happened to me and what I was going to do next. My only thoughts were "Catch this man; you really must catch this man."

At this time, the police were very reassuring to Linda, promising her that if the assailant was still in the state, they would soon catch him, and that if he had left the state, then he could not reach her and could not harm her again. They further reassured her that since they knew his identity and had staked out his mother's house, where he was staying, there would be no problem in apprehending him. Linda remembers suddenly thinking at this time how frightening it would be for the 11-year-old daughter of her landlord if the police should suddenly appear at her door and start asking questions, and she hoped that the child would not be the one to answer the door when the police did arrive. Linda was also upset at this time because the police informed her that they had to give out the information regarding the assault to some reporters, and that it would be broadcast on the news at 6:00 P.M., but she was assured that her name would be withheld from the report at that time. Linda felt strongly that it was important that she tell her parents personally about the incident.

The police offered to call them for her, but she declined, feeling that the information should come from her. However, she did not yet feel up to making the phone call to inform them.

When Linda was brought to the police station after lunch, a police photographer took pictures of the bruises on her neck, after which she was introduced to Detective Johnson, the man assigned to handle her case. The detective did not strike an empathic chord in Linda. She felt overpowered by his extreme height and his overly quiet manner; both characteristics were somewhat reminiscent of her assailant.

Detective Johnson drove Linda and Ellen back to Mark's house, where they were going to spend the night. It was a 45-minute drive, and the detective spoke very little during the entire trip. By this time it was approximately 5:30 in the evening and getting dark. Ellen was sitting in the back seat while Linda sat in front with Detective Johnson, and she began to feel overwhelmed and frightened by what she perceived as this man's "mysterious" manner:

I started to feel that I didn't trust this guy; very scared of him.

Her fears, however, eventually proved groundless, and she feels that Detective Johnson really did work hard to help her prove her case.

At Mark's house, Linda found two other friends awaiting her return. One was Carol, another woman who had a room in the same house in which Linda and Ellen lived, and the other was Mark's roommate, Harry. The presence and the sympathetic reactions of these friends were an additional comfort to Linda. Linda and Ellen stayed to rest while the other three drove to the farmhouse to pick up some of their belongings, since none of the women planned to return to that house again. The two remaining students, although not close friends of Linda's, also moved out of the house immediately afterwards. At approximately 6:00 P.M., while Linda and Ellen were awaiting the return of Mark and the others, the police telephoned and informed Linda that her assailant had been apprehended. Linda reports that although this news greatly relieved her, the actual terror of the entire ordeal began to register on her consciousness at this time. She tried to call her parents, but there was no answer. She tried to watch television but could not concentrate. It began to appear to her and Ellen that the others had been gone much longer than necessary:

> We started to get scared about being alone in Mark's house. Even though the man was caught, we just felt that anybody else could just come and break in and attack us.

The others finally returned after what seemed an interminably long time. They explained that they had been talking with Linda's landlord and his family about the incident, and they reported that although the landlord believed Linda and felt very upset and sympathetic toward her, his children refused to accept the fact that their idolized "Marine-hero" brother-in-law could have done such a thing. Linda remembers feeling "shattered; really, really low," at the realization that there would be people who didn't believe her.

At approximately 8:30 P.M., Linda finally reached her parents by telephone. They were shocked by her news and wanted to come to her right away, which was at least a three-hour drive from where they lived. Linda reassured them that the assailant had been apprehended and that she was with friends and would be all right, and she convinced them to wait until morning. They agreed to wait but said that they would be there at 9:00 A.M., when Linda was scheduled to meet again with Detective Johnson. Try as she might, Linda did not sleep at all that entire night.

Prior to her parents' arrival the next morning, Linda felt that the worst was over and that she had a grip on herself. But when she saw them face-to-face, she broke down again. However, she did feel comforted having them with her. They drove to the police station, where Linda was questioned by Detective Johnson. Her story was tape-recorded, and through it all, for several hours, a bright light was kept shining in her face, which made her feel like a criminal under interrogation. She was finally dismissed but was advised to return at 3:00 P.M. that afternoon, at which time a lineup had been scheduled to see whether she could identify the man who had raped her. Her immediate reaction was one of terror at the thought of seeing him again face-to-face, but she was advised that the identification would take place through a one-way mirror and that the assailant would not be able to see her:

> It still freaked me out; that's all that was on my mind for the rest of that afternoon, the fear of seeing him again.

When Linda entered the room with the one-way mirror, through which she was to view the men in the lineup, she was given the incredible information that because her assailant had such a distinctive type of haircut, he would have to be disguised before she was allowed to view him. The further victimization to which Linda was then subjected defies all reason. Had the men in the lineup all been selected so that they all had blond hair with identical crew-cut haircuts, that would have been only as expected and within the rights of the accused. Instead, Linda was advised that the men in the lineup would be presented to her with towels draped over their heads. Despite this disguise, Linda was expected to make a positive identification of her assailant if her credibility was to hold up. Furthermore, the mirror through which she was to view the line-up was high up in the wall. Linda is 5' 1" tall. Although a chair or a stool could have been provided for her to stand on, this was not done. Therefore, in order to see through the mirror, she had to stand on her toes and hold her balance while the men, with their heads draped in towels, were shifted around in different positions. What she was confronted with, then, was the bizarre spectacle of five tall, powerful-looking men, any one of whom might be her attacker, all parading around with white towels draped over their heads—a nightmare in itself:

> I stood up on my toes to look, and I started to cry. It was just a shocking, horrible scene; five men with white towels over their heads, standing there, moving about, being shifted around, each one holding a big piece of cardboard with a number on it. I got very upset, and I started crying.

Needless to say, a positive identification under such conditions was not possible. Although the police tried to reassure Linda that the lineup itself "doesn't mean that much," since they had so much additional evidence as to who her assailant was, she nevertheless felt that her case was already lost.

That night, Linda returned to her own home with her parents. Apparently, her parents had informed several of their close friends and relatives of what had happened, and Linda was greeted with much emotional support:

> I just felt very awkward. By no means did I feel shameful or any-
> thing like that; I just didn't know really how to deal with it. I had
> a lot of close friends at home I really wanted to tell, but I didn't
> know how.

The following day Linda had her mother call these friends, and when they arrived, she told them in detail what had happened. She found that sharing this information with her close friends helped enormously. Linda also contacted a rape-crisis worker who helped her greatly in understanding her own feelings and reactions as well as those of people around her:

> I remember telling her my problems at this point were my parents,
> that my mother seemed to be constantly talking about the incident to
> people on the telephone. The rape-crisis worker helped me to under-
> stand that my mother, too, was going through a trauma, and talking
> about it was a need of hers at this time. So I grew to understand
> that, and that was all right. The worker also gave me some titles of
> books to read, and I became very interested in reading more about
> rape and showing some concern about self-defense.

While at home, Linda had a complete physical examination by her mother's gynecologist, who also treated her with penicillin to ward off the possibility of venereal disease.

Linda reports that her two brothers reacted quite differently to her experience. The older brother, who is five years older than she, is married and living in his own home: "He was really affected by it, I guess. He was crying." Regarding the brother closer to her in age, who was then 22, and from whom she had expected the most support, she seemed to receive the least. First of all, she was surprised to learn that he had several friends who had been raped. Second, instead of offering support, he seemed to dwell more on the rights of the defendant with which Linda would be confronted at the time of the trial, should she pursue the matter that far. Linda states:

> This is not what I needed to hear at that time. I know I had his
> support, but he just wasn't really on my emotional level, whereas
> other people were, and this surprised and disappointed me.

Linda's parents drove her back to school a week later. She felt ambivalent about returning but also felt that she had put too much work into her schooling not to finish out the one month remaining in the semester. However, she was frightened about returning to the scene of the assault and by the added pressure of finding a new place to live in the area. When she returned, she met with Detective Johnson and was informed that a preliminary hearing on her case had been set for the following week. She was also told that her assailant was free on bail:

> All of a sudden I wanted to turn around and leave. It really didn't matter how much people reassured me that he wasn't going to take the chance of making contact with me because he would lose his bail. I still felt very unsafe in that area.

However, Linda did stay, and she and Ellen rented an apartment together for the balance of the school semester. Linda's father drove up to school to be with her at the time of the hearing, and she was also accompanied by a counselor from the local rape-crisis center with whom she had made contact in the interim. Although Linda had not met with the prosecutor previously, she was scheduled for only a brief 20-minute meeting with him just prior to the hearing, which she felt was insufficient for all the questions pressing on her relative to the procedure and what would be expected of her. At her own request, however, this time was extended, and she was allowed 40 minutes in which she met with both attorneys. At this time, she was informed that she was going to be required to testify and to tell her whole story to the judge, that she would be cross-examined, that the defendant would be in the courtroom, and that she would be asked to identify him. After receiving these instructions, Linda waited outside the courtroom for her case to be called, and all her feelings of terror at the thought of again seeing the man who had assaulted her returned:

> I was really, really frightened about seeing this man again; I just did not want to see him, and I was a wreck. I had my composure about me, but I was very nervous in anticipation of seeing him.
> We were sitting outside the courtroom, and this man passed by, and I said to the rape-crisis worker, who was sitting next to me, "That's him! He's wearing a wig!"

The assailant had appeared for this hearing wearing a wig with long dark hair to cover his identifying short, blond haircut, and he was not asked to remove this wig during the court hearing. Nevertheless, Linda had no difficulty in immediately recognizing and identifying him.

During the hearing, Linda was submitted to the further indignity of the defense attorney's tactics. In an attempt to unnerve and disarm her, he used the tactics of pretending to be unsure of details, even going so far as to call Linda by the defendant's last name. His treatment aroused Linda's contempt rather than her anger, so that she did not fall into his traps, and she felt that the hearing went rather well for her case. What was damaging, however, was the fact that Linda's identification of the assailant at this hearing was disqualified on the basis of a bizarre technicality. At one point during his conversations with Linda, Detective Johnson, in his quiet way, had casually handed some snapshots to her without any comment at all. She immediately recognized them as pictures of her assailant and said so. It was now determined that having seen these snapshots "aided" her in identifying the assailant, which invalidated her courtroom identification at this hearing. The court ruled that Linda would not be allowed to identify the assailant during the actual trial, that identification could be no part of her case, and that the entire case would have to be tried on the basis of circumstantial evidence.

After this preliminary hearing was over, Linda tried to concentrate all her energies on finishing out the school semester:

> I was used to walking around by myself, and suddenly I was afraid to go anywhere alone, even driving. Somebody had to go with me at all times, even to the library on campus to do my studying. I was making a lot of demands on my friends at school, especially Ellen, to be with me at all times when I went somewhere. In fact, Ellen seemed to be experiencing the same reaction of not wanting to be alone at any time.

Linda realized that her demands on other people's time were unfair and should not continue, so the following semester she did not return to school, using this time, instead, to concentrate on coming to terms with her feelings. She did a great deal of reading about the topic of rape and felt that she was coming to a better understanding of the underlying dynamics of this crime. She feels that as a result of her new understanding, she was able to allow her feelings to begin to emerge:

> I was beginning to understand a lot of it. I was building up an anger, getting more in touch with my feelings on the whole subject.

Linda now began to feel a compulsion to share her experience with other people. Previously, she had talked about it with close friends, but now she began to tell others:

> I was telling more people about it, people that I normally wouldn't be that close to. I really felt it was part of me now and that it was having a direct effect on the course of my life; I was changing because of this experience. I also felt a kind of obligation to tell other women about it, to make them aware that it could happen to them, to urge them to be a little more cautious.

Linda finds that even today, a year after the incident, she is still often suddenly overcome with unnecessary fears. She did contact a female psychiatrist, during the semester she took off from school, with whom she met once a week, and she found these sessions helpful in overcoming some of her irrational fears. Some, however, are still with her. She drives alone now, but sometimes when she is stopped at a red light and sees a man sitting in the car next to hers, she feels panicky:

> If I have to park my car and walk somewhere, even in the daytime, I'm often very frightened the whole way in my car, just thinking about it. Then I always run to where I have to go. Then I run back to the car holding my keys between my fingers.

Although Linda could have made the decision to drop her case following the preliminary hearing, she made the decision to take the case to trial, despite the fact that she knew the experience would be extremely painful for her:

> This man had to be punished. He violated me, he changed my life; I wasn't going to let him get away with it. I didn't want to kill him, I didn't want him put away for life, but I did not want him to get off scot-free, because I felt he would just do it again; he's not going to understand that he did anything wrong unless somebody stops him now. And I felt that I had to be the one to do that.

While at home, Linda saw a male friend, Allen, who was in town for a visit. Although they were close friends, they had kept up only infrequent contact while Linda was away at school. Allen was the first man Linda "dated" following her assault, and she felt that she had to tell him about it. He was very supportive, and she experienced no qualms about discussing her experience with him.

The uncertainty of when the trial would come up now permeated Linda's life. She had planned to spend part of the spring traveling with friends but could not finalize these plans. Instead, she got a job as a cashier in a market and waited. She did accept a job as a camp counselor beginning at the end of June. Linda was really looking forward to this job, to the chance of getting away to an area of the country that she loved, away from all the pressures besetting her. She also made the decision during the spring to return to school in the fall. Her education was important to her in her future life plans, and she was determined not to let the rape experience disrupt her entire life. However, she did choose to transfer to a school in a different state, much farther from home:

> I think I really wanted to test myself, test my strength about being away and kind of facing the real world.

Linda describes some of her feelings and reactions at this time:

> The whole experience taught me a lot. I all of a sudden couldn't trust people. Not that I was necessarily naive before that point, but until I had this real contact with crime, a violent crime of this nature, I think that I was kind of oblivious to it. Now I'm very conscious of it; I'm reading about its happening all the time—rape seems to be an epidemic. Since that time, I've felt a need to do something about it, but I have to face it too. So, by moving away from all my securities, my friends, my family at home, it lets me kind of step into it alone. I just kind of felt like it was a healthy move, something that I had to do for myself. So I chose to go away to a school several hundred miles from home and in a different state.

The trial date was finally set for June. As the day approached, Linda felt that she was well prepared since all she had to do was tell the truth. She felt that she had gained strength through the ordeal of the preliminary hearing, and her background and upbringing in the beliefs of justice had not prepared her for the fact that justice does not always prevail. In no way was she prepared for the acquittal which followed the trial, even though she had tried to convince herself of its possibility:

> I found that there was no way, prior to the acquittal, that I could really prepare myself for it. I knew it might happen, but I couldn't anticipate the effect it would have on me: it was like a second rape; he got away with it twice. There was so much evidence that despite

the fact that I was not allowed to identify him in court, it still seemed like it was enough to convince anybody that he was guilty.

The day of the trial, the defendant arrived in full military uniform, looking clean-cut and impressive, with his wife clinging to his arm. He was a local boy, and his family and that of his wife were both well known to the rural townspeople. Linda, on the other hand, was definitely an outsider, a big-city girl from a relatively affluent background as well as a different ethnic background, and all these factors were emphasized by the defense attorney during the trial. Linda feels in retrospect that her composure during the trial had an adverse effect on the jury, who apparently felt that a woman who had been raped should be hysterical on the witness stand. She also feels that the appearance presented by her friends, Ellen and Mark, may have made an additional negative impact. They were "those college kids from outside," with long and somewhat unkempt hair and a different style of dress, with whom the local townspeople never seemed to feel comfortable:

> It just left me feeling so sick about the whole judicial system. Was the jury listening to the evidence that was being presented, or were they judging me on my composure and on my being an outsider and "different"? I suppose there's no way I'm ever going to know just what went into their decision. All I know is that there were about six police officers just loaded with evidence, and they had a full confession from the assailant that he gave when he was first being held. None of this stuff made sense to me; it still doesn't make sense to me, and it seems so unfair.

Perhaps one of the most upsetting factors in the trial was the fact that the defense attorney emphasized in his closing statement that Linda had not pointed out and specifically identified the defendant as her assailant, despite the fact that personal identification had been explicitly forbidden following the preliminary hearing. Although Linda's attorney objected, it is impossible to believe that an unsophisticated jury was not influenced by this argument, particularly since they were not informed of any of the factors in the preliminary hearing and were not told that a personal identification at this trial had been expressly forbidden. What effect, then, could the objection of Linda's attorney have had?

> I was left feeling very helpless. All I wanted to do was stand up and say, "He did it! He did it! I'm not lying! He did it, and it's your duty

to somehow make him pay for his crime just as it was my duty to
press charges!"

The trial went on for two days, and the jury deliberated for about
five hours and brought in a verdict of "not guilty." Linda's attorney, in
breaking this news to her and expressing his sympathies, commented
that this was the fifth rape trial in that county where the man was
acquitted despite the evidence pointing to his guilt.

Linda left the next day for her job as a camp counselor feeling
frustrated, angry, and bitter, but she felt that she had to hold in these
feelings since she was going to be working with young children whose
needs must come first. However, the day after she arrived at camp she
felt "really sick to my stomach" with suppressed rage and explained
what had happened to the camp director. She was given the day off and
contacted Allen, who lived in that area:

> Allen and I went to these falls, and I just screamed and cried and just
> let my emotions flow with the water. I cried a lot and he listened a
> lot. It felt a lot better to release the anger, but this second injustice
> that was done to me, this second rape, it just left me with this
> helpless feeling that still exists now, a year later.

After the summer, Linda involved herself in her studies at her new
school. She also became a volunteer worker at the local rape-crisis
center. She expresses great concern that despite the beginning progress
which has been made in the understanding of the crime of rape, not
enough people are aware of the problem except on a superficial level:

> Not enough people understand what rape is, and, until they do
> become aware of it, not enough will be done to stop it. I don't
> completely understand it yet myself. I've learned a lot more about
> the nature of the crime itself and the makeup of a rapist, and all the
> myths about who it can or can't happen to have been erased from
> my mind. But so many people still carry around those misconcep-
> tions, and, until they're made aware of it, nothing can be done. I still
> have the feeling that it can happen to me again; I'm walking around
> on guard 24 hours a day. It's not that this thought is always upper-
> most in my mind, but generally I feel not too safe. I can't walk down
> the street by myself without looking behind me every five minutes. I
> get this frozen feeling when some man honks his horn when I'm
> walking down the street, even in the middle of the day; if I pass a
> strange man on the street, I want to run. I'm really scared so much of
> the time, and that's kind of where it's left me now, a year later. It

made me realize, and I can't express this enough, how unfair it is to be a woman and of not being able to sustain my independence, not being able to walk around freely if I just want to take a walk. I'm particularly afraid to go out alone at night, even to a movie on campus, because something could happen on the way, and that's so unfair. I can't schedule night classes because of my fears. And guns terrify me now. I never thought much about guns before, but now even a picture of a gun upsets me. These are all new and real fears that I don't know I can work out, that I really believe I have to live with now. And then the whole thing about the court proceedings, and how trials aren't fair. It's a real, real helpless feeling. I can't stress that enough.

Linda now lives in a dormitory room at school. She keeps her door locked at all times and has told her roommate of her experience:

Her reaction shows me that she just doesn't understand it; there's no way I can get her to understand it. I've told her all the details, but she just has the impression that it's not going to happen to her, and she doesn't really concern herself with it much.

Linda tries to encourage those who will listen to her not to go places alone if rapes have been reported in that area and to have a possible plan of action in mind should they be confronted with such a situation. But she realizes that for most women, the feeling still is that it simply will not happen to them:

I guess until it happens to you, you just don't believe that it can or will.

Linda had planned to take a self-defense course when she enrolled in her new school, feeling that the knowledge and skill she would derive would give her an added sense of security, but she did not seem to find the time to fit this type of program into her busy schedule.

Linda did not suffer many physical reactions following the assault, aside from not being able to sleep for the entire night after it happened. She recalls no nightmares, her eating habits were not disrupted, and she was not given to hysteria or excessive crying spells. The basic and lingering reaction that she reports is her fearfulness:

I feel threatened so much of the time; it's really screwed me up emotionally as far as the way I can scare myself.

Minor noises, such as the usual creaking house noises that most people are barely aware of, cause Linda to "visualize strange men lurking around." Socially, disruptions have consisted of making her very distrustful of all unfamiliar males:

> The most important point I would like to emphasize, and I can't emphasize it enough, is that women must be made to realize that rape can happen to them. It was never too real to me before, and maybe it can't be until it actually happens to you, but I wish there was some way of making women understand the extreme ease with which they could become victims of this crime. I remember discussing an article on rape with a friend a few years ago, when I was 17, and of being very unsure of how to react in such a situation, whether you should scream and make a lot of noise and try to attract people's attention or whether to submit to get it over with as quickly as possible and then report it later. Every situation is different, but I think it's important for every woman to have at least a type of plan in mind of how she would react if it happens to her and also to have a few alternate plans for different situations. I know I didn't give enough thought to it prior to the attack, and neither did I read very much about it. Rape was just something that I knew existed but about which I felt only vaguely concerned. Again, it apparently can't seem real to an individual until it actually happens to her. My attitudes have changed, but my physical behavior is pretty much the same as before. I think only time will tell to what extent my entire life has been affected by the rape experience. I'll probably discover things from time to time throughout the course of my future life which I will recognize as a result of this experience and the long-reaching effects it has had not only on my physical being but also on my social, emotional, and sexual life.

Rape is a crisis both for the offender and for his victim. In examining the crisis aspects, we find the offender responding to an internal condition (failure in psychological control) and his victim reacting to an external event (loss of self-determination). Both are in a state of crisis and responding to stress. The offender asserts control and expresses hostility through his assault. The offense impacts on his victim in two basic ways: powerlessness and vulnerability. Persons who subsequently come into contact with the victim must be particularly careful not to compound the core issues underlying the trauma of being raped. It is crucial that the individual (police officer, examining physician, family member, etc.) not be angry with the victim for having been victimized, that is, not blame her for the assault. It is equally important that she be permitted to have as much opportunity as possible to be self-determining again and to have some say in the subsequent series of events, activities, and decision-making processes that come into play following the attack. By capitalizing on these opportunities, much can be accomplished in helping the victim to restore her sense of competency, adequacy, and self-worth. Failure in this regard will not only retard recovery from the psychic injury done the victim but will also compound and perpetuate her victimization more seriously.

In dealing with a rape victim, cues can be derived from the type of rape assault that has occurred, which should help the counselor to ascertain the most immediate, the most pressing, and the most disturbing aspects of victimization and can help guide the counselor into focusing on these target issues in working with victims. Some basic clinical knowledge about the men who rape may prove helpful in this respect. Just as it is important to dispel myths and stereotypes about victims, it is equally important—especially for the victim—to dispel myths and stereotypes about the offender, since such misinformation and impressions may reinforce fear and continue her sense of intimidation and victimization.

Clinical Aspects of Rape

In addition to the motivational factors underlying rape, there are a number of correlates to such behavior that need to be examined for a fuller understanding of the dynamics of the offender. What activates his assault? What determines his choice of victim? What is his subjective reaction to the sexual offense? In short, what are the bio-psycho-social components of his assaultive sexual behavior?

Sexual Dysfunction[1]

It is commonly—and mistakenly—assumed that men who rape do so either because they are sexually aroused or because they are sexually frustrated, or both. In fact, as we have seen, the motives underlying such assaults have more to do with issues of anger and power than with pleasure and desire. Rape is a pseudosexual act, a distortion of human sexuality, symptomatic of personality dysfunction in the offender, rather than a sexually gratifying experience.

This conceptualization is supported by an examination of the offender's physiological functioning during his sexual assault. If rape is symptomatic of psychological conflict and anxiety, it would be expected that offenders would evidence more sexual dysfunction in their assaultive sexual acts than in their consenting sexual acts. They in fact do. In our clinical work with identified rapists, we found that one out of every

[1]This section is an expanded version containing excerpts of A. Nicholas Groth and Ann Wolbert Burgess, "Sexual Dysfunction during Rape," *New England Journal of Medicine* 297, no. 14 (October 6, 1977): 764–766. Copyright 1977, Massachusetts Medical Society. Reprinted by permission.

three offenders reported experiencing some sexual dysfunction during their offense, and we believe this to be a conservative estimate.

Impotency

The ability to achieve and sustain an erection is a prerequisite for sexual penetration, and partial or complete failure is referred to as *erective inadequacy* or *impotency*. Masters and Johnson[2] subdivide impotency into (1) *primary*, where an erection for intercourse has never been accomplished, and (2) *secondary*, when there have been prior successful erections during intercourse. The offenders in our study fall into the latter category. Although they are not impotent in their consenting sexual encounters, they report having difficulty attaining or sustaining an erection during the assault. In some cases the offender must masturbate himself in order to become erect:

> I hit her and pulled her slacks down, and at this time, I found that I couldn't get an erection. So I tried to masturbate in every way possible, trying to get a hard-on, but I just couldn't, so I even had her masturbate me . . . you know, maybe arouse me some more, but I still couldn't. So I tried to penetrate her anyway, but I just got it in a little and then quit.

Other offenders describe what we term *temporary* or *conditional impotency*, since they find they are able to achieve erection only when the victim acts in some specified way. That is, tumescence occurs only when the rapist's victim resists him, or is forced to perform fellatio on him, or is subjected to physical abuse, and so on. Sexual potency is contingent upon such acts. The following case illustrates such erective dysfunction during sexual assault:

> I had been riding around, and I saw a woman sitting in the living room of her house. It had been in my mind to rob a place, and when I saw her, I thought of both robbery and rape. I broke in through the cellar and walked upstairs to the living room. She was sitting in a chair drying her hair. She asked me what I wanted, and I asked for money. She went into her bedroom and handed me her pocketbook. I had a knife. I put my hands on her and said, "I want you." I undressed her. She asked me about her kids asleep in the next room,

---

[2]William H. Masters and Virginia E. Johnson, *Human Sexual Inadequacy* (Boston: Little, Brown & Co., 1970), p. 137.

and I told her as long as she cooperated, nothing would happen to them. She asked me to put the knife down, which I did, and then I got undressed. I couldn't get an erection, so I had her go down on me. It ended up with her sucking me off, but it wasn't a normal erection and ejaculation. There was no sense of pleasure. In all my rapes, I never got hard until my victim serviced me orally, then I'd have intercourse with them.

Premature Ejaculation

Premature ejaculation usually refers to reaching a climax just prior to or immediately after achieving intromission. The variance among clinicians in defining this dysfunction is in the number of seconds following penetration before ejaculation occurs. Some diagnose premature ejaculation if it occurs within 30 seconds after penetration. Masters and Johnson include sociocultural components and consider a man a premature ejaculator if he is unable to control his ejaculatory process a sufficient length of time to satisfy his partner in at least 50% of their sexual activity.[3] We are dealing here with victims, not partners, so therefore the operational definition of premature ejaculation was a subjective judgment on the part of the offender: Did he find he ejaculated faster than usual and/or before he wanted to during the sexual assault? One offender described his experience in this way:

> I think I hit her once when she refused to take off her shirt—she didn't do what she was told. I was feeling nervous and shaky. I had her play with my cock, and after it got hard, I had intercourse with her, but this lasted a real short time. I came off real quick. Actually, when it came to having sex with her I was afraid, and I was embarrassed—I didn't feel I was worth a damn.

In addition to ejaculating quickly upon penetration, the offenders in some cases reported ejaculating during the assault but prior to any actual intercourse. We refer to such an experience as a *spontaneous ejaculation.* The following case illustrates this form of sexual dysfunction.

Bill, age 24, made sexual advances toward a 20-year-old woman whom he knew casually. She objected and struggled to free herself, but Bill choked her with his forearm until she almost became unconscious. He then undressed her and attempted to sexually penetrate her. His victim was not sure whether or not she had been penetrated, but Bill

[3]Ibid., p. 92.

reported experiencing a spontaneous ejaculation from the excitement of the assault, discharging partly on the victim and partly on the car seat:

> At first she was real friendly, and I got turned on. When I started taking the initiative, she got turned off, and I wasn't prepared for that. She started struggling with me, and I overpowered her, but I had some problems getting into her. I had only half a hard-on, because I already shot my load. I came off during the struggle.

Retarded Ejaculation

Difficulty in or failure to ejaculate during intercourse is referred to as *ejaculatory incompetence* or *retarded ejaculation*. In the spectrum of male sexual dysfunction, such retarded ejaculation is the reverse of premature ejaculation. In both conditions, erection is achieved, but the variance is in the amount of time required to elicit ejaculation. Masters and Johnson report that an incompetent ejaculator can continue 30–60 minutes of steady intravaginal penetration without climax.[4] The following case illustrates this type of ejaculatory dysfunction in a rapist.

Bruce, age 30, picked up a 26-year-old woman in a singles bar and drove to the beach, where he began making sexual advances. Bruce wanted to have intercourse, and when the woman refused, he hit her with his fist, ripped off her dress, and performed oral sex on her while forcing her to reciprocate. He then made her submit to intercourse. He later reported, "I felt numb... got nothing out of it. I kept forcing it, kept pushing, but couldn't come off." Bruce then sodomized his victim, explaining, "I kept trying harder and harder to have a climax." He swore at the woman and cursed her and repeatedly raped her until finally, after almost an hour, he abandoned the assault without ejaculating.

In some such cases the offender does not ejaculate. In other cases, he eventually does but only after prolonged intercourse. In some instances, following sexual penetration without ejaculation, the offender masturbates himself and ejaculates outside of the victim. Such dysfunction in some cases accounts for the offender's raping two or more victims in succession in the same offense and/or committing multiple sexual assaults on one victim during the offense.

Larry broke into a house and found the victim at home with her husband and two children. He locked the husband and children in a

[4]Ibid., p. 128.

closet and took the wife to a bedroom, where he committed sodomy on her and forced her to submit to genital intercourse.

He then sodomized her a second time. This lasted for about a half hour, and Larry threatened to kill her husband and children if she made any outcry. He then tied up his victim and searched the house for money. After a short period of time, Larry returned to the bedroom and forced her to have sexual intercourse with him again. He left the room a second time but again returned and made her take his penis in her mouth and perform fellatio for about 15 minutes. Following this, he then forced her to submit to intercourse with him, after which he again sodomized her. Larry then tied her to the bed, robbed the house, and left. Over a period of two hours, he had sexually invaded his victim seven times.

When the possibility of retarded ejaculation is not taken into account, the victim's version of such multiple and extended assaults may be greeted with doubts and skepticism. Police investigators, judges, jury members, and others may find it difficult to believe that any male could be capable of such extensive and prolonged sexual activity. Instead, the victim may be accused of exaggerating or dramatizing or even fabricating her victimization.

Our data indicate that approximately 34% of men who rape, or one out of every three offenders, shows clear evidence of some type of sexual dysfunction at the time of the offense, either erective inadequacy (impotency), premature ejaculation, or ejaculatory incompetence (retarded ejaculation). Since 20% of their offenses were incompleted attempts at rape, either because the sexual act was not one involving penetration, or the assault was interrupted by someone coming to the victim's aid, or the victim successfully resisted her attacker, the obtained incidences of sexual dysfunction during rape can be considered a conservative estimate.

Importantly, *such dysfunction appears specific to the assault*, since very few of these offenders complained of inadequate sexual performance in their regular and consenting sexual experiences with their wives or girlfriends. Only 25%, or one out of every four, of the identified rapists we worked with showed *no* erective or ejaculatory dysfunction during the sexual offense.

Incidence

Sixteen percent of the offenders experienced some degree of erective inadequacy (impotency) during the assault, usually during the initial stage of the rape. In contrast, Katchadourian and Lunde reported that erective impotence affects only about 1% of males under the age of 35 (the age range of the offender sample) and that such inadequacy is chronic and totally incapacitating in only a few of the men.[5] In comparing the incidence of impotency among the offenders on whom data were retrievable to the other forms of sexual dysfunction, we find it ranks first and constitutes 46% of the cases. Masters and Johnson also reported that impotency ranked first among 448 patients seen in regard to sexual dysfunction in consenting relationships, accounting for 55% of their cases.[6]

Five (3%) of the rapists experienced ejaculatory dysfunction in the form of a premature ejaculation during the rape assault. Katchadourian and Lunde pointed out the difficulty in defining a premature ejaculation operationally, noting that there is no absolute scale against which to evaluate male sexual performance.[7] To a large extent, premature ejaculation is defined on the basis of the person's subjective dissatisfaction. Also, it is more difficult to ascertain the occurrence of this type of sexual dysfunction than that of impotency or retarded ejaculation. The victim may not witness such reactions. We must rely completely on the self-admission of the offender. Therefore, it is conceivable that spontaneous ejaculations may account for part of those offenses in which there did not appear to be any attempt at penetration of the victim. However, even if this is so, premature ejaculation still ranks last among the types of sexual dysfunction experienced by the rapists, constituting only 9% of the cases. In the Masters and Johnson study, it ranked second, constituting 41% of their cases.[8]

Twenty-six (15%) of the convicted rapists experienced ejaculatory incompetence in the form of a retarded ejaculation during the sexual assault. This finding contrasts sharply with the rate of incidence reported in the literature. Katchadourian and Lunde stated that "failure to ejaculate is very rare and affects no more than one in seven hundred men of all ages."[9] Masters and Johnson encountered this form of sexual dysfunction so infrequently that they felt it did not warrant delimiting categories.[10] In contrast, in the offender sample, retarded ejaculation

---

[5]Herant A. Katchadourian and Donald T. Lunde, *Fundamentals of Human Sexuality* (New York: Holt, Rinehart, and Winston, Inc., 1972), p. 307.
[6]Masters and Johnson, p. 137.
[7]Katchadourian and Lunde, p. 307.
[8]Masters and Johnson, p. 92.
[9]Katchadourian and Lunde, p. 307.
[10]Masters and Johnson, p. 117.

was reported almost as frequently as impotency. It ranked second by only a single case and constituted 45% of the incidence of sexual inadequacy.

In the prosecution of a rape case, the defense often attempts to impeach the victim's credibility with the fact that her medical examination revealed no evidence of sperm. Representative of this type of situation is a letter we received from a prosecutor in Alaska who wrote:

> I recently had a rape trial in which the victim testified that she had been raped two times in a three-hour period, with no ejaculation from the assailant. Between these two assaults her attacker had forced her to perform fellatio, though no ejaculation occurred then either. The toughest part of the case was convincing the jury that the lack of semen was not dispositive.[11]

To complicate matters even further, although rape is a legal concept, not a medical one, we have found physicians at times overstepping their boundaries and concluding in their medical reports that the victim's condition was inconsistent with rape since, among other things, no sperm was found.

The absence of sperm does not counterindicate sexual assault. To the contrary, our data suggest that this absence is consistent with the nature of rape and can be expected to be the case in the majority of rape assaults. Only if one mistakenly assumes that rape is a supersexual, comfortable, and pleasurable experience for the offender would the absence of sperm appear puzzling—unless, of course, the offender wore a condom or had a vasectomy (and such conditions we found were almost nonexistent in our men who sexually assaulted adult victims).

From a clinical perspective, rape is in fact symptomatic of psychological conflict in the offender. Subjective emotional distress in the form of anxiety, rage, depression, and the like is more closely correlated with the psychological experience of rape than is sexual gratification. The absence of sperm in many cases of rape can be accounted for by the impact of the rapist's psychological frame of mind on his physiological functioning during the assault.

In gang rape, as well as in single-assailant rape, there may be ejaculatory dysfunction on the part of one or all of the rapists. The following victim account[12] illustrates sexual dysfunction on the part of all three assailants during the offense:

---

[11]Personal communication from Victor C. Krumm, Bethel, Alaska, October 17, 1977.
[12]Ann Wolbert Burgess and Lynda Lytle Holmstrom, *Rape: Crisis and Recovery* (Bowie, Md.: Robert J. Brady Co., 1979).

The first man took me into my closet, saying "he couldn't fuck in front of his friends." He closed the door and told me to spread my legs. I was shaking with terror and said, "I can't." He began to choke me and knocked the wind out of me and said, "Do you want to fuck or die?" He unzipped his pants and pulled out his penis, but it wasn't hard. That infuriated him, and he said, "If you won't fuck here, I'll throw you on the bed and we'll all have you." So the second one was now in the position to prove his toughness to his friends, and he said he would take me first. He unzipped his pants... he wasn't on top of me for long. He got up in digust and said, "I can't get off on this stupid white cunt." He zipped up his pants and walked off to the hallway.... The first one had his penis out, but it wasn't hard... he told me to put it in my mouth. The third guy got on me, ordered me to suck the first guy and to keep my eyes shut. He was on and off in a short time, and they all laughed at how fast he was. The first one told the others to leave and ordered me to manually stimulate him.

In this assault, each type of sexual dysfunction is exhibited: impotence (first offender), retarded ejaculation (second offender), and premature ejaculation (third offender).

It is significant to note that medical examination of a sample of 23 women who were victims of multiple assailants detected no evidence of sperm in half (50%) of the cases.[13]

Etiology

Masters and Johnson point out that human sexual behavior is a complex set of learned and instinctive phenomena which impact with hormonal factors, personality dynamics, and sociocultural influences. Sexual functioning, like any other physiological function, can be disrupted by physical and psychological stress.[14] The etiology of sexual dysfunction may be organic, psychogenic (intrapsychic or interpersonal), cultural, or some combination thereof. Organic insult and aging were uncharacteristic of the offender population. Physically, they constituted a relatively young and healthy group of males. The cultural attitudes and modes of the offender sample also encouraged and supported heterosexual intercourse as the only nontaboo mode of gratification. It

[13]A. Nicholas Groth and Ann W. Burgess, "Sexual Dysfunction during Rape," *New England Journal of Medicine,* 297 (October 6, 1977): 766.
[14]William H. Masters and Virginia E. Johnson, "Principles of the New Sex Therapy," *American Journal of Psychiatry* 133 (May 1976): 538-554.

therefore appears that the etiology of their sexual dysfunction may be understood as primarily psychological. The psychological causes of sexual malfunctioning, Katchadourian and Lunde pointed out, are innumerable and not specific to types of disturbances: the same conflict may cause sexual apathy in one man, impotence in another, and premature ejaculation in a third.[15]

In the Masters and Johnson study of sexually dysfunctional men, two major etiological factors of erective impotency were cited: a prior history of premature ejaculation and a history of alcoholism.[16] The former condition did not appear in the sexual histories of the offender sample, and although the latter condition does obtain, it occurs consistently for both the dysfunctional and the nondysfunctional subjects. Crider reported the presence of one or more negative emotions (hostility, guilt, anger) in conflict with the patient's sexual intent as an underlying factor of impotence.[17] This finding is consistent with our understanding of the dynamics of rape, in which sexuality becomes a means of expressing anger, power, identity, and status.

The psychological literature comments on the relationship of power and premature ejaculation. Salzman pointed out that

> The symptom may represent many aspects of a patient's problems, such as fear of feminine aggressiveness, unconscious jealousy, injured feelings, expressions of contempt, fear of women's genitals, concern over conception, etc., but operationally it is used as an instrument of power and manipulation in interpersonal relations . . . it appears to be present only in an interpersonal context where the participants are engaged in some form of struggle, whether for status, prestige, or dominance.[18]

There is a minimal amount of psychiatric literature on retarded ejaculation. Ovesey and Meyers related retarded ejaculation to rage, which they interpreted as being instantly mobilized by any threat to the rapist's concept of himself as a man.[19] Friedman cited a fear or a disinterest in women as a major dynamic underlying this experience which combines with various unconscious destructive dangers associated with ejaculation and which is followed by a fear of retaliation.[20]

---

[15]Katchadourian and Lunde, p. 307.

[16]Masters and Johnson, *Human Sexual Inadequacy*, p. 160.

[17]B. Crider, "Situation Impotence," *Journal of Clinical Psychology* 2 (1946): 384–389.

[18]L. Salzman, "Premature Ejaculation," in M. F. DeMartino (Ed.), *Sexual Behavior and Personality Characteristics* (New York: Citadel Press, 1963), pp. 317–319.

[19]Lionel Ovesey and H. Meyers, "Retarded Ejaculation," *American Journal of Psychotherapy* 22 (1968): 185.

[20]M. Friedman, "Success Phobia and Retarded Ejaculation," *American Journal of Psychotherapy* 27 (1973): 78.

In summary, the psychiatric literature relates sexual dysfunction to psychological mood states of anxiety, depression, and anger and to psychogenic conflicts regarding sexuality as something negative or dangerous and/or as a measure of strength, power, and adequacy. We view these same factors as underlying determinants in rape.

The underlying dynamics of sexual dysfunction in the rapist are consistent with and reaffirm our conceptualization of rape as a distortion of human sexuality. Just as the rapist's assaultive behavior reflects underlying motives of power (control) and anger (hostility), so too are these conflict issues expressed in the significantly high rate of sexual dysfunction that occurs in these assaults.

Conclusions

The medicolegal aspects of a physician's role in the treatment of the rape victim has been receiving increasing attention in the literature as there is more focus on sexual violence in our society. The medical record can play a crucial part in the criminal justice process, and thus there is a need for precise and objective recording of laboratory findings. From such data, interpretations are made to support or contest the allegation of rape. It is important to recognize, therefore, that in a large number of cases, sperm may not be present because of the high incidence of sexual dysfunction exhibited by rapists during the assault. Careful interviewing of the victim might explain the absence on this basis. The absence of sperm, in and of itself, does not contradict sexual penetration. We need to appreciate what happens physiologically in fact during rape to interpret more clearly what the results of a physical examination of a victim indicates—specifically, that negative findings do not counterindicate sexual assault and penetration—and to clarify the interpretation of negative findings in the prosecution of such offenses.

SUBJECTIVE RESPONSE

Rape is commonly misperceived as a crime of passion and is sometimes even believed to be a supersexual event. It is commonly assumed that the act of rape is a sexually pleasurable experience for the offender. And the rapists themselves—those who premeditate their offenses—similarly anticipate that the crime will prove sexually rewarding. In reality, however, this is not the case. For the most part, offenders report finding little if any sexual satisfaction in the act of rape. Their subjective reactions range from disappointment to disgust. When asked to rate the amount of sexual pleasure they experienced during their offenses on a scale of 1 (little/none) to 10 (extremely satisfying), the large majority of rapists gave the sexual assault a rating of 3 or less. Some offenders reported disappointment in that the offense did not live up to their expectation:

> It still didn't seem to give me the satisfaction I was looking for. I don't think I could ever define what I was looking for. I felt at the time that it was sex, intercourse itself, that there was somehow a way the woman could do something that would make it fantastic, but it was always the same old thing. I was disappointed and just that much more frustrated. It made me feel sick, because I went through all of this and to no avail at all. It disturbed me that I went to such ends and it didn't do any good.

Others reported ejaculating without orgasm:

> Right after I penetrated her I felt disgusted because, believe me, the girl was not attractive at all. It was just blah! I guess I was humping her for half a minute and then I rolled over. I shot my load, but I didn't get any pleasure out of it. I didn't enjoy it.

Still other offenders had no awareness of even ejaculating, let alone experiencing an orgasm:

> It was all so vague, and it all happened so fast. I couldn't say if I came off or not.

Some offenders attribute the lack of pleasure to the use of force:

> It was like animal sex, hard and rough, not gentle. There was no foreplay. I felt sick and disgusted about it after it was over. I knew this wasn't necessary. I was having sex regularly with three or four girls I knew at the time. I don't know why I did it.

Others cite being in a negative frame of mind and conflicted over their actions:

> I was in a big dilemma. I knew what I was going to do to my victim was wrong and I shouldn't do it—yet I was so angry at the world, at life, at women. I didn't want to do it and I wanted to. The anger won out. I finally managed to get it up. I masturbated myself and concentrated on her in a sexual sense. After it was over, I felt a big letdown. It just wasn't worth it. The sex wasn't any good at all,

and I didn't prove anything. I felt sick over what I did. I had the girl all shook up and bent out of shape. All the purpose that was there before the offense came down, what drove me to it, that was gone. We sat there for a few minutes. I wanted to say I was sorry—it was nothing against her—but I didn't say anything.

Some others found intercourse physically difficult or uncomfortable:

I found it hard to come off, because I couldn't penetrate her all the way. I did come off, but it took a while, and she kept asking me was I finished yet. She was dry, and the sex was no good at all.

Those few offenders who did rate their rape assaults as pleasurable generally cited nonsexual components of the experience as the reason for the gratification:

It was one of the most satisfying experiences I've ever had. I got more pleasure out of being aggressive, having power over her, her actions, her life. It gave me pleasure knowing there was nothing she could do. It like built me up. I had been driving around thinking about sex and searching for someone. I was looking for someone I could get my feelings out on. My feelings were a mixture of sex and anger. I wanted pleasure, but I had to prove something, that I could dominate a woman. I felt exhilarated during the rape. It was so intense that it took away from the sex itself. The sex part wasn't very good at all.

Some of the offenders reported that they had no memory of the details of their assaults or of their subjective reactions during the sexual acts.

None of the offenders felt that the rape experience was sexually more rewarding than their consenting sexual encounters. It was something they felt they had to do, and, even though it did not prove gratifying or fulfill their fantasy expectations, it was nevertheless something they found they would again contemplate carrying out:

I felt that I had to have it, just like a man who is starving to death feels that he has to have something to eat.

Conclusions

It is not sexual pleasure and satisfaction that leads to repetition; it is desperation. Not finding what it is he is seeking in the sexual assault, and unable to find it because he is looking to sexual activity to gratify a need or resolve an issue that is basically not sexual, the rapist becomes caught up in a self-perpetuating and self-defeating cycle of behavior. His sexual offense does not reassure him of his manhood, nor resolve the conflicts and resulting angers that he experiences in his interpersonal relationships, nor provide any significant amount of physical gratification for him. It may serve to discharge some tensions or frustrations, but this is only a temporary and transitory experience, and, in terms of physical sexual gratification, rape is no more satisfactory to the offender than it is to the victim.

INTOXICATION

Over 40% of the rapists we worked with had a history of chronic drinking, usually dating back to their early adolescence. About one-third of them were steady but moderate drinkers, and one out of four reported only minor or occasional alcohol abuse. As a group, then, these men tended to be relatively heavy drinkers, and in 50% of the cases, they had in fact been drinking and/or using other drugs (usually marijuana) immediately prior to their assaults. It was typical for many of these offenders to attribute their offenses to the influence of alcohol:

> It was a big accident, a big mistake. It wasn't planned. The condition
> I was in, I was drunk and didn't know what I was doing.

However, careful examination of those instances in which alcohol and/or drugs were associated with the commission of rape revealed that the amount of drinking and/or drug use engaged in by the offender at the time of his offense did not constitute a significant departure from his customary drinking or drug habits. As one offender succinctly described it:

> The rape happened on a Saturday night, and I had been drinking
> more than I should have—which is typical of me on Saturday nights.

The use of alcohol, in and of itself, is insufficient to account for the offense. Although some offenders were to some extent intoxicated at the time they committed their assaults, these same men were more often not sexually assaultive when intoxicated. Our data suggest then that alcohol may at most serve as a releasor only when an individual has already reached a frame of mind in which he is prone to rape.

Intoxication serves to reduce an individual's inhibitions, to impair such cognitive functions as reasoning and judgment, to distort his contact with reality, and to increase his insensitivity to the impact of his behavior on others. In this way, it may contribute to the releasing of rape impulses or assaultive tendencies in some offenders:

> My drinking was not to forget my problems but to give me the courage to do what I did.

Although alcohol and/or drug abuse may thus in some instances diminish an individual's rationality or bolster his assaultive urges, it is not what causes him to commit his offense. In certain cases, it may be a necessary component in the process that evolves into an assault. In other cases, it may serve as a catalyst in this process. But in still other cases, alcohol abuse and sexual abuse may constitute two parallel but independent symptoms of personality dysfunction. Here, the symptom of alcohol abuse would signify that a process of decompensation is under way in the psychological functioning of the offender. As one man described his experience:

> I had stopped drinking for a long time. I had my confidence back, so I went out trying to find work. You're supposed to be honest, so I told the truth—I was on a methadone program—and I was refused one job after another for a lot of bullshit reasons. I couldn't deal with that and got mad. I knew better, but I just picked up a drink and started drinking. I felt like a dog. I just gave up. I wouldn't go home, or to the methodone program, or to friends. I slept outside in cars and cellars. I just couldn't deal with anything. I went to a party. I was drunk and got mad there about something. I was just angry at everything. The last thing I remember is being at the party and then waking up in jail with the shakes. I had signed a confession that I raped a woman. I probably did it, but I don't know why. I didn't have rape on my mind. I never did anything like that before. I'm ashamed of what I've done. It makes me think I'm crazy. I know when I'm drinking I have a lot of problems.

Conclusions

In examining the relationship between alcohol/drug abuse and rape, we found no significant difference between the offender's characteristic pattern of drinking and his use of alcohol/drugs at the time of his crime. Although as a group identified rapists tended to be relatively heavy drinkers, this can be understood as an independent but parallel symptom of their psychosocial dysfunction. Some rapists are also alcoholics, but they do not commit their offenses only when intoxicated or always when intoxicated. For other offenders, the effect of alcohol may be to disinhibit underlying assaultive impulses. It gives them the courage to act. At most, however, alcohol and/or drug abuse plays a contributing role, not a causative one, in the commission of a sexual offense. It may diminish the offender's controls but never his responsibility for his actions.

Symptom Choice[21]

Rape is sexual contact without consent. Legally, it is a criminal offense, and clinically, it is a symptom of psychological dysfunction. Like the dynamics of any symptom, it serves to gratify an impulse, to defend against anxiety, and to express an unresolved conflict. One of the intriguing aspects about forcible sexual assault is the question of symptom choice. Why does sexuality become the mode of expressing power and anger and of discharging tension and frustration? What developmental factors or experiences play a part in the etiology of this form of sexual psychopathy?

Symptom formation is complexly determined and may involve such factors as genetic defects, constitutional vulnerabilities, parental deprivations, pathogenic family patterns, social pathology, and developmental traumas. In this section, the latter factor is addressed. Specifically, to what extent do sexual aggressors (rapists and child molesters) have a history of sexual trauma during their formative years?

Sexual trauma is defined as any sexual activity witnessed and/or experienced that is emotionally upsetting or disturbing. Evidence of some form of such sexual trauma was found in the life histories of about one-third of the offenders we worked with. This statistic appears significant in comparison with the finding that only one-tenth of adult males (nonoffenders) report similar victimization in their lives.[22] The incidence of sexual trauma appears to be consistent for both rapists and child molesters.

---

[21]This section is adapted from A. Nicholas Groth, "Sexual Trauma in the Life Histories of Rapists and Child Molesters," *Victimology: An International Journal* 4, no. 1 (1979). Copyright 1979, Visage Press, Inc. Reprinted by permission.
[22]David Finkelhor, *Sexually Victimized Children* (New York: The Free Press), 1979.

Type of Sexual Trauma

A little less than half (45%) of those offenders who experienced a sexual trauma during their formative years described being the victim of a sexual assault. As one child molester described his experience at age 5:

> I was walking down an alleyway in the wintertime when a drunk approached me and asked me about somebody who lived in the building. Then he grabbed me and tore the crotch of my ski-suit open. He tried to kiss me and play with me and get me to play with him. All the time, I was screaming, and he let me go when someone started coming down the stairs in the building. I ran home and told my parents, who telephoned the police. The police drove me around town for two hours trying to locate the man, but without success. Later that same day, however, I was walking downtown with my brother when I spotted him coming out of a store. I got scared and ran into the doorway of another store and hid in a corner. I was so scared I couldn't talk. I kept pointing. When the man disappeared, I got my voice back and told my brother that that was the man.

About one-fifth (18%) of the victimized subjects were pressured into sexual activity by an adult; that is, the adult occupied a position of dominance and authority in regard to the child and enticed or misled the child into the sexual activity. For example, one subject who raped an elderly victim reported that he was introduced into sexuality by his mother at about age 8. She would take him into her bed and have him perform oral sex on her. This involvement continued until he was 16 years old:

> I knew it was wrong. I didn't want that, but that was the only way I could feel close to my mother—the only time I felt anyone would touch me—so I did it. I gave in because of my need to have somebody in my life at that point. My father wasn't home much, and when he was home, he would beat me. My dad was a bum.

Another one-fifth (18%) of the subjects participated in a sex-stress situation where the anxiety resulted from family reaction to the discovery of the subject's involvement in sexual activity. For example, the parents of one subject had him circumcised at age 14 because "he handled himself too much," and in another case, the subject at age 13 was severely punished and made to go to confession when his father learned he had had sexual relations with a prostitute.

Some (3%) of the subjects witnessed upsetting sexual activities, usually on the part of their parents. One subject reported that when he was 5 years old, he would be in bed with his parents and they would engage in intercourse: "I thought my father was hurting my mother." At age 12, this same subject learned that his mother was engaging in sexual relations with a friend of the family: "I was disgusted with her, and I was really torn between wondering if I should tell my father or remain loyal to my mother." In a number of these cases, the mother was a prostitute or the father would bring other women into the house for sex, and, in one case, the subject's father was a rapist and would have his son take part in the sexual assaults.

A few (2%) of the subjects suffered some sexual injury or physiological handicap. One subject, for example, suffered from an endocrine deficiency. His testes did not develop, and no male hormones were secreted. Then, at age 12, this subject began to develop breasts and had to undergo corrective surgery. Another subject, as the result of a motorcycle accident, had to be fitted with a penile prosthesis since he could not sustain an erection.

In examining the relationship between the subject and his assailant, it was found that about one-half (47%) of the offenders who had assaulted our subjects were members of the subject's family: parent, sibling, or family relation. One-third (33%) were close associates: friends, neighbors, teachers, and the like. A smaller number (12%) were essentially strangers, and in a few (8%) of the cases—those involving physiological injury—this factor did not apply.

The majority (68%) of the subjects were victimized as preadolescents (before the age of 13), and, of this group, 15% were preschoolers (age 6 or less). Less than one-third (31%) of the subjects were young adolescents between the ages of 13 and 15. (Age of victimization could not be determined for one subject.)

Many (42%) of the assailants were adult males; a little more than one-quarter (27%) were adult females; 9% of the incidents involved a male peer; and 14% involved a female peer. Of the situations reported, 8% involved only the subject.

In examining the age relationship between the subject and his assailant, it was found that in one-fourth (23%) of the cases they were more or less age-mates; 18% of the assailants were 5–10 years older than the subject; one-third (37%) were 15–20 years older; nine (8%) were about 30 years older; and five (5%) were 40 years older. No data were available in three (3%) of the cases, and this issue did not apply in eight (8%) of the subjects.

For half of the subjects, the sexual trauma appears to have been a single event, but one-quarter of the subjects experienced multiple (two or more) but independent sexual traumas during their development, and another one-quarter were involved in an ongoing traumatizing sexual situation. In 9% of the cases, the subject was sexually victimized by more than one assailant at the same time; that is, he was the victim of a gang assault.

In contrasting the pattern of victimization for men who sexually assaulted adults with that for those who sexually assaulted children, the following differences emerged. The most prominent type of traumatic event for the rapist appeared to be a sex-pressure/sex-stress situation, whereas for the child molester it was a forcible sexual assault. More rapists reported witnessing disturbing sexual activity on the part of their parents than did child offenders. Although for both groups their assailants were mostly familiar persons, for the rapists they were predominantly family members, whereas for the child offenders they were not. The character of the rapists' early sexual victimization, then, was much more incestuous in nature (for example, see the case of Derek, p. 18), and females outnumbered males as their assailants. The opposite was true for the child molesters. Although the age of trauma for both rapists and child molesters was predominantly preadolescent, 40% of the rapists had reached adolescence when they were sexually traumatized, whereas this was so for only 25% of the child molesters. There did not appear to be any significant differences between the rapists and the child offenders with respect to the age disparity between them and their assailants or the duration of the victimization.

Two other clinical observations may be of some significance. In comparing those sexual offenders who showed a persistent and exclusive preference for children with those whose involvement with a child was a clear departure, under conditions of acute stress, from their preferred, adult-oriented, sexual relationships, twice as many (46%) of the former group reported being sexually victimized than the latter (23%) group. For those subjects who did not appear to have been victims of sexual trauma during their early development, a much larger number of rapists than child molesters had an older, more experienced, consenting adult partner initiate them into genital sexuality (intercourse).

Discussion

In examining the developmental histories of repetitive sexual aggressors (rapists and child molesters), about one-third of these men appear to have experienced some type of sexual trauma during their formative years. This may be a conservative estimate since such data were not retrievable for 12% of the subjects. Furthermore, when asked if they were ever the victim of a sexual assault as a child, a number of subjects gave the curious response, "It might have happened, but if it did I don't know it." They were unable to elaborate or explain why they felt this was a possibility. Also, since many of the subjects were undergoing evaluation for disposition of their cases, a number of them may simply have denied victimization out of concern about how such information might be viewed. In any case, for one offender out of every three, there appears to be a high incidence of sexual victimization, especially when compared to a nonoffender peer group. Although obviously not the only factor that may play a part in the determination of symptom choice, its significance should not be overlooked.

The predominant type of sexual victimization of child molesters was forcible assault, whereas for rapists it was a pressure–stress situation. The psychological impact of the former may be more one of fear (especially of adults) and of the latter one of anger. This hypothesis would be consistent with the child molester's turning away from adults and directing his interest toward children, who are safer and less threatening. Since rapists were victimized more by females than by males, this may in part explain the victim selection of women as targets of their hostile sexual offenses.

Although this investigation into sexual trauma in the life histories of rapists and child molesters is not a rigorous, highly detailed, and tightly controlled study, but more retrospective and reconstructive in design, its findings nevertheless encourage further study and warrant closer attention to several implications of these data: forcible, repetitive, sexual assault can be understood to be more a result of internal, psychological determinants in the offender than external, situational factors in his environment. The offender's adult crimes may be in part a repetition and an acting out of a sexual offense he was subjected to as a child, a maladaptive effort to solve an unresolved early sexual trauma. It can be observed, especially with reference to the child molester, that his later offenses often appear to duplicate the aspects of his own victimization, that is, age of victim, type of acts performed, and the like. Most of the professional work to date with victims of sexual assault has concentrated on the female victim. Our data underscore the importance of also attending to the sexual victimization of young males in order to better understand and assess the impact and consequences that such experiences may have. Furthermore, the results of this study would suggest that the incidence of sexual offenses against children perpetrated by adult women is much greater than would be suspected from the rare instances reported in crime statistics. Finally, in regard to the treatment of sexual aggressors and the prevention of sexual aggression, it may be that for identified offenders, one facet of their treatment–rehabilitation that needs to be taken into consideration is the assessment and treatment of unresolved sexual trauma. There is also, then, a need to train providers of social services to identify symptoms of sexual trauma and to develop and support victim service programs to provide therapeutic intervention in such cases.

Although the complex social problem of sexual assault cannot be reduced to merely the result and perpetuation of early sexual trauma, the sexual assault of children and adolescents poses an issue that should not be ignored and underscores the need of intervention services to prevent any long-range aftereffects, whether these be sexual dysfunction, sexual aversion, sexual aggression, or other nonsexual problems.

Diagnostic Classification[23]

In the realm of sexual behavior, the legal concept of *sexual offense* and the clinical concept of *sexual deviation* overlap, but they are not synonymous. A sexual offense is any sexual act prohibited by law. *Sexual deviation* is an ambiguous concept referring to a personal attribute in which there is a persistent preference for sexual behavior that departs from prevailing social standards. It is a condemnatory label connoting psychopathology. Although there are some sexual behaviors that are regarded as both offenses and deviations, such as sexual relations between an adult and a child, which constitutes the crime of carnal abuse–risk of injury and the deviation known as *pedophilia*, not all outlawed sexual behaviors are regarded as deviant or abnormal. For example, the crimes of adultery, fornication, or unnatural acts (i.e., fellatio) are not indicative of pathological sexuality. Nor are all unconventional sexual behaviors considered illegal. For example, fetishism, sadomasochism, and transvestism are not found in the criminal codes regulating sexual conduct. Therefore, the concepts of sexual offense and sexual deviation are not identical.

[23]This section contains excerpts from A. Nicholas Groth and Ann Wolbert Burgess, "Rape: A Sexual Deviation," *American Journal of Orthopsychiatry* 47, no. 3 (July 1977): 400–406. Copyright 1977, American Orthopsychiatric Association, Inc. Reprinted by permission.

Rape is recognized as a sexual offense, but it has yet to be officially listed as a sexual deviation. Probably because of the ambiguity surrounding the concept of deviation and the absence of clinical data pertaining to the psychology of rape, the rationale for its inclusion under the category of sexual deviation has not been apparent. Rather than being understood to result from inner psychological determinants within the offender, rape is more often viewed as the outcome of external situational factors. It is ironic that there is an abundance of psychological literature pertaining to what is essentially unconventional but consenting sexual behavior and a paucity of information about those forms of sexual behavior that jeopardize the safety of others.

Sexual Deviation

In our culture, a sexual deviation has traditionally been identified as any persistent departure from genital intercourse with a single partner of approximately the same age and the opposite sex. Sexual deviations have generally been defined in regard to a number of variables: the sexual object (e.g., pedophilia), the mode of gratification (e.g., exhibitionism), the intensity of the drive and the frequency of its gratification (e.g., nymphomania), and the context within which the impulse is aroused and gratified (e.g., sadomasochism). The concept of sexual deviation has become practically synonymous with the concept of abnormal and pathological behavior. The terms *deviation* and *perversion* are judgmental, disparaging, and stigmatizing. The human being is an adaptive and resourceful creature, capable of a wide variety of sexual behaviors and a broad spectrum of sexual expression and gratification. Unconventional sexual behavior is not pathological if it is consensual, and traditional sexual behavior is not normal if it is engaged in through coercion.

Rape is a legal term, not a diagnostic one. It refers to the crime of sexual penetration without consent. From a clinical perspective, however, the act of rape may be regarded as dynamically equivalent to a symptom in that it serves to express an unresolved conflict, defend against anxiety, and gratify an impulse.

Rape is a dangerous distortion of human sexuality. It is sexuality in the service of nonsexual needs. It is the sexual expression of needs or wishes that are not primarily or essentially sexual in nature and that jeopardize the physical and psychological safety of another individual. Rape is the sexual expression of hostility and aggression. It is a behavioral act, not a psychiatric condition. It is always symptomatic of personality dysfunction, but it is not in and of itself a diagnostic category any more than is, for example, suicide. At one extreme, the act of rape may reflect a transient reaction to extraordinary stresses that temporarily overwhelm an individual's psychological resources, which, under ordinary circumstances, are usually sufficient to negotiate his life demands. At the other extreme, the rape behavior may result from a more internal state of affairs in which the offender's psychological resources are developmentally insufficient to cope with the successive and increasing demands of his life, and a crisis is activated when this individual advances to an age where he becomes personally responsible for managing his life. The former individual has conflict-free areas of psychological functioning, whereas the latter individual has few or no conflict-free areas of functioning. In either case, rape becomes the symptom equivalent of his psychological distress.

In theory, anyone could commit a rape, just as anyone could, for example, commit suicide or go insane if the right combination of pressures and stresses impacted on him or her at a critical moment. However, for the majority of people, it would most likely require extraordinary circumstances for such behavior to occur. For example, it is conceivable that in warfare, under the stress of life-endangering combat, where the victim is perceived as a foreign enemy, and where hostility and aggression are socially sanctioned, a serviceman might commit a rape and yet never do so as a civilian during peacetime. Such an assault would be an exception to his characteristic behavior and would be understood as a temporary regression or decompensation under unique, external stress conditions to more primitive behavior. Similarly, it is conceivable that an individual might, under less unusual circumstances, commit a rape but, as a result of realizing its impact and aftereffect and the moral, social, legal, and psychological consequences of such behavior, self-correct and not repeat such an offense. Such a reaction would be comparable to that of a person who avoids again becoming intoxicated because of the negative effects of his first such experience.

In fact, although anyone might commit a rape, the majority of people do not. And, although some individuals may learn from experience and commit only one such offense, the alarming incidence of forcible rape in our society appears to be more the result of a core group of highly repetitive or chronic offenders than simply the accumulation of widespread but solitary events. For at the other extreme from the offender who may rape under extraordinary situational stresses is the individual for whom the ordinary demands of everyday life are stressful and overwhelming. This is the repetitive or chronic offender who turns to sexual assault as the means of rectifying or undoing his failure to resolve major life issues and cope with life demands in an adaptive fashion. Rape is symptomatic of defects in human development. Although there is a wide variety of individual differences among men who rape, there are certain general characteristics that men who are prone to rape appear to have in common. Although his cognitive abilities appear intact, his actual behavior appears inconsistent with his rational functioning. Although intellectually competent, he tends to exhibit poor judgment, especially when he is emotionally aroused or under stress. He does not anticipate the consequences of his behavior. He acts without thinking and fails to appreciate how his behavior is self-defeating. He does not seem to realize how he is mismanaging his life, how he is not acting in his own best interests, and how he creates situations that can only end unhappily for him. Or, if he does show some awareness of consequences, he seems powerless to change the course of events, to self-correct. Consequently, he fails to modify his behavior on the basis of prior experience.

Although his perception of reality is not distorted, his interpretations of his perceptions are. He tends to misread the feelings of others and to misinterpret their motives, largely because of his tendency to project his own characteristics onto others. He does not differentiate well among people or separate his own interests from theirs. He finds it hard to appreciate that other people may have needs, feelings, attitudes, and values that are separate and distinct from his own. Lacking empathic skills, he has no point of reference except himself and, consequently, attributes his own attitudes and motives to others, with the result that he feels threatened and victimized by them.

He tends not to be introspective and exhibits little capacity for self-observation. Insight and self-awareness tend to be lacking. He is not very much in touch with his own needs and feelings, and, except for anger, his emotional life appears impoverished. He is not comfortable with and does not know how to express tender feelings, such as warmth, trust, and affection. He seems to identify such feelings with weakness and tends instead to equate sex with closeness and personal worth. Yet, although sex may provide him physical satisfaction, it does not gratify his affectional needs. Emotions are troublesome for him. He tends to experience himself as being controlled by his feelings rather than being in control of them. He does not know how to identify his feelings or how to modulate or discharge them in an appropriate and adaptive fashion. Nor can he cope with frustration. He cannot delay or redirect his impulses but, instead, seeks immediate need-gratification. This behavior tends to interfere with his capacity to persist in the face of frustration and to pursue long-range objectives. He fears that formulating new goals will only lead to further setbacks. Anxiety and restless dissatisfaction with the existing circumstances of his life and/or with unfulfilled emotional needs result from a feeling of powerlessness. He feels menaced by his circumstances and helpless to remedy the situation. The use of humor to cope with life difficulties is noticeably absent.

The result is that his life appears to hold little pleasure and to offer few rewards. His overall mood state, then, is dysphoric, characterized by dull depression, underlying feelings of fear and uncertainty and an overwhelming sense of purposelessness and hopelessness.

At the root of all this are deep-seated doubts about his adequacy and competency as a person. He lacks a sense of confidence in himself as a man in both sexual and nonsexual areas—a feeling that is often unacknowledged since he exhibits little capacity for self-awareness. His tendency to take offense where none is intended, his defensiveness about his personal flaws or shortcomings, the premium he puts on toughness and strength, and the extremes to which he will go to avoid facing himself all seem to be efforts designed to counter painful feelings of worthlessness and vulnerability. Low self-esteem, coupled with a poor self-image and little self-respect, reflects a tenuous sense of identity. Since he does not value himself very much, he does not value others, and he then anticipates that others will not care about or be considerate of him but will, instead, exploit his unadmitted vulnerability. For this reason, he is apprehensive of being submissive, he finds inactivity bothersome, and he has difficulty in dealing with authority figures. Operating from the premise that others are his adversaries, he relates to them in a provocative and alienating fashion, which elicits negative and rejecting reactions from them that then serve to confirm his original presumption.

As a result, he has difficulty in establishing and maintaining intimate and mature interpersonal relationships. He is, by and large, socially insensitive, unaware, or indifferent to the feelings and needs of others and tends to see only himself and his own needs as important. Other people tend to be regarded as obstacles to be overcome or objects to be used or manipulated for his own need gratification. Qualities such as mutuality, reciprocity, and sharing are not prominent characteristics of his relating, and, consequently, he does not achieve close, stable, and enduring relationships. He tends instead to remain psychologically distant from others, a loner who has few real friends. Manipulation and exploitation are more characteristic of the way he negotiates his interpersonal relationships than reciprocity and sharing.

The result of such maladaptive attitudes and actions is that typically such an offender finds that he has achieved few or no genuine accomplishments in his life. He takes no pride in or finds little satisfaction in his work, in his recreation, in his possessions, in his relationships, and the like. Having developed few other avenues of personal expression, he attempts to rectify the situation, to establish a sense of well-being, and to ward off disturbing and painful doubts about himself through sexuality and aggression.

Sexuality, however, is also anxiety-producing for him. He tends to be sexually uninformed and may have experienced some significant and unresolved sexual trauma during his development. He himself tends to have a somewhat ambiguous or poorly developed sense of sexual identity. He is not a sexually comfortable and secure male. Instead, he tends to be handicapped by stereotyped impressions of what are appropriate male and female role behaviors and expectations. The feminine social role has a strong attractiveness in that the offender tends to perceive women as persons who are fully differentiated from others, able to take independent action, capable of handling disappointment, and stronger and more stable under stress than males. Negatively, women are perceived as seductive, depriving, manipulating, and powerful—even dangerous. He tends to dichotomize women into good and bad, virgins and whores. Good women are asexual; sexual women are no good. For males, it is just the reverse. They are dichotomized into strong or weak, "studs" or "queers," and his perception of the masculine role is one of incurring increasing and massive obligations and responsibilities to an extent that will prohibit any independent choice of activities. He sees his task as one of conquering women and competing with men. Moreover, he has adopted a value system that is highly conservative and confining in regard to what is acceptable sexual activity, but uninhibiting and nonconfining in regard to what is acceptable aggressive behavior. Such distorted attitudes and perceptions lead to problems in negotiating successful and satisfying sexual encounters. For him, a sexual encounter is getting something rather than sharing something. "I always thought sex was something you did *to* a woman; not something you did *with* a woman." Sexuality may be regarded as something basically impure, humiliating, and degrading, or it may be misidentified and equated with love and acceptance. The result is that sex may be used by him to agress against another, or it may offer him physical but not affectional satisfaction.

His tendency to regard others more as objects or obstacles than as persons, as symbols or stereotypes more than as individuals, serves to mitigate against a genuine sense of remorse for his offense. He characteristically employs a system of psychological defenses that serves to exonerate him from a sense of personal responsibility for his offense and allows him to experience himself instead as a victim of an unfair, uncaring, and hostile world. Projection, rationalization, and minimization are prominent defense mechanisms, and he tends to overemphasize what he perceives to be wrongs done him and to be relatively insensitive to the impact of his behavior on others. His sense of victimization, his reliance on sexual aggression as a way of counteracting his distress, and the failure of sexual assault to remedy the situation makes the likelihood of this individual's being a repetitive offender very high.

These are very general characteristics and not unique to men who rape, but they are characteristic of the chronic offender. The act of rape itself is complex and multidetermined. It cuts across the whole spectrum of conventional psychiatric nosology and can be found within all diagnostic categories.

Among identified rapists, neurotic reactions appear to be underrepresented, accounting for only about 3% of the offenders we worked with. Clinical evidence of some psychotic process operating at the time of the offense was apparent in 10%. The majority of offenders (56%) were diagnosed as belonging to various types of personality disorders (inadequate, antisocial, passive–aggressive, borderline, and the like).

Rape is a distortion of human sexuality, and it becomes a repetitive pattern of behavior when it derives more from the internal, psychological dynamics operating in the offender than from external, situational events occurring outside of him. It is here that treatment of the offender becomes a critical issue—incarceration may be necessary but, in and of itself, it is insufficient to reduce recidivism.

Patterns of Rape

The focus of this chapter is on major patterns of rape and the identification of some of their unique or distinguishing characteristics. In most cases, these characteristics are based on a systematic study of 170 men who were convicted of sexually assaulting adults and 178 men who were convicted of sexually assaulting a child and who comprise a random subsample of all the offenders we have worked with to date.

GANG RAPE

Although the majority of men who rape act alone in committing their assaults, in some cases the offender may have one or more codefendants who take part in the offense. Such assaults are referred to descriptively as *pair rapes*, if no more than two assailants are involved, or *gang rapes*, if three or more assailants are involved.

Norman is a 17-year-old, single male and an only child. Although he comes from an economically advantaged home, he is not close to his parents, who regard their son as stubborn and argumentative. Norman sees his father as irresponsible and promiscuous and his mother as distant and inattentive. His perception of other people is that they are there either to hurt or to gratify him. Norman himself is basically a loner who, with one exception, tends to confine his social relationships to female peers. He has a steady girlfriend with whom he has been sexually active. However, Norman finds that he is impotent following arguments with his girlfriend.

Norman's only male friend is Rick, a boy his own age, whom he has known for two years, and who is his codefendant in the rape of a 20-year-old woman. The offense occurred while Norman and Rick were out on a camping trip. On a number of previous occasions, Rick had expressed an interest in committing a rape. When they met a woman hiking along a trail, Rick found the opportunity he had been waiting for. He grabbed the woman and called for Norman as he and the victim began to scuffle. Rick wrestled the woman to the ground and ordered Norman to tear her clothes off, which he did. Rick forced the woman to perform oral sex on him and then ordered Norman to perform intercourse on her. When Norman hesitated, Rick called him "chicken":

> I didn't like being called "chicken," so I got undressed. I didn't have an erection, but I got in her anyway. She was skinny, and I didn't feel turned on. I was shaking and afraid of getting caught. Rick whispered to me during this that afterwards we would kill her. I didn't want to be thought of as chicken, but I didn't go for hurting her. After I climaxed, Rick had intercourse with her. When he finished, she ran naked into the woods, and I told Rick to let her go.

In a study of 348 men who were convicted of sexual assault, we found that in 30 (9%) of the cases, the offense involved more than one assailant. However, the greater the number of co-offenders who participated in the assault, the lower the incidence of such offenses. Twenty-four (80%) of these sexual assaults were pair rapes, in which the offender studied had one codefendant. Six (20%) of these sexual assaults were multiple-offender rapes in which the assailant studied had two or more codefendants, five (17%) of these men had two co-offenders, and one (3%) had three co-offenders.

The large majority (27 or 90%) of the gang rapes were committed against a single victim. In 2 (7%) of the cases, two victims were gang-raped, and 1 (3%) case involved three co-victims. The offenders ranged in age from 10 to 34, with the majority (77%) falling in the age range of 17–27. Most (26 or 87%) were white; 4 (13%) were black. However, all co-offenders in any given case were of the same race. The victims in all these multiple-offender assaults were white. Consequently, there were 4 (13%) interracial assaults. The victims ranged in age from 5 to 40, with most (23 or 77%) of them being in the 16–28 age range. Although in general these gang assaults tended to be peer rapes—the average age of the offender being 23 and the average age of the victim being 22—in 6 (20%) cases, the victim was a significantly younger person, a preadolescent child. The majority (26 or 87%) of the gang assaults were against female victims; 3 (10%) of the cases involved a male victim; and in one (3%) case both a male and a female were co-victims. Most (19 or 63%) of the offenders targeted complete strangers as their victims; the rest (11 or 37%) of the victims were known in some way to at least one of the gang offenders: 4 (13%) of the victims were casual acquaintances; 5 (17%)—all child victims—were friends; and 1 (3%) was a relative (wife). The assaults took place in a variety of locations, both indoors and outdoors, in rural and in urban settings, in isolated and populated areas, and it appeared that a vehicle (car, van, truck) played a role in a little over one-third (11 or 37%) of the offenses. At the time of the offense, all the offenders were actively engaged in consenting sexual relations. Half of the men were single and the other half were married, although eight of the married men were either separated or divorced at the time of their assaults.

In examining the dynamics of men who commit gang rapes, it becomes evident that in any given case, the co-offenders may play different roles and participate for different reasons. Although in a few instances it appeared that the sexual assault was a mutually arrived-at plan of action or decision, in most cases one of the offenders emerged as the originator of the assault. Of the men we studied, 17 (57%) were the instigators of the rape. It was their idea to commit the offense, and, typically, they took the initiative in raping the victim; that is, they were the first to sexually assault her. What role do codefendants play in the dynamics of such offenders? In part, they provided the offender with additional courage to commit the assault:

> Having a partner is like having something to drink. I felt braver. I felt stronger. This gave me the courage to do something I might not have done on my own.

Five (17%) of these offenders had codefendants who were accomplices to the rape but did not actively participate in the sexual assault of the victim. However, not only did none of these codefendants do anything to discourage the assault or alleviate the plight of the victim, instead they aided and abetted the instigator in achieving control over the victim. Their presence alone was intimidating—not only is the victim at a disadvantage in comparison to the physical strength of the men, she or he is also outnumbered—and, in a number of cases, the accomplice actively assisted the rapist by holding the victim or restraining her or him in some fashion. In the remaining 12 cases, the codefendants of the instigator also took part in the sexual assault. This feature of gang rape satisfies the need of the instigator to feel in charge and in control. It is an indicator of his power. Not only does he feel in control of the victim, he also feels in control of his cohorts: they are following his orders. He derives a sense of power from being the leader. He feels in charge of his codefendants as well as of the victim, and this reinforces feelings of strength and mastery. Interestingly, the majority (10 or 71%) of the 14 offenders who were instigators of a gang rape against an *adult* victim had at least one prior conviction for sexual assault. Half of these recidivists had committed solitary, or individual, sexual assaults on victims, and half had co-offenders participating in their previous offenses.

Thirteen (43%) of the gang offenders we studied appeared to be more followers in the offense rather than instigators. Although they participated in the sexual assault, their involvement seemed to be a response to the actions of the initiator. They reported that the offense was not their idea but that they were persuaded to go along with it. They were talked into it, pressured to take part, or forced to participate. In the dynamics of this type of offender, the presence of codefendants diminishes their sense of personal responsibility for the sexual offense. They may take part out of a sense of indebtedness or emotional dependency, or as a way of validating their manhood, or in order to retain membership in a peer group:

Kurt is a 23-year-old, white male. He is married and has three children. All his assaults involved his buddy, Pete:

> I always looked up to Pete and felt second-class to him. I felt I owed him and couldn't chicken out on the rapes. I worshipped him. He was the best fighter, lover, water skier, motorcyclist I knew. Taking part in the sexual assaults made me feel equal to him. I thought I was doing him a favor for all the good things he done for me. I didn't have any friends and felt like a nobody. He was five years older and was almost like a father to me. He brought me into his bike club. He made me a somebody.
>
> I'd go to a shopping center and find a victim. I'd approach her with a knife or a gun and then bring her to him. He'd rape her first, and then I would. When it came to my turn, I usually felt too frightened to get a hard-on, so I'd force the girl to suck me, and then I'd fuck her. Pete would watch me when I was having sex with the girl, but I never watched him. We raped about eight girls together over a four-month period. They were all between 16 and 30 years old.

Through participation in the gang rape, the follower seeks to find or confirm his masculinity, achieve recognition, and/or retain his acceptance with his co-offenders. In regard to the recidivism among this group, we found it to be only slightly lower than that evidenced by the initiators: six (67%) of the nine offenders who were followers in a gang rape against an *adult* victim had at least one prior conviction for sexual assault. However, five (83%) of these six recidivists had co-offenders in their previous offenses, and only one (17%) committed a previous assault on his own. In this latter case, the victim was a preschool child. Therefore, it appears that the majority of participants in a gang rape are likely to repeat their offenses irrespective of whether they are the instigators or the followers in the assault. However, the pattern of recidivism appears to differ between these two groups. The followers essentially commit sexual assaults only in the context of a gang, whereas the instigators are just as likely to commit individual rapes as they are to commit gang assaults.

The power factor appears obvious in the dynamics of gang rape, and the anger component may also be evident in some assaults. This is especially true where the offenders tend to view women as virgins or whores and believe that all females, once they experience sex, are prone to become whores. As a result, in some gang rapes each offender in turn becomes more aggressive than his predecessor and forces more degrading acts onto his victim, in part to prove his toughness to his cohorts, but also because it seems that, in his eyes, the victim is a whore because she is having sex with all the men in the gang. The fact that she is submitting under duress seems irrelevant. The fact that she is submitting sexually to a number of men confirms the offender's view of her as a whore, and whores are legitimate targets for abuse and mistreatment. They are to be punished for their sexuality, and sex becomes the punishment.

Vic, a 20-year-old married man, and two of his buddies were driving around town when one of the guys spotted a girl, age 18, named Kim, whom he knew slightly. They invited her to go to the beach with them, and she accepted. As they walked across the sand dunes toward the ocean, Vic said to her, "Now that we're here, we're going to have an orgy." Kim started to laugh, but Vic grabbed her by the shoulders and threw her to the ground:

> I told her we wanted to lay her and for her to take her clothes off.
> She agreed to cooperate, but I couldn't get hard, so I had her blow
> me. Then I got in her. I was the first, and then the other guys had
> her. I kept holding her down by the shoulders and knew that I was
> really mad. I thought she was a cock teaser, going down for every
> Tom, Dick, and Harry. Then I took her again, and when she pro-
> tested, I slapped her hard across the face a few times and called her a

cunt. I warned her that if she told anybody about what happened
we'd kill her.

Vic and his buddies left, and Kim contacted a friend who took her to her
doctor, who treated her for lacerations, bruises, and abrasions on her
face, neck, arms, and legs.

In another case, a 21-year-old woman was walking along the street
when she was approached by four adult males who grabbed her and
dragged her into a van. They drove to a deserted area, where all four
men started ripping off her clothes and punching her in the face and
body until she gave in. Then all four offenders had intercourse with her
a number of times. The driver of the van was the last to have intercourse
with her and asked her if she was enjoying this. She swore at him, and
he pulled her hair and punched her. Then he had sex with her again and
began choking her, telling the victim that "the thrill" was over and it
was time for him to kill her. At this point, the other three men took him
out of the van, and the victim managed to escape.

In gang rape, as in individual rape, sex becomes an expression of
power and anger to compensate for feelings of inadequacy, depression,
and vulnerability and to retaliate for feelings of humiliation, hostility,
and frustration. It is a multidetermined act. However, one of the unique
dynamics in gang rape is the experience of rapport, fellowship, and
cooperation with the co-offenders. The offender is not only interacting
with the victim, he is also interacting with his co-offenders. In fact, it
appears that he is using the victim as a vehicle for interacting with the
other men. He is behaving, or performing, in accordance with what he
feels is expected of him by them. He is validating himself and participating in a group activity. This is sometimes misinterpreted as an expression of a latent sexual interest on the part of the men in the gang toward
each other. In fact, gang rape does not appear to have any such hidden
meaning any more than, for example, two men who rob a store uncon-
sciously want to rob each other, or than a group of guys who go hunting
together have a latent wish to kill each other. For a number of men to
share a sexual activity with a woman (consenting or forcible) is different
from such men's wanting to have sex with each other. The former is a
social need more than a sexual need, and for men whose social skills are
deficient, an offense offers them one framework in which they can interact with others, compete, and validate themselves.

The offenders we saw who committed gang rapes, by and large, did
not exhibit much interest in the actual sexual activity or performance of

their co-offenders. In only one case, for example, did the codefendants participate in simultaneous sexual acts with the victim. In this single exception, one offender forced his victim to perform fellatio on him while his codefendant performed intercourse on her. In all the other cases, the sexual assaults were successive, each offender in turn engaging in individual sexual acts with the victim. In half of the gang rapes, the sexual assault by one offender was witnessed by the co-offender(s), and in half the cases, it was not. In these witness situations, it appeared that most such observation was more unavoidable than deliberate or intentional, as, for example, in a gang rape where one assailant held the victim down while the other had sex with her. In a few cases, there did appear to be some interest on the part of some offenders in watching their codefendant(s) and the victim engage in sex. Although it is difficult to ascertain that such interest is focused specifically on the sexual activity of the male, even if this is the case, to be interested in male sexuality is not identical to having a sexual interest in males. Men do not rape women out of a sexual desire for other men, but they may rape women, in part, as a way to relate to men.

In many cases, it is obvious that the offender wants to impress his codefendants and feels that they are evaluating his performance. One offender in a pair rape alleged the following:

> I'm balling her, and she says to me, "You're either good or it's been a long time since I've had it." I said, "Tell that to my cousin [the codefendant]." After we had her, we asked her who was the best.

Men compete with each other to win recognition and esteem. Similarly, criminals compete in antisocial acts, and, for the gang rapist, the sexual assault is the product of both internal motives and group dynamics.

In the cases of gang rape that have come to our attention, we have found all the assailants to be power or anger rapists. We have not yet seen a case of sadistic rape or mutilation-murder that involved codefendants. Such offenders appear to be solitary assailants. Gang rape also seems to be a sexual offense directed more against adults than against children.[1] It appears to be especially prominent among adolescents. Recent research[2] indicates that the rejection rate for complaints of gang rape is twice as high as for complaints of rape by a lone attacker. Since

---

[1] See the section of this text entitled "Sexual Abuse of Children," p. 150.
[2] Lorraine Clark, "Conference Focuses on Gang Rapes," *Sexuality Today* 2, no. 1 (October 23, 1978): 2.

sexual assaults by juvenile offenders tend to be taken less seriously than sexual assaults by adult offenders, it may well be that gang rape is more common than would be expected from criminal justice statistics. In any case, it would appear that age-mates, or peers, are more likely to be victims of gang rape than are significantly younger persons. In our sample of 30 cases of gang rape, 25 (83%) of the offenses were against age-mates and only 5 (17%) were against children. Relatively speaking, gang assault constituted 15% of a sample of 170 rape assaults studied, whereas it accounted for only 3% of a sample of child molestations studied. The few cases we saw involving adult offenders and a child victim were all pair rapes. All but one of these offenders had a previous record of similar offenses, and typically the codefendants in these cases were related in some fashion—in a few cases, they were husband and wife.

Hal and his wife Edna are in their early 30s and have been married for six years. Hal stated that he and his wife have had a satisfactory sexual relationship and that she became aware of his sexual interest in preadolescent boys early in their marriage. For the past two years, they have baby-sat for a boy named Billy and had him sleep overnight in their home. On these occasions, beginning when Billy was 8 years old, Hal brought the child into bed with him and his wife, exposed himself, and had Billy perform fellatio. Then Hal and his wife engaged in intercourse, and, after they were finished, he made Billy get on top of Edna, and she showed him what to do. On other occasions, Edna performed oral sex on Billy, and sometimes Hal tried to sodomize him. After each incident, Hal warned Billy not to say anything to anyone about what had happened or he would cut his throat. Billy ultimately disclosed these assaults when another young boy, who was being simultaneously victimized by Hal and his wife, reported the incidents.

One of the unique features of the sexual assaults against a child involving codefendants was the repeated victimization of the same child over time; subsequent offenses were directed toward the same victim. In contrast, in the cases of gang rape of adults, none of the recidivists assaulted the same victim. That is, the pair or gang targeted a different adult victim in each offense. There seems to be a stronger voyeuristic component in the pair sexual assaults against children. One offender closely watches the sexual activity of the child with his codefendant and sometimes photographs the acts. Also, the child victim is usually well known to the offenders and repeatedly victimized by them, whereas in the cases of gang rape of adults none of the recidivists assaulted the same victim.

In contrast to the offenders involved in the pair or gang rape of adults, alcohol or drug use played no part in the multiple assaults of children. Dynamically, there appears to be less a need for acceptance and approval operating in regard to the interaction between the co-offenders in the pair rape of a child and more investment in victim participation, response, and cooperation.

Conclusions

In cases of rape involving a single offender, we are faced with the dynamics of an individual, but, in cases of gang rape, these dynamics become compounded by the interactions among co-offenders. The anti-social behavior is given peer sanction, support, and validation. Unresolved life issues revolving around such needs as dependency, affiliation, peer recognition and esteem, and group membership and status become especially salient in gang assaults, in addition to the multiple factors typically underlying rape: power, anger, vulnerability, and the like. Sexual gratification is neither the motive nor the reward in gang rape any more than it is in rape by a single individual. More likely, a primary motive in gang rape is camaraderie with the other members of the group, and the sexual aspects of the crime are the means of such interaction. It becomes one way of relating and/or competing.

MALE RAPE

Introduction

Although an increasing amount of attention is being paid in the professional literature to forcible sexual assault with regard to both the dynamics of the offender and the trauma to the victim, this interest has focused almost exclusively on offenses against adult women and against children in terms of victim choice. Except for a few articles on the sexual assault of male inmates in an institutional setting,[3] there is almost no attention given to the forcible sexual assault of adult males. The litera-

---

[3]A. J. Davis, "Sexual Assaults in the Philadelphia Prison System and Sheriff's Vans," *Trans-action* 6, no. 2 (December 1968): 8–16; and C. Weiss, and D. Friar, *Terror in the Prisons* (New York: Bobbs-Merrill), 1974.

ture is silent on the topic of male rape in the community. The assumption appears to be that the adult male does not get raped unless he has the misfortune to wind up in prison, and that once he has reached adulthood, a male is safe from sexual assault.

Police statistics would appear to support this impression. For example, in Boston in 1976, out of 355 reported rapes, only four victims (1%) were males 17 years old or older.[4] Likewise, a survey by the Philadelphia WOAR (Women Organized against Rape) rape crisis center revealed that of 382 client contacts over an eight-month period in 1977, 22 (6%) of the victims were male, but of these only 1 (0.3%) was over the age of 16.[5] Yet, such statistics may be unreliable in trying to estimate the actual incidence of such offenses since, perhaps even more than women, the stigma of being sexually assaulted discourages men from reporting such events.

In our professional work, we have had some access to a number of offenders who raped adult males, or male age-mates, and to a number of victims of such assaults. In spite of the small number of such cases in our study, we feel that it is important to examine male sexual assault both in regard to the descriptive characteristics of the offense, the dynamics of the offender, and its impact on the victim in order to discover similarities and differences, if any, between male rape in the community as compared to male rape in a correctional setting, and in regard to male and female rape.

Information was obtained on 20 males who sexually assaulted other males and on 7 men who identified themselves as rape victims, for a combined sample of 27. The offender and victim samples were independent and unrelated. Information in regard to the nature of the offenses, the dynamics of the assailants, and the reactions of the victims were retrieved through interviews with the subjects and, where available, examination of their clinical records. The rapists were, with one exception, convicted offenders referred for evaluation. The victims were either self-referred or referred to us by police and/or hospital personnel. Of the men in the offender sample, 16 assaulted their victims in the community and 4 of them raped their victims in a prison setting. In regard to the victim sample, 6 of the men were assaulted in the community and 1 was

---

[4]P. Sadler, personal communication, Boston, 1977.
[5]B. Lakey, WOAR Data Report, December 21, 1977; personal communication, February 21, 1978.

raped while in prison. None of the offenders of the male victim sample was convicted. Data, then, were obtained on a sample of 22 cases of community rape and 5 cases of institutional rape.

Descriptive Characteristics

Age. The offenders ranged in age from 12 to 41, with an average age of 24 for the offenders who committed their offenses in the community and an average age of 21 for those who committed their sexual assaults in a correctional institution. Of these subjects 3 were juvenile offenders between the ages of 12 and 16; the majority (18 or 72%) were young adult males. These ages are comparable to those of men who rape women, where adolescence and young adulthood appear to be times of stress that activate the potential in males who are prone to rape.[6]

Race. The majority of offenders (21 or 77%) and victims (26 or 96%) were white. Five (18%) of the offenders and one (4%) of the victims were black. One (4%) of the offenders was Puerto Rican. Five (18%) of the assaults were interracial, and the victim in each of these cases was white. Two (40%) of the five institutional assaults were interracial, whereas only three (14%) of the community rapes were interracial. Again, these statistics are consistent with female sexual assault, in which the majority of cases are found to be intraracial.[7] Although our institutional sample was small in number, our findings were consistent with those reported by Davis,[8] who found that a greater proportion (56%) of institutional rapes are interracial, involving a white victim.

Social Relationship. The majority of offenders (15 or 56%) were total strangers to their victims. In one-third of the cases (9 or 33%), which, by definition, included the five institutional assaults, the offender and the victim knew each other casually. Two (7%) of the victims were raped by close friends; for example, in one case the assailant was the victim's employer; and in one assault (4%), the offender and his victim were brothers. Again, this distribution appears comparable to what is reported in regard to the sexual assault of females.[9] It is significant to note that this distribution is consistent for both the convicted offender cases

[6]R. Rada (Ed.), *Clinical Aspects of the Rapist* (New York: Grune & Stratton, 1978).
[7]See, for example, Menachem Amir, *Patterns in Forcible Rape* (Chicago: University of Chicago Press, 1971), p. 13.
[8]Davis, p. 15.
[9]A. W. Burgess and L. L. Holmstrom, *Rape: Crisis and Recovery*, 2nd ed. (Bowie, Md.: Robert J. Brady Co., 1979).

and for those in which the offender was not convicted, since it is sometimes speculated that the closer the social relationship the greater the reluctance to prosecute and/or the greater the likelihood of acquittal.

Access to Victim and Place of Assault.   In eight (30%) of the cases, the victim was hitchhiking, and the offender gained access to him by offering him a ride. In one additional case (4%), the victim was a passenger in his offender's car. In eight (30%) other cases, the victim engaged in some out-of-doors activity, such as swimming at a beach or hiking in the woods, when the offender approached him, and in two (7%) instances, the victims were walking along the street headed for a specific destination. Two (7%) other victims were gained access to in the offender's home, and five (19%) were housed in the same correctional facility (jail) as their offenders. One victim (4%) was a customer at his offender's place of employment (barroom).

The vast majority (24 or 89%) of the sexual assaults took place in the same locale that the offender encountered his victim, but in one case (4%), the offender accosted his victim in a parking garage, raped the victim in the victim's own car, then commandeered the vehicle and drove around the city with the victim held captive. In another case (4%), the offender encountered his victim on the street and forced him into a vacant building, where he sexually assaulted him. In a third case, one (4%) offender, after offering the victim a ride, drove him into a wooded area, tied him to a tree, and sexually assaulted him, then drove the victim to the offender's apartment and again sexually assaulted him there.

As in cases of female rape, men are assaulted where they live, work, travel, and relax. They appear to be at greater risk when engaged in solitary activities, are hitchhiking, or are in prison.

Style of Attack.   The offender gained control over his victim through three major methods: entrapment, intimidation, and/or physical force. Three (11%) of the offenders entrapped their victims by first getting them drunk and then taking advantage of the victims' intoxicated state to sexually assault them.

One victim, Bud, was at an office party and had too much to drink. His boss offered to drive him home, and Bud passed out in the car. A short time later, he awoke to find himself on the back seat of the car, completely naked, and his boss sodomizing him.

A more common style of attack, however, was through some sort of intimidation. Twelve (44%) of the offenders intimidated their victims into submission either by threats of physical harm and/or by brandishing a weapon.

One victim, Todd, was hitchhiking and was offered a ride by four men. He got into the back seat of the car, and, as they drove off, one offender put a knife to Todd's throat and told him he was going to have to give them all some "head," which he did.

An equally frequent approach was an unanticipated attack in which the offender approached the victim by suddenly striking or physically overpowering him. Twelve (44%) of the offenders employed this blitz style of attack.

Barry was asleep in his cell when he was awakened by his assailant, who said he wanted to do something with him. He punched Barry in the chest and stomach and knocked him to the floor. Then he picked him up, threw him on his bunk, held Barry face down on the bed, and sodomized him. When he was through, he called to another inmate, who came into the cell and also sodomized Barry.

Although it is commonly believed that a male is powerful enough to defend his sexual zones from invasion, he is, in fact, susceptible to the same techniques by which assailants gain control over their female victims. In many cases, a combination of entrapment, intimidation, and brute strength were employed in the commission of the assault, but there were some noticeable differences between the community and the institutional assaults. As might be expected, the use of intoxicants and weapons was confined to those assaults that occurred in the community, since such items are contraband in correctional settings and thus are less easily available. On the other hand, there was a greater incidence of codefendants (gang rape) in the prison setting: four (80%) of the five cases involved between two and seven assailants. Generally, the gang assaults were of single victims, but in one case, four inmates each committed multiple and simultaneous sexual assaults on two co-victims. In contrast, of the assaults that took place in the community, less than one-third (7 or 32%) involved codefendants, and in two (7%) of the community assaults, a single offender sexually assaulted more than one victim during the same offense.

Types of Sexual Acts

The sexual acts demanded of or performed on the victim were distributed as follows:

6 (22%) of the offenders sodomized their victims.
5 (19%) of the offenders sodomized the victims and forced them to

perform fellatio. In addition, in two of these offenses, the victims were forced to perform annilingus on their assailants.

2 (7%) of the offenders sodomized and masturbated their victims.

1 (4%) of the offenders sodomized and performed fellatio on his victim.

3 (11%) of the offenders forced their victims to perform fellation on them.

2 (7%) of the offenders performed fellatio on their victims and forced their victims to reciprocate.

4 (15%) of the offenders performed fellatio on the victims.

1 (4%) of the offenders forced his victim to masturbate him.

2 (7%) of the offenders forced one victim to perform a sexual act on a co-victim while the offender watched.

1 (4%) of the offenders sexually abused his victim and attempted to penetrate the victim with an instrument.

In 19 (7%) of the assaults, the offender sexually penetrated his victim in some fashion, whereas the offender accepted penetration in only 7 (26%) of the assaults. The most common type of sexual act committed during the offense was sodomy. In half (14 or 52%) of the cases, the offender performed anal intercourse on his victim. Fellatio was the next most frequent act. In over a third (10 or 37%) of the assaults, the victim performed oral sex on the offender. Obviously, differences can be expected between male and female rape in regard to the type of sexual acts committed. However, it appears that multiple sexual acts are demanded in a greater number (12 or 45%) of male rapes in comparison to female rapes, in which the sexual assault is frequently limited to a single act: vaginal intercourse.

Those offenders who raped their male victims in prison confined their assaults to the sexual penetration of the victim. In three cases, the offender sodomized his victim, in one case he forced his victim to perform fellatio on him, and in one case he penetrated the victim both anally and orally. This can be understood as an extension of the exaggerated "macho" prison code in regard to sexual encounters among inmates: if you are the sexual penetrator and make no effort to satisfy your sexual partner or bring him to orgasm, then you retain your manhood.

In contrast, there appeared to be a substantial effort made by those offenders who assaulted their victims in the community to get these victims to ejaculate. This occurred in nine (41%) of the community offenses. Such efforts may serve several purposes. In misidentifying ejaculation with orgasm, the victim may be bewildered by his physiological response to the offense and thus discouraged from reporting the assault lest his sexuality becomes suspect. Such reaction may serve to impeach his credibility in trial testimony and discredit his allegation of nonconsent. In addition, in the psychology of the offender, such reaction may symbolize his ultimate and complete control over his victim's body and confirm the fantasy that the victim really wanted and enjoyed the rape.

Sexual Lifestyle

At the time of their offenses, all the men who sexually assaulted other men in the community were actively engaged in consenting sexual encounters or relationships. Six (27%) of these men confined their consenting sexual activity to members of the opposite sex, and half of them were married. Seven (32%) of these offenders engaged in consenting sexual encounters with both men and women, but three of these men were extremely conflicted over their sexual activity with other males. As one offender expressed it, "I'm bisexual, but I'm not a faggot." Two of these seven men were married. Two (9%) of the men in this community-offender sample confined their consenting sexual encounters almost exclusively to other men, but none was committed to a permanent union in this regard. No data were available in regard to seven (32%) of these offenders.

The offenders who were incarcerated at the time of their assaults had access only to masturbation or same-sex encounters as an outlet for their sexual needs. None of these men acknowledged any sexual interest in other males, although a few admitted they would accept being serviced by inmates whom they identified as homosexuals. In regard to their pre-institutional sexual behavior, three (60%) of these men confined their sexual activity exclusively to women, but none of them was married, and no data were available for the other two (40%) inmate offenders.

No data were available in regard to the unapprehended offenders of the men in the victim sample.

It would appear then that one-third (9 or 33%) of the men who sexually assault other men were heterosexually oriented. One-quarter (7 or 26%) of them could be described as bisexual, and a small minority (2 or 7%) appeared to be homosexually oriented. These designations, however, address only the direction, not the quality, of their sexual lifestyle.

To define the sexual lifestyle of these offenders as heterosexual or homosexual is not actually an accurate description of their sexual orientation, since, in general, their interpersonal relationships lacked such qualities as empathy, mutuality, and reciprocity. Instead, with one or two exceptions, they tended to possess a rather ambiguous and undefined sexuality that was more self-centered than interpersonal. Their relationships to others, both sexual and nonsexual, were based more on exploitation than on sharing.

Recidivism

With regard to the offenders who raped males in the community, the instant offense constituted the first conviction for a sexual offense in only 3 (14%) of the 22 cases. One (5%) of the subjects in this sample was in fact never arrested and had no criminal record whatsoever but voluntarily admitted to having committed such an assault on two occasions. Since none of the assailants of the victims we interviewed was apprehended, no data were available in regard to the question of recidivism in 6 (27%) of the community cases. Of the remaining 12 offenders who had a prior criminal record of sexual offenses, 6 (27%) of them had previously committed sexual assaults against other males; 4 (18%) had committed sexual assaults against females; and 2 (9%) had sexually assaulted both male and female victims. In these prior offenses, 7 of the offenders sexually assaulted age-mates, 4 adult offenders assaulted adolescent victims, and 1 adult offender assaulted a child. Apart from their sexual offenses, 9 (41%) of the community offenders had no criminal record; 7 (32%) had a serious criminal history in addition to their sexual offenses; and no data were available for 6 (27%) of these subjects.

In regard to the 5 offenders who raped other men in a correctional setting, no information was available in regard to one of the subjects; 3 of the remaining 4 men had been previously convicted of a sexual assault—in every case, the victim was a female age-mate—and 1 of the subjects had no record of any previous sexual offense. All 5 of these men, however, did have a serious criminal record in addition to their sexual offenses.

In cases of male rape outside of prison, one might assume that the gender of the victim is an important and psychologically significant determinant of victim choice as compared to sexual assaults in institutional settings where there is no option in regard to the sex of the victim. It does appear from our data that for the offender who rapes other men in prison, the assault may be a counterpart to his sexual offenses against women in the community and that the selection of a male as his victim, to a significant extent, is situationally determined. Many of the men in our sample who raped other men in prison raped women in the community.

However, those offenders who raped males in the community divided equally into two groups. For one-half of these subjects, the gender of their victims did not appear to be of special significance. They appeared, instead, to be relatively indiscriminate with regard to victim choice; that is, their victims included males and females, adults and youngsters; in essence, anyone could be a target of their sexual assaults. This lack of discrimination would tend to suggest an undifferentiated or multisexual orientation. For the other half of these subjects, males appeared to be the specific targets of their sexual offenses. All of these offenders appeared to be sexually active with other males. Two of them led predominantly homosexual lifestyles, and the selection of a male victim would constitute a counterpart to the selection of a female victim by a heterosexual rapist. The other four offenders led bisexual lives but were extremely conflicted over and uncomfortable with their sexual attraction to and involvement with other males. The selection of a male as the target of their sexual assault can in part be seen as an expression of this unresolved aspect of their lives. The victim may symbolize what they want to control, punish, and/or destroy—something they want to conquer and defeat. The assault is an act of retaliation, an expression of power, and an assertion of their strength or manhood.

Dynamics

Rape is a complex and multidetermined act serving a number of psychological purposes for the offender. In this study of men who rape men, we found their dynamics to be similar to those of men who rape women. What is immediately apparent about the sexual assailants is that none of them had to rape for sexual gratification. The adult offenders were all sexually active men who had access to consenting relationships at the time of their offenses, and even the juvenile offenders had established some consenting, age-appropriate sexual encounters prior to their assaults. Sexual desire, then, did not seem to be the paramount force prompting their assaults. Instead, rape could be understood as the sexual expression of aggressive issues and motives. Rape by its very nature is nonconsenting and, therefore, a hostile act. It thus serves a variety of aims in the psychology of the offender simultaneously:

1. *Conquest and control:*   All assaults served as an expression of power and mastery on the part of the offender.

Mike is a 22-year-old, single, white male on the wrestling team of his university. One evening he and some buddies were having a beer party at a beach when some local working-class young men crashed the party:

> There was this one guy, very good-looking, who kept giving me these hard looks. The tension between the groups was building, and a fight was inevitable; when it started he went right for me, and we rolled down the sand dunes. We struggled, and it was immediately quite sexual, and I grabbed him by the genitals. He said, "Let go, get your hands off me," but I had him pinned down. I pulled off his shorts, greased him with suntan oil that I had in my pocket, and fucked him. While I did that I reached around and masturbated him. I know this sounds like a rationalization, but I felt he really wanted this but had to make a show of resistance. When I started balling him he said, "No, don't," and then he started to whimper, but as I masturbated him vigorously, he got very, very hard and came off. Afterwards he had tears in his eyes and said something like, "I hope you're satisfied," or "I hope you got what you wanted," and I felt kind of funny, because he was so upset. What was really exciting, though, was that all during the assault I felt in total control of him.

Sexual conquest, possession, and exploitation serve to reassure the offender of his strength and authority and to compensate for feelings of inadequacy and vulnerability. The ultimate form of power is seen as being able to control the victim's sexual responses, even against his will. It is for this reason that a number of offenders attempt to get their victim to ejaculate. They misidentify ejaculation, a physiological reaction, with orgasm, a psychological response, and view this as evidence of the victim's really enjoying, even welcoming, the assault. In addition, they tend to misinterpret such physiological reaction as indicating that the victim is homosexual and, therefore, a legitimate victim.

2. *Revenge and retaliation:*   In some cases of male rape, the offense is activated by anger on the part of the offender toward his victim and is regarded by him as a form of retaliation.

Carlos is a 25-year-old Puerto Rican male who had served time in prison for raping a 20-year-old woman. He violated his parole and was returned to jail. While there, he raped a 23-year-old fellow inmate:

He was talking about my race, calling me a Puerto Rican pig and a punk. He made comments about my mother. I told him I'd get him when I had the chance. Two days later I cornered him in the showers and said, "You think I'm a punk? I'm going to prove you are what you called me!" He was real scared and said, "Forget about what I said," and then he asked me if I wanted a hand job. I said, "What do you think I am, a homo?" Then I told him, "You're going to give me some ass," and I fucked him. It wasn't for sex. I was mad. I wanted to prove who I was and what he was.

3. *Sadism and degradation:*   For some assailants aggression itself becomes eroticized, and they find excitement and gratification in the sexual abuse and degradation of their victim.

Frank, age 18, described his assault on a 16-year-old student as follows:

> I said, "How would you like someone to make you blow him?" and I picked him up and carried him across the street into the woods, and I threw him to the ground five or six times. I kept on doing it. The more he pleaded to stop, the more I did it. I wanted to hurt him. He was scared, so the more I kept on doing it—to tease, to see him plead. Something came over me. I undressed him and tied a garrison belt around his ankles. I squeezed his balls and threatened to shove a stick up his ass unless he blew me. I had the guy so frightened, I could have made him do anything I wanted. I didn't have an erection. I wasn't really interested in sex. I felt powerful, and hurting him excited me. Making him suck me was more to degrade him than for my physical satisfaction.

Sexual sadism may be evidenced by bondage, ritualistic torture, and coprophilic acts. In extreme cases, it may lead to lust murder, but for a variety of reasons, such male homicides may not be identified as sex-related.

4. *Conflict and counteraction:*   Another component in some male rapes is an attempt to punish the victim as a way of dealing with unresolved and conflictual sexual interests on the part of the offender.

Jon, age 20, drove around a city block where male hustlers cruised and picked out a guy about the same age as himself. They drove to a roadside area and parked:

> I fucked him and then made him blow me. After I came, I dragged him out of the car and punched him out and called him a punk and a

> shit. I told him I was going to kill him. Then I threw his clothes out of
> the car and took off. I was angry at him. I don't know why. At what I
> was doing, I guess, is what I was really angry at.

Such offenders seem caught in a bind: unable, on one hand, to admit interests in sexual encounters with other males and unable, on the other hand, to abandon pursuing some such encounter. They do not feel comfortable or secure with themselves in regard to their sexual identity or orientation. Such an offender is conflicted over and fearful of his homosexual urges, and he projects these feelings onto his victim, perceiving him as a provocative seducer. The offender then acts out of his anger and repulsion towards this aspect of his sexuality by assaulting the victim. He rapes and beats him as a means of punishing him. Hustlers or male prostitutes may particularly be target victims of such assaults.

5. *Status and affiliation:* In gang rape, some offenders feel pressured to participate to retain status and membership with their peers. In addition to other motives, validation by one's codefendants becomes a dynamic in group rape, and mutual participation in the assault serves to strengthen and confirm the social bond among the assailants.

Chuck, a 20-year-old inmate in a county jail, and his 19-year-old cellmate were victims of gang rape:

> The two of us were in our cell, and four black dudes came in. They
> said, "We're the Black Power," and they started beating on us. After
> they had worked us over, they said, "Now we are going to give you
> full initiation." One guy pulled out his cock and told me to suck him
> or he would kill me. He reached a climax and blew a load into my
> mouth. While I was blowing him, I had to massage another guy's
> cock; then this guy screwed me up the ass. All four guys took turns
> on me and my cellmate. When they were finished, they said, "Now
> you know who's boss. If you rat on us we'll break your arms and
> legs." The first guy then dumped a pot of piss on me, and they left.

The status and membership dynamic was evident in all seven gang rapes but seemed especially pronounced in the prison setting. In prison rape, participation in gang assault serves to confirm one's position of superiority and masculinity.

As in the case of the sexual assault of females, the sexual assault of males, whether it occurs in the community or in a prison setting, is prompted more by aggressive needs than sexual ones. More paramount than sexual gratification is the assertion of power and the discharge of anger.

Larry is the third oldest of seven siblings. During his childhood his family existed on public welfare funds. Both his parents had serious drinking problems and neglected their children. At age 12, a 16-year-old male friend engaged Larry in sexual activity, and this secret relationship continued for two years. In his late teen years Larry became sexually active with girls his own age and found his continuing sexual interest in males troublesome. Although of superior intelligence, Larry did poorly in school and dropped out in the 10th grade. He worked at unskilled, low-level jobs and supplemented his income by tending bar part time.

His first offense occurred at age 25 against a 22-year-old victim:

> I was working as a bartender, and it was closing time, and there was this real good-looking guy there. I had been checking him out all evening, and I was really attracted to him. I was drinking, and by the end of the evening, I was feeling good. I really wanted to get into this guy's pants, so I'm trying to figure out a way to get him downstairs into the cellar. He's straight, and I know I can't lure him, so I'm going to have to force him, and then I remember there's a shotgun behind the bar. All the customers had left, but he was still shooting pool, so I got the gun and forced him downstairs. I wanted to see his body and told him to get undressed. He kept refusing and then turned and ran upstairs. I was angry that he wouldn't cooperate and afraid that he would tell others about me, and I pulled the trigger. I shot him in the hip, and he fell. He grabbed a beer bottle and hit me over the head with it, but I dragged him back down the stairs, undressed him and myself, and went down on him. Then I laid on top of him and masturbated against him until I shot my load. He told me that he was hurt and that he would not tell anybody if I let him go. I suddenly realized what I had done. There was blood all over both of us. I realized the seriousness of it, and I really felt scared. "God, what am I going to do?" He was turning white, and the thought flashed through my mind to kill him or let him die, but then a little feeling, a little compassion set in towards him—he was a person, someone who was hurt—and I called an ambulance.

Larry's next offense followed his release from prison. He was 32 years old, and his victim was 21, a male prostitute:

> The only guys I had sex with were hustlers, because I felt if I was paying for it they wouldn't tell my secret. Yet, I felt attracted to straight guys, and I would get emotionally involved with a guy in the kind of relationship where I was sure to wind up feeling used

and rejected. I'd pick up a hustler, but this didn't satisfy me, because he wasn't who I really wanted to be with—this was like having to settle for something less than I wanted. I'm feeling that if I proposition the guy I really wanted to be with, it would be a total rejection, and then the other feelings I have would come out: the anger at being rejected. That's what happened in this case. I really did a number on the hustler. I was vicious. I beat him up, tied him up, and raped him—he didn't want to take it up the ass, but I made him.

Larry's parole was revoked, and he had to serve out his sentence. The next sexual assault occurred when he was 34. His victim was a 20-year-old hustler:

I was really hung up over a guy named Jim. It was a bad day, and I was upset because my relationship with him was going down the drain, and it seemed like I was the one he was taking most of his anger out on, for whatever reasons, and I got upset by it—angry and depressed, but the depression was greater than the anger. I hadn't drunk for a couple of months, and I called Jim and asked him to come over, and he said he couldn't do it this weekend. I could really feel the rejection, so, after I hung up the phone, I just picked up a drink and said, "The hell with it." I went out to a bar and met some guy there, and we went to a hotel and made out. Then I went back to the bar and drank some more until they closed. It was about two in the morning, and I met this hustler, a kid in his 20s, in the area of the bus station. He wasn't all that attractive, but basically, he was the best of those around. I felt excited. I know when I'm out looking like that I feel a little excited. I don't know if that's anxiety or anger. I was thinking just in terms of sex. I gave him $20 and said I wanted to ball him and promised him $50. We took a cab back to my place. I felt angry, but it wasn't focused on this guy. I was thinking about Jim, but now this guy's going to become my outlet. I knew something was really wrong. I was depressed and angry. As much as I knew I had all these feelings, I couldn't like say, "You know, you've got to stay away from this guy because these feelings are going to come out even though they have nothing to do with him." So we went in and got undressed and started making out. I was doing him but thinking about Jim. We had sex for about an hour, and then he wanted to stop, but I didn't want to. He wanted to leave, and I said, "No." At that point I hadn't come off, and I felt if I paid $20 I had a right to. He said, "No, no way," and we ended up having a fistfight, and I really punched him out. About a half hour later, I glanced outside and saw two cops and the kid coming toward the house. The kid told them I had kidnapped him at knifepoint and beat him up, fucked him up the ass, jumped up and down on him, and kicked him or kneed him in the balls, that I had tied him up, and that this had gone on for over an hour. The cops asked me what happened, and I told them I picked him up and agreed to pay him, and I guess it wasn't enough money or something. In the meantime, they were checking up on me, and my record came back.

As Larry describes his offenses, what starts off apparently with sexual intent winds up in an assault:

> That's because I'm using sex as an outlet—I'm pretty sure of that—whether I feel sexually aroused or not. It's got to be that. I'm still uncomfortable about feeling turned on to guys. I don't like that, and I don't know what to do about it. The more depressed I get, the more intense my sexual needs become, and the more aggressive my sexual fantasies get, and the thought of actually hurting someone becomes stronger. In my fantasy, I'm blowing a guy who's not wanting it, not willing. His reaction is one of fear. He's afraid of me, and then I've got him under my control. He doesn't like getting sucked, and I feel excited by that. Then I hurt him—punch him, stab him, shoot him—whatever. The whole thing really is kind of scary, because the fact is that the fantasies have gone so far that I'm a walking time bomb, and I know it. I'm more vulnerable now than I have ever been, because now it's a matter of if I do something, my paranoia or whatever is going to say, "Well, Jesus, you know you're going to be in serious trouble, real serious trouble," so the risk of me really hurting someone is much more serious.

When a person feels powerless in regard to controlling his life, he can defend against the discomfort of such an experience by asserting control over someone else. In this way, he comes to feel more powerful than his victim and thus compensates for his feelings of inadequacy. This is particularly evident in prison rape, where the offender's tenuous sense of identity, personal control, and self-esteem are further diminished by his incarceration. Sexual assault becomes a means of compensating for his sense of helplessness and vulnerability and of retaliating for his feelings of resentment and anger.

Tony, a 36-year-old inmate who was serving time for an armed robbery, described the prison experiences as follows:

> I felt no sexual attraction to other men, but I got angrier and angrier as time went by. You see other guys, and you fall into testing them. You challenge the other guy to fight—if he does, it doesn't matter whether he wins or loses, you leave him alone. If he doesn't fight, then he's got to service you and your buddies. The sex itself is not that important; it's being in the position to control: "You're going to

give it up whether you want to or not." If the guy doesn't fight, his only option is to get a protector, but then he has to service this guy in exchange for the protection.

Sex in prison becomes one of the few ways inmates express who is in control and who is controlled.

The power to degrade the victim by subjecting him to the indignity of a sexual assault retaliates for what the offender perceives to be mistreatment, put-downs, rejections, or injustices dealt him by others or by life events. In some extreme cases, the dynamics of mastery and revenge combine in a sadistic assault. Aggression itself becomes eroticized, and the offender literally becomes a powerful and cruel master over his victim with the ability to punish and destroy him.

Satisfaction and pleasure in male rape appear to be experienced in the sense of power, the discharge of anger, and the eroticization of aggression, more than in sexual release. It seems to validate the offender's manhood, since he equates it with being in control, being aggressive, and being the penetrator or in charge in regard to the sexual acts. Some offenders wish to control; others to control and to degrade; still others to control, degrade, and destroy. Sex becomes an instrument of power, control, retaliation, debasement, and punishment. In some cases, especially institution rape, the selection of a male as the victim seems less significant than the choice of sex as the means of domination and retribution. In expressing his contempt and anger through sexual assault, the offender symbolically emasculates his victim or, in prison argot, "robs him of his manhood." In other cases, the selection of a male as the victim may be understood as his being symbolic of a target group (such as homosexuals) whom the offender finds disturbing and/or a life issue that he has not resolved. In those few cases where the offender is himself homosexual (admitted or unacknowledged), the sexual assault of another male can also be understood as a counterpart to heterosexual rape.

Victim Impact

Sexual assault can have the same biopsychosocial impact on male victims as it does on female victims. Burgess and Holmstrom[10] have identified four areas of life disruptions in rape-trauma syndrome: physical, psychological, social, and sexual.

[10]Ibid.

Roy, a man now in his late 20s, recounted his victimization at age 17:

> I was hitchhiking home from a high school dance. I was picked up, and we were riding down the street, and I told the guy which direction I was headed in. We were driving along, and I wasn't saying anything, we weren't talking, and he suddenly grabbed my left hand. I told him to let go. He didn't say anything. His grip got tighter, and he started pulling my hand toward his groin area. I tried to pull back, but he was strong, and I couldn't do it. I just froze. I got really scared, and I said, "Let me out of the car." He didn't say anything and kept right on driving. He kept holding my hand between his legs. He had an erection. Then he let my wrist go and began to grope me. I just thought to myself, "I've got to get out of here," so I pushed his hand away and jumped out of the car. I got bruised from hitting the street, but I didn't break any bones or anything. There was a state police barracks nearby, and I walked there and reported it. The police drove me to the hospital, and my parents picked me up there.

This was Roy's first sexual encounter with an adult. Prior to this he had engaged in some consenting sexual activities with peers:

> I used to jerk off with a couple of guys in school, but that was it.

Following the attempted assault,

> I had difficulties in sleeping, and I couldn't go into any public restrooms—I still don't like to go into public restrooms alone. It would take me a longer time to get to sleep, and I had to apply myself a little harder to do my schoolwork. I stopped hitchhiking, and I don't hitchhike even today. My sexual activity also ended. I didn't have sex with my friends anymore. I completely knocked that off. In fact, I didn't have sex with anyone for almost eight years. When this happened, I didn't think of myself as gay, but about three years later, I realized I felt more attracted to men than to women. This incident had nothing to do with my becoming gay, but, as a result of it, I found it was awfully hard for me to go to a gay bar and socialize with the older men there. I had a fear of men—even my men teachers—and it was an awful long time before I would go to bed with a guy. I went to gay bars for a long time before I ever went home with anybody or had a sexual contact. Also, I had a fear of anyone under the influence of alcohol—I remember that the guy who tried to assault me smelled of alcohol.

Roy never hesitated about reporting the incident. He felt that the police treated him fairly, but they did suggest that he had been looking for some sexual activity:

> I said no, I wouldn't have jumped out of the car if I had wanted it. I felt they didn't believe me. My parents did, but their attitude was, "Just forget it; don't say anything about it." My friends would ask me what happened, and I would just say, "He tried to get funny with me and I jumped out of the car." I was kind of embarrassed, because they would then ask, "Well, did he *do* anything?" and I would say, "No," and I felt like they didn't believe me when I said no. They would pursue it: "Nothing else happened? Come on, you can let me know, I won't tell anybody." I felt no one believed me that he didn't do anything or that I didn't do anything to him. I think from then on I kind of got away from having friends, too. This broke up some of my friendships.
>
> What frightened me about the incident was that I felt my life was on the line. I thought he was crazy, that there was definitely something wrong with him. He was a big guy, and I felt helpless. I was shaking. I think I had a vision of me being kidnapped. I thought of him as a person who was going to do me in.
>
> I feel it would have helped if I had had someone to talk to about the incident, but I didn't know who I could talk to that would understand, so after a few weeks I decided I was just going to block it out of my mind, and I did block it out. I never thought about it, but I still don't like to be alone, and I still have a fear of going into public restrooms. I feel like somebody is going to bust through the door and accost me.

Roy's reactions illustrate each major type of disruption: physical (sleeping difficulties); psychological (difficulties in concentrating on schoolwork and phobic reactions to male strangers and public restrooms); social (termination of friendships); and sexual (cessation of consenting sexual activity). Moreover, they tend to reflect some difficulty in long-term reorganization, which might have been facilitated by rape crisis counseling.

One of the pronounced reactions to sexual assault that we have noted among many male victims has been intense anger and plans to avenge themselves:

> I was about 17 or 18, and a guy I knew invited me to a party. We were members of a motorcylcle gang, the Gladiators, and we went to this party. I wound up getting really smashed. They got me drunk or

some damn thing, and they were chasing me around the apartment. There were three or four guys in their 20s, and they were chasing me around. I remember going to a bathroom with an alternate door to another room. I remember running through there, but they grabbed me eventually, and I wound up getting, I guess you'd call it, raped. One of the guys fucked me in the ass. I was just kind of sick about it. All I remember was walking around the streets that night, pretty pissed off that that happened, figuring out how I could get back at them. This happened 10 years ago, and I remember I was walking around feeling sick and angry and trying to figure out how I could get back at them in some way. I don't remember whether there was any retaliation towards these particular individuals. There may have been, but I don't want to talk about it.

Another coping strategy adopted by some male victims has been to concentrate on their work as a way of validating their competence and to resume their usual lifestyle as quickly as possible. Brett is a 22-year-old graduate student:

It was late at night, and I was going to my car, which was parked in an underground garage. I didn't see anybody or anything, and I got in and shut the door and put the key in the ignition when this guy came running down the ramp toward my car. I locked the door, and he stood by the window saying, "Let me in, let me in." I wasn't going to let him in. I was afraid he was going to steal my car, so I tried to hide the ignition keys. He saw I was stalling, and he said, "If you move I'll kill you. I have a gun." I wasn't going to let him in anyway, but, unfortunately, one of the back doors was unlocked, and he got in and crawled over the seat and said, "Don't move or I'll kill you." Then he said, "You're going to suck my dick." So he took his pants off, and I started sucking. This went on for five minutes or more, because he couldn't get off. He said, "You're not sucking hard enough. What's wrong with you?" I could smell alcohol and knew he was drunk. I thought, "My god, what's going to happen! This guy is probably going to get frustrated because he can't get off." I said, "I've never done this before," but I was afraid he would think I was just bullshitting him and he would get mad at me. He kept pushing my head down on his cock and kept saying, "You can suck better than that," and I said, "I can't do this, I'm choking," but he kept it up saying, "Suck harder, suck harder or I'm going to fuck you," so I sucked harder, but he couldn't come. After another 5 or 10 minutes he said, "Take your pants off"—he kept threatening to kill me—so I did, and he put his cock up my ass and started to fuck me. This went on for a long time, maybe as much as 10 minutes, and it was really gross. I'm really uncomfortable, and he's on top of me, and I've never been fucked in the ass before, and it hurt. He still couldn't come, so he got up and told me to suck him some more, so I did. Then it was sort of off and on. He'd make me suck him awhile, and then I'd stop awhile, and then he'd say, "Okay, suck again," and I'd do it. I'd say this happened three or four times, and he still couldn't get off. So then he sucked me. I don't know why—maybe to turn himself on or something, or maybe to humiliate me. I felt repulsed. I didn't feel horny at all, and I couldn't get off. He asked, "Why can't you get off?" And I was afraid to hurt his feelings, so I said, "Well, I beat off a couple hours ago." Then he tried masturbating himself and had me suck him some more, but he still couldn't get off. So finally he said, "How would you like to go find a couple of girls?" And so I go, "Yeah," figuring it was a good way to get out of this. I put my pants on, and he insisted on driving the car. He was driving really wild, because he was drunk, and I was really scared. He said, 'Don't worry, I'm not going to hurt you," and he got friendly all of a sudden and asked me my name and what college I was going to and what I was studying. I tried to be really friendly toward him and said, "Listen, this whole thing was cool. I didn't mind at all. I think it was all right. I'm sorry if you didn't get off. I was trying my best. I just don't want to get hurt," and he offered me a cigarette and said, "Don't worry, you're not going to get hurt, and you'll get your car back, and we're going to find a couple of women, and you might even make some money too." That implied we were going to go out and maybe rob some place. It was totally bizarre. It reminded me of Patty Hearst. I didn't press him on it. I was very nervous and thought, "Well, maybe he's just being nice to relax me and he's really going to hurt me. He's just putting me at ease so I won't get scared and do something." I thought he was planning to kill me, and, when he slowed down enough, I opened the door, jumped out, ran down the block and into an alley, and hid under a car. I was really scared and stayed under the car for about a half hour, and I got really cold, so I crawled out and walked around until I came to a grocery store that was open, and I got directions to the nearest police station. I walked into the station and there was this old guy, and I think, "Oh, my God. This is going to be amazing just telling this guy what happened." He must have been 50 or 55, not the kind of guy who would understand at all anything like this. And I told him, and he was pretty cool about it. He took all the information down and then arranged to get me to a hospital to get checked over.

This happened in the early hours of the morning, and I had a 10 o'clock class, and it's really an intense school, and if you don't stay on top of things, you're dead. I got back to my dorm and took a shower, and I was thinking during the shower, "What should I do?" And I thought the one thing I'd better do is keep my shit together. I tried to get all organized: "I'm going to get dressed. I'm going to my 10 o'clock class. I'm going to practice at least two hours a day and get everything done so I don't get totally behind."

Brett shared this incident with his sister and a few male classmates:

> My sister asked me how I felt about it and told me she had been raped once herself and she felt really, really badly after it. I didn't feel as badly. I wasn't as shaken up by it as she was. In talking with her, I kind of got my thoughts together about it: it was like the police had found my car, I had been shot full of penicillin, I didn't think I had VD, I wasn't experiencing any pain, so my attitude towards it was it was an awful thing to do to somebody, but it wasn't that awful for me to go through it, the sex, but I *was* scared. The guys I told were fairly mature and took it in the sense that it was an accident. I still felt a little funny telling them. It's like telling another guy you masturbate. It's something you usually don't do, and it's embarrassing. It's the same with this. It's sort of embarrassing to tell a guy you've been raped.
>
> The dumbest thing—what I should have done when the guy crawled into the car was to have asked to see his gun. I just took him at his word. In the back of his mind, he's probably laughing at me, thinking, "What a stupid shit! He sucked my dick, and I didn't even have a gun. What an ass!"

Some men, however, report that the impact of rape has been so devastating that it has permanently affected their life:

> I was 19 years old when I was sent to the county jail on a larceny conviction. I was a skinny little kid, and I was sexually hounded by everybody in prison. I was forced to go down on guys and give them my backside and jerk guys off. I was threatened that they'd kill me if I didn't submit to it. I didn't know anything about this until I came to prison. I was the one who had to give sex to the others—no one gave me any sex. One guy tried to make me into his wife, and, when I refused, he stabbed me with a ballpoint pen. I finally reported it to the deputy warden and was transferred to a work farm.
>
> I'm 38 now, and I still have flashbacks about it. It still upsets me. I've been thinking about this ever since I was in prison, and I don't think it'll ever let me go. I've got to live the rest of my life with these memories.

To appreciate the situation of the male rape victim, it is important to understand several factors that are somewhat unique to male rape. Most important is the strategy to get the victim to ejaculate that is frequently employed by many offenders in their assault. People mistakenly think that if a man is in a state of fear or anxiety, he cannot achieve erection or ejaculation. Further, in misidentifying ejaculation with orgasm, the victim himself may not understand his physiological response and may come to doubt his own sexuality. The victim may be troubled with wondering why he was selected and whether there might be something about his appearance or behavior that singled him out for sexual assault. A male also tends to equate manhood with independence and control, and when such control is lost, as it is in rape, and when another male gains sexual access to him, there may be a feeling of loss of manhood in the victim. He feels less of a man. As one victim put it:

> A woman isn't expected to be stronger than a male assailant, so it's no reflection on her if he overpowers her and she fails to resist the assault, but for a man it's different. It's a humiliation to get beaten and an even greater disgrace to be used sexually.

Women victims do not report that they feel less of a woman for having been raped, but men victims do often state that they feel that the offender took their manhood. Whereas a female victim may develop an aversion to sexual relations following assault, a male victim may show increased need for sexual activity with a woman to reestablish and reaffirm his manhood. Because of existing social values, sexual contact with another male, even though coerced, may be stigmatizing for the victim, since now his manhood has been tampered with, and he himself may fear labeling or even actual conversion, especially if he is not secure in regard to his sexual identity.

Male victims who are assaulted in a correctional setting are faced with the additional concern that their assailant has continuing surveillance of and access to them. They are also bound by the prison code that on one hand, you don't report such incidents to the authorities lest you be identified as an informer and, on the other hand, that if you do disclose, you will be put into protective custody, which means additional loss of privileges and increased security restrictions. Also, in prison, there is practically no privacy, and word of an inmate's sexual victimization quickly becomes common knowledge, which, in turn, increases the likelihood of attempts by other inmates to gain sexual access to him. This sometimes leads to drastic measures on the part of such victims to escape such a dilemma; for example, rather than report his being raped, Chuck (see above, p. 129) broke a light bulb and cut his wrists in the hope of being removed from the jail and sent to a hospital and thus put out of reach of his assaulters.

Conclusions

There is no way of knowing how representative our limited sample is with regard to all instances of male rape, and, consequently, we must be cautious in reaching conclusions based on these data. Therefore, we regard our observations more as suggestive than definitive, but the impression that emerges from our data is that the similarities between male and female rape in regard to the characteristics of the offense, the dynamics of the offender, and the impact on the victim are greater than the differences.

As with any subject about which little dependable information has been accumulated, a number of popular notions or assumptions develop to account for or explain the event. This is true of male rape. For example, since the victim is the same sex as the offender, it is commonly but mistakenly assumed that the perpetrator is homosexual and that his motive is one of sexual gratification. Likewise, it is commonly believed that a male can defend his sexual zones from invasion if he really wants to, and that if he is a victim, then he must have in some way encouraged the assault.

Rape is first and foremost an aggressive act, an assertion of power on the part of the offender—the power to control, to hurt, and to degrade activated by a feeling that power over one's own life has diminished. Imprisonment, in particular, has such an impact. The inmate is confronted with intense external controls, a restriction of his activities, a loss of self-determination, and an undermining of his sense of personal worth and identity. Prison, therefore, becomes a high-risk setting for male rape. However, the same thing can also happen in the community. A sense of powerlessness may be activated by confrontation with unresolved life issues or demands that overwhelm the individual. Equating manhood with being in control, the offender compensates for his feelings of vulnerability by gaining physical and sexual control over another. Rape is not an act of passion but a crime of aggression, and, therefore, being a man is no safeguard against being a victim. The rape of a male is often regarded by both the offender and his victim as a symbolic defeat and emasculation. It is unfortunate that the misidentification of rape with sex and the stigma associated with sexual acts between males have the result that male victims of sexual assault feel pressured to bear the burden of their victimization alone and in silence. The courage of women in speaking out against their sexual victimization has resulted in an increased awareness of this issue and in concentrated efforts to combat this serious social problem. It is important for male victims to do likewise. Rape is a problem that everyone, men and women alike, needs to combat.

SEXUAL ABUSE OF CHILDREN

Adults are not the only victims of sexual assaults. Infants, preadolescent children, and teenage girls and boys are also frequent targets of sexual assault. The sexual exploitation, misuse, and abuse of underage persons has been recognized for some time by law enforcement and child welfare agencies. It is a problem of increasing concern to health service providers and other professionals whose work brings them into contact with such victims and/or offenders.

In adult relationships, sexual encounters occur in three ways: through negotiation and consent, through pressure and exploitation, or through force and assault. The first method is regarded as a healthy and mature manner of relating sexually to another person. In the second method, one adult takes sexual advantage of another, usually through a position of dominance, and the subordinate person agrees to the sexual activity in order to achieve some other, nonsexual goal. The third method, legally termed *rape,* involves the threat of harm or injury and/or actual physical assault to establish sexual contact. The second method is dishonorable, and the third method is criminal and pathological. Only through negotiation and consent can sexual relations properly be achieved. However, negotiation and consent are precluded in encounters between an adult and a preadolescent or underage person because such a youngster has not developed sufficient knowledge or wisdom to be able to negotiate such an encounter on an equal basis with an adult. Although the youngster may be sexually mature, she or he is not psychologically equipped to deal with sexual situations on an equal basis with an adult and can therefore be easily taken advantage of by an adult without regard for the impact of such victimization on the child's psychosocial development. By definition, children are immature; thus, adults can capitalize in self-serving ways on this immaturity and can exploit the child in a variety of ways: physical, social, psychological, and emotional.

Sexual Encounters between Adults and Children

There are two basic ways in which the offender gains sexual access to the child. One is by pressuring the child into sexual activity through enticement, encouragement, or instruction, and the other is by forcing the child into the sexual activity through threat, intimidation, or physical duress.

In the *pressured* situation, the offender initially establishes a non-sexual relationship with the child in which the child comes to trust and to feel comfortable with the offender. Then, the offender influences the child to engage in sexual activities through the offer of some type of reward, such as candy or money; or by misrepresenting moral standards, such as telling the child that "all boys and girls do this—it's fun"; or through trickery and deception, for example, "This is going to be a game, and we're going to wrestle." The most commonly used technique of luring the child into this pressured sexual activity is by capitalizing on the child's need for attention, approval, and human contact. In such situations, the offender spends considerable time with the child, gives the child a lot of attention, and makes the child out to be special or a favorite. Children respond to attention and are taught to be obedient, so the intended victim cooperates and goes along with sexual demands of the offender in order to secure the promised rewards, or because the child is somewhat confused and does not fully appreciate the ramifications of the situation or does it for approval and recognition. In describing his selection of a victim, one offender explained:

> I can look at the kids in a school yard and tell you who is an easy mark. It will be the child alone and off by himself, the one who appears lonely and has no friends. The quiet kid—the one that no one is paying any attention to—that's the one who'll respond to some attention.

In pressured sex encounters, the offender does appear to have a high emotional investment in his victim and uses the child to gratify unmet needs for approval, recognition, and affiliation in his own life. He describes his attraction to children as an expression of his own need for affection and explains that what is important to him about the sexual relationship is that it makes him feel important or special to the child; he feels loved and looked up to by the child. In essence, the offender states that the child makes him feel good. He does not find satisfaction for such needs in his adult relationships, but in his encounters with children, the sexual activity serves to validate his worth as a person. When this is the dominant motive, the offense is characterized by a relative lack of physical force in the commission of the offense, and, in fact, the offender generally behaves in counteraggressive ways. Such offenders typically describe their victims in positive terms, such as innocent, clean, loving, open, warm, affectionate, attractive, and undemanding. They feel safer and more comfortable and secure with children. They entice the child into the sexual encounter and are usually dissuaded if the child actively refuses or resists. They do not resort to force but instead seek out another, more cooperative or accommodating victim.

In the *forced* situation, the offender gains access to the child through intimidation in the form of verbal threats, for example, "Do what I say and you won't get hurt"; or physical actions, such as grabbing hold of the child; or through the use of a weapon, for example, brandishing a knife. Or the offender resorts to physical force to overcome the child's resistance and, in some cases, derives pleasure from hurting and sexually abusing the child. Here we are dealing with situations that are comparable to rape. In these assaults, sexuality becomes an expression of power and anger. Such offenders describe the victim as small, weak, helpless, unable to resist, easily controlled, and vulnerable. They feel stronger and more dominant in regard to a child. Any resistance on the part of a child may result in increased aggression on the part of the offender; he does not take no for an answer and will er force his sexual demands. In the majority of these cases, whatever for ce is used is directed toward having control over the victim, but in a small number of cases, the aggression itself is eroticized, and the offe ider experiences excitement and pleasure in hurting the child.

The sexual abuse of children encompasses a wide variety of sexual interactions, extending from one extreme, in which there may be no actual physical contact between the offender and the child (such as when the adult exposes his genitals and masturbates in full view of the child or persuades the child to be photographed in the nude), through incidents of child molestation, in which the offender engages in sexual activities such as kissing, hugging, fondling, sucking, and masturbating the child but does not sexually penetrate the victim, to episodes of child rape, in which the adult sexually penetrates the child and, in some extreme cases, murders and mutilates the victim.

Such sexual victimization of children is a serious social issue that is currently receiving widespread attention in both the popular and the professional literature.[11] However, many myths and misconceptions continue to abound about the perpetrator of such assaults. Without an accurate understanding of the child molester, however, one cannot fully appreciate what the victim is a victim of.

In Massachusetts, serious attention to developing a statewide program for the diagnosis and treatment of dangerous sexual offenders came into being as the direct result of the sadistic sexual homicide of two preadolescent children by an offender who, only a few weeks earlier, had been released from a correctional institution following the expiration of his sentence for an almost identical but nonlethal offense. A forensic mental health facility was created to which anyone convicted of a sexual assault could be sent for diagnostic assessment. If he was found likely to repeat a sexual offense that would jeopardize the safety of his victim, the offender could then be committed indefinitely in lieu of or in addition to a fixed prison sentence. In examining a sample of 148 offenders who sexually assaulted underage persons and were referred to this facility for diagnostic evaluation, it became evident that many popular notions about men who sexually assault children do not correspond to their actual biopsychosocial characteristics or traits.

The Child Molester: Myths and Realities[12]

Myth 1: The child offender is a "dirty old man." The sexual attraction to children is sometimes attributed to senility. In fact, we found that the offenders ranged in age from 14 to 73, with the majority (105, or 71%) of the subjects referred to us under the age of 35. Only two (1%) of the subjects were over the age of 55, and neither showed any evidence of senility. It is important also to realize that no one under the age of 14 would be referred to the diagnostic program, since in Massachusetts, as in other jurisdictions, adolescent offenders are typically dealt with by a special youth services agency. This would, of course, affect the lower end of the age distribution of the pedophilic offenders in our sample.

---

[11]A. W. Burgess, A. N. Groth, L. L. Holmstrom, and S. M. Sgroi, *Sexual Assault of Children and Adolescents* (Lexington; Mass.: D. C. Heath, 1978).

[12]This section is adapted from A. Nicholas Groth, Ann Wolbert Burgess, H. Jean Birnbaum, and Thomas S. Gary, "A Study of the Child Molester: Myths and Realities," *LAE Journal of the American Criminal Justice Association* 41, no. 1 (Winter/Spring 1978): 17-22. Copyright 1978, American Criminal Justice Association/Lambda Alpha Epsilon. Reprinted by permission.

Another factor in this regard is the finding that about three-quarters (110, or 74%) of the offenders in our study sample had one or more prior convictions for a sexual offense against a child. At the time of their first known pedophilic offense, 122 (82%) of these men were under 30 years of age, and 10 were, in fact, under the age of 13, or preadolescent—in other words, they were still children themselves!

Myth 2: The offender is a stranger to his victim. Often parents caution their children not to talk to strangers in the hope of protecting them from sexual victimization. The irony is that only 43 (29%) of the offenders who were studied selected victims who were complete strangers. In the majority (105, or 71%) of cases, the offender and the victim knew each other at least casually, and in 20 (14%) of the cases, the offender was a member of the child's immediate family (father, brother, or grandfather). Further, it is reasonable to assume that when the offender is a family member or a close friend, there may be less willingness on the part of the family to prosecute him, and our data on the familiarity between the offender and his victim may, therefore, be a conservative estimate.

Myth 3: The child molester is retarded. It is sometimes thought that the child offender is of low or defective intelligence and therefore doesn't know any better. On the basis of their performance on a standard intelligence test, the Wechsler Adult Intelligence Scale, there was no significant difference between the convicted child offenders and the general population in regard to intellectual ability: 111 (80%) of the subjects fell within the normal range of intelligence. Only 10 (7%) subjects scored within the defective range, and clinical observation indicated that this retardation was more a function of an extremely limited, disadvantaged, and deprived developmental history than of a genuine impairment in cognitive skill. At the other extreme, 8 (6%) subjects scored within the bright to superior range of intelligence. No data were available for 10 (7%) of the subjects. With regard to their formal schooling, the majority (89, or 60%) had achieved less than a 10th grade education; 34 (23%) had graduated from high school, and of these, 3 (2%) had completed college. Although the child offenders studied appear undereducated in regard to their intellectual ability, their scholastic achievements do not appear significantly different from those of nonoffenders from the same socioeconomic backgrounds.

Myth 4: The child offender is alcoholic or drug-addicted. Some offenders themselves allege that the offense happened only because they were in a state of intoxication, and people commonly believe that alcohol and/or drugs play a part in the commission of sexual offenses against children. Drug use was essentially nonexistent among our subjects, and less than one-third (45, or 30%) of them would be described as alcohol-dependent. The majority (98, or 66%) did not abuse intoxicants, and 50 (34%) essentially abstained from their use. There did not seem to be any particular significance to the incidence of alcohol use at the time of the offense, since such use was consistent with their general pattern of drinking. In other words, those offenders who were intoxicated at the time of their assault were just as frequently or more often not assaultive when intoxicated.

Myth 5: The child offender is a sexually frustrated person. It is sometimes thought that children are turned to because the offender has no other outlets for his sexual needs or no other opportunities for sexual gratification. We found that approximately as many child offenders were married (70, or 47%) as not (78, or 53%). In fact, the sexual encounters with children coexisted with sexual contacts with adults. For example, in the incest cases, we found that the men were having sexual relations with their daughters or sons in addition to, rather than instead of, sexual relations with their wives. Those offenders who confined their sexual activity to children did so through choice. There was no one for whom no other opportunity for sexual gratification existed. In describing the frustration they experienced, the child offenders described it less in terms of sexual needs and more in regard to feelings of intimacy, competency, and adequacy. In a previous study,[13] it was determined that a distorted expression of identification and affiliation needs, power and control issues, and hostile and aggressive impulses, rather than sexuality, were the underlying issues in pedophilia.

Myth 6: The child molester is insane. One of the most frightening stereotypes of the child offender is that of the demented "sex fiend." Fortunately, it appears that such cases are rare exceptions: only 7 (5%) subjects showed clinical evidence of some psychotic process operating at the time of their offense. However, it was not of the nature or extent to render the offender incompetent to stand trial or to be found not guilty on the basis of insanity. The majority (141, or 95%) of the subjects were not psychotic. Although it could be argued that the more bizarre and frankly psychotic pedophiles would be committed to an institution for the criminally insane rather than being referred to a diagnostic pro-

[13]A. N. Groth, and A. W. Burgess, "Motivational Intent in the Sexual Assault of Children," *Criminal Justice and Behavior* 4, no. 3 (September 1977): 253–264.

gram, an informal exploration of that possibility did not support the assumption.

Myth 7: Child offenders progress over time to increasingly violent acts. The statement is often heard, "Well, the kid was lucky he wasn't hurt, but who can tell what will happen next time?" The assumption that the child offender will repeat is a legitimate one. Although about one-fourth (38, or 26%) of the subjects referred for evaluation were "first offenders" according to the law, it was a rare exception where the first conviction constituted the first such incident in the offender's life. Child offenders do not spontaneously abandon their sexual involvements with children. However, there does not appear to be any reason to assume that an offender will necessarily become more dangerous over time; this was not evident in the majority of cases. Only a small number (27, or 18%) of the subjects exhibited an increase in force over time.

On an absolute scale, a minority (13, or 9%) of the offenders had committed a violent sexual assault, one marked by an excessive force and brutality that put the victim's life in jeopardy. In fact, only 2 (1%) cases resulted in the death of the victim. The majority of offenses did not result in serious physical injury to the victim. In 87 (59%) cf the situations, the offender gained sexual access to his victim through deception and enticement. In 18 (12%) cases, he used verbal threats; in 8 (5%), he used intimidation with a weapon; and in 16 (11%) cases, he used minimal force (grabbing the victim by the arm or putting his hand over the victim's mouth) to make a show of strength. In 6 (4%) cases, more than moderate force was used (striking the victim, binding the victim, etc.). This overall relative lack of violence or physical trauma to the victim by child offenders is even more encouraging with the realization that only those offenders who had some physical contact with their victims were referred for diagnostic evaluation. If the extent of the offense is one of the offender's exposing his genitals in the presence of the child (indecent exposure or exhibitionism), he would not be referred to the program, and it appears reasonable to assume that many of the reported incidents of sexual encounters between adults and children are confined to exhibitionism.

In 1976, four children—two girls and two boys, ages 10–12—were individually abducted from a suburb of Detroit, Michigan; kept for varying lengths of time; then murdered and their bodies left in visible locations in Oakland County. A special task force was assembled under First Lieutenant Robert H. Robertson of the Michigan State Police to coordinate the investigation into these suspected sex-related homicides. As one of its projects, the task force analyzed 1,252 sex offenses against children reported to the police during the preceding two years.[14] They found the most frequently reported incident to be indecent exposure, which accounted for 482, or 38%, of the total reported crimes. Offenses involving sexual penetration of the victim accounted for only 148, or 12%, of the crimes. It would appear, then, that although children may be targets of rape, this is not the most prominent type of sexual abuse of children. Instead, the majority of child victims have witnessed inappropriate sexual activities on the parts of adults or have been pressured into sexual activities with adults that stop short of penetration. This is not to imply that we should not be concerned about the traumatic impact that such noncoital sexual encounters may have on some children, but at least their physical safety is not in jeopardy.

Myth 8: Children are at greater risk of sexual victimization from "gay" (homosexual) adults than from "straight" (heterosexual) adults. It has been alleged that homosexual males are especially prone to actively recruit and indoctrinate young boys into their lifestyles. In fact, 75 (51%) of the men in our sample selected only female children as their victims; 42 (28%) selected only male children; and 31 (21%) selected both boys and girls as their victims. Female children were victimized almost twice as often as male children. Further, it is a faulty assumption that if an adult male selects a young boy as his victim, his sexual orientation is homosexual. We found that some (73, or 49%) offenders responded exclusively to children—boys, girls, or both—and showed no interest in adults or age-mates for sexual gratification. These men were pedophiles in the true sense of the word. Other (75, or 51%) offenders showed no persistent sexual preference for children but turned to them as the result of conflicts or problems in their adult relationships. Although this group regressed to sexual encounters with children, their predominant sexual orientation was toward adults. In examining the *adult* sexual lifestyle of this latter group, it was found that the large majority (62, or 83%) of these subjects led exclusively heterosexual lives, and the remaining subjects (13, or 17%) were bisexually oriented—that is, their adult sexual activities involved both female and male partners, although here, too, their preference was for women. It appears, then, that the heterosexual adult constitutes more of a threat of sexual victimization to the underage child than does the homosexual adult. The offender who selects young

---

[14]J. L. Tobias and T. Gordon, "Special Projects: OPERATION VICTIMIZATION," Oakland County Homicide Task Force, 1977, p. 3.

boys as his victims has either done that exclusively in his life or does so having regressed from adult heterosexual relationships. Offenders attracted to boy victims typically report that they are uninterested in or repulsed by adult homosexual relationships and find the young boy's feminine characteristics and absence of secondary sexual characteristics, such as body hair, appealing.[15] Their focus remains on the male child as opposed to the female child, however, because they identify with the boy. As one offender expressed it:

> I was a boy, so I know what to do with boys, what they like. I can relate to them better. I was never comfortable relating to females.

Another offender stated:

> At first, I was interested in boys and girls, but little girls talk a lot and little boys don't, and I became happier with boys; the girls were more demanding.[16]

The observation that boys are less likely to report sexual victimization than girls is supported by the work of the Oakland County Homicide Task Force. In their review of sexual offenses against children reported to the police, they found that the overwhelming majority (74%) of the victims were female, although a sizable number of males (17%) were also victimized.[17] (No data were available for 9% of the cases.) However, when the task force established a program in conjunction with local schools in which counselors or teachers acted as contact persons for the schoolchildren (grades 4-9) to assist them in reporting and documenting any incidents in which they were approached by adults, over a one-year time frame it was discovered that 51% of the 782 reported contacts were directed toward females and 46% were directed toward males. (There was no information for 3% of the incidents.) Such data would suggest that the actual at-risk potential for children in this age bracket (10-13) is equal for both sexes.[18]

---

[15]A. N. Groth and H. J. Birnbaum, "Adult Sexual Orientation and Attraction to Underage Persons," *Archives of Sexual Behavior*, 7, no. 3 (May 1978): 175-181.

[16]Burgess, Groth, Holmstrom, and Sgroi, p. 12.

[17]Tobias and Gordon, p. 3.

[18]J. L. Tobias and T. Gordon, "Special Projects: Operation LURE," Oakland County Homicide Task Force, 1977, pp. 3-4.

Miscellaneous Observations

In examining other variables within our convicted-offender study sample, a number of additional characteristics were apparent. First, the child molester appears to act alone: 140 (95%) of the offenders had no codefendants in regard to their assaults, as compared to 8 (5%) cases in which there was more than one offender. Group sexual assault, then, appears to be uncharacteristic of child offenders.

Child offenders appear to be fairly specific in regard to the age of their victims: 20 (14%) selected children who were only 5 years of age or younger; 68 (46%) chose victims between the ages of 6 and 11; 49 (33%) selected young adolescent victims between the ages of 12 and 15; and only 11 (7%) of the offenders selected victims of various ages.

The type of sexual act performed during the offense also appeared to be specific and consistent: 58 (39%) of the offenders confined their activities to foreplay types of acts where no penetration was involved (fondling, masturbating, sucking, kissing, etc.); 46 (31%) sexually penetrated their victim in some fashion (orally, anally, or vaginally); and 19 (13%) performed both types of acts during their assault. (No data were available for 25 (17%) of the subjects.) Again, the offenders who were referred to the diagnostic program were those who had some kind of physical contact with their victims. As the Oakland County Task Force discovered, the most frequent type of sexual encounter between an adult and a child is one confined to genital exposure, and we found that 30 (20%) of the subjects in our sample had at some point in their sexual histories exposed themselves.

Race and religion appeared to be insignificant variables. The majority of our sample (123, or 83%) held unskilled or semiskilled jobs, and individuals in the white-collar professions were underrepresented. Less than half of the sample (59, or 40%) had no criminal history apart from their sexual offenses. More than half (91, or 61%) had never entered military service. Of those (57, or 39%) that had, 33 (58%) had received an honorable discharge; 8 (14%) a medical discharge; 7 (12%) a general discharge; and 9 (16%) a dishonorable discharge. The overall impression is that our sample of convicted child offenders are a group of men who, in large part, have multiple life difficulties.

It is important to separate fact from fiction in regard to the sexual molestation of children and to dispel the stereotypes and myths pertaining to the offender that have developed in the absence of systematic inquiry. An accurate understanding of the characteristics of such assailants will improve one's ability to work with both offenders and victims in whatever capacity, legal, medical, clinical, or the like. The reality of this social problem is serious enough. Myths and misconceptions can serve only to alarm us out of proportion and obstruct dealing with this issue in a rational, thoughtful, and effective manner. It is important to realize that not all child offenders are alike and that there is a great deal of variation in what they do, how they do it, and to whom they do it. The risk they constitute may be gauged from this study of convicted child offenders, who can be regarded as falling within the more danger-ous spectrum of sexual assailants since they were sent for evaluation and possibly indefinite commitment to a maximum-security treatment center. The impression that emerges is that, contrary to popular opin-ion, the child molester is a relatively young, heterosexual man who is neither insane, nor retarded, nor sexually frustrated. He seeks to control the child more than to injure him/her and most of the time poses more of a psychological than a physical risk to the victim. His behavior is highly repetitive, often to the point of a compulsion, rather than being the result of a temporary lapse of judgment while in a state of intoxication. His crime is a symptom, and imprisonment alone is insufficent to remedy the underlying causes for his problem behavior.

Rape versus Pedophilia

Adult sexuality is threatening, for a variety of reasons, to both the rapist and the child molester. However, they react differently to this threat. The rapist counterattacks, whereas the child offender retreats. The rapist denies his fears by striking out at the adult, whereas the child molester avoids the threat by turning to a safer substitute. Both are maladaptive attempts to deal with unresolved life issues, but, in con-trasting offenders who pressure the child into sexual activity with offend-ers who rape their victims, a number of comparative differences emerge. There seems to be a stronger erotic component in pedophilia, and the child offender appears to have a high emotional investment in the vic-tim. He seems to regard the victim less as an object and more as a per-son, with whom he identifies. He is interested in maintaining an ongo-ing relationship with the child so that there is repeated sexual access to the same victim over time, and his investment appears to extend beyond the sexual activity. There is much more lovemaking and foreplay, kiss-ing, caressing, etc., in such encounters. Pedophilia appears to be more equally distributed across all socioeconomic, educational, and professional levels, and it does not appear to diminish with time. Rape, on the other hand, appears to be much more a hostile act. The victim is more of an object or a symbol to the offender than a person. Rather than committing repeated assaults against the same victim, the rapist, instead, attacks different victims in his successive offenses. The victim is not regarded positively but instead is an object of contempt—someone to be vanquished—in the eyes of the rapist, and there is greater risk of physical injury in such assaults. Most such attacks are directed toward achieving sexual penetration of the victim, and the sexual activity is devoid of affectional, emotional involvement. Rape appears to be more class-related, with offenders from disadvantaged socioeconomic backgrounds being overrepresented and, as can be observed in regard to other crimes of violence, such offenders appear to "mellow" or "burn out" with time. Active rapists tend to be relatively young men. It is uncommon to find many such offenders who are beyond their late forties.

Child Rape

The emphasis in the remainder of this section is on the rape of the child. Although such offenses are not as prominent as incidents in which the child is pressured into sexual activity by an adult, they are not uncommon, and their impact may be more devastating to the victim. Descriptively, child rape is the use of force on the part of an adult to gain sexual access to an underage victim. The selection of a child as the target of a sexual assault is multidetermined. An adult is physically superior to a child, and the offender may feel stronger and more powerful in regard to a child victim as compared to an adult victim. The child does not pose as much of a physical or psychological threat. The child is sexually immature and inexperienced, and the offender may feel that there is less risk that his sexual performance will be compared to that of others. He may not feel as sexually inadequate with a child as he would with an adult. Since the child may not have matured sexually, she or he may be seen as sexless, and the offender is not confronted with adult or mature sexuality. In some cases, the child may be experienced more as a peer or an equal with someone who has difficulty forming relationships with age-mates, and in other cases, the child may symbolically represent everything that the offender negatively feels about himself, and the rape may in part serve to punish the victim for the offender's self-hatred and guilt. Or the child may be a means by which the offender attempts to control or retaliate against another adult.

Cory is a 40-year-old man who was convicted of sexually assaulting his 11-year-old son. Cory is a college graduate and an excellent athlete. He has a good military history and is a very successful businessman. He has no prior criminal history. Cory has been married twice. His first marriage ended in divorce, allegedly because of his wife's lack of interest in sex. He remarried within a year, this time to a woman considerably younger than himself, and they had a very active sex life, which resulted in four children, all boys. Cory describes this marriage as ideal until his wife started working. He worked days and she worked nights. He felt that she became overinvolved in her work, to his detriment, and serious arguments erupted. Cory felt that their work schedules interfered with their sexual relationship. He became jealous of the men she worked with, and he began to experience some problems with impotency. Cory also quarreled with his wife because of her friendship with a neighbor, whom he claims was lesbian.

Cory states that he always enjoyed a close relationship to his sons and would engage in sports activities with them. He claimed that he planned his sexual offense against his son, Bud, as a means of forcing his wife to give up work. He says he assumed Bud would tell his mother, after which she would stay home to protect the child from further recurrences:

> She favored him. Everyone did. He was the cutest. I loved him. He's the youngest. I told him what I was going to do and told him to undress. I used my mouth on him, and then I laid him. He never said no or showed he was afraid of me. This happened about a dozen times.

Cory admits that he knew his son did not like what he was doing to him but states that he never hurt the boy. After Bud first disclosed the assault, Cory was placed on probation with the stipulation that he move out of the house. He and his wife continued to see each other and ultimately reunited. Shortly afterwards, the sexual victimization of Bud reoccurred, because

> nothing had changed. My wife continued to work. She thought more of her job than of being a wife and mother.

Although the sexual assault of a child is complex, serving a number of purposes in the psychology of the offender, the dynamics of anger, power, and sadism are prominent features. Those offenders who rape children exhibit the same motivations as those offenders who rape adults.

Anger Assault

Sex may become a weapon and a means of discharging anger and frustration when it plays a part in the battering of a child. The intent is to hurt the victim, and the rage of the offender is expressed through both a physical and a sexual assault. Sometimes, the sexual components of such attacks are overshadowed by the general physical brutality directed against the victim. In other cases, the assault may be a predominantly sexual one, and the child may be a substitute for the individual the offender is actually angry at. Although the child may not have been the target of battering in the past, she or he is brutally raped in an effort to retaliate against the parent of the child. For example, following an argument with her lover, a 30-year-old divorced woman terminated her relationship with him, and in retaliation, he kidnapped her 8-year-old daughter and savagely raped her.

Power Assault

Sex may come to serve as an expression of power when the offender uses threat, intimidation, and force to capture, command, and control the victim. Such offenders capitalize on the relative helplessness of a child to coerce her or him into the sexual activity. A child is targeted as the victim because the child is physically small, unable to resist, weak, and vulnerable. Although it is not the specific intent of such offenders to hurt their victims, resistance on the child's part may release hostility or increased aggression on the part of the offender. He will not take no for an answer and shows a lack of concern for the consequences of his behavior. He does what he feels is necessary to get the victim to submit to his demands. The demands are sexual ones, by which he hopes to compensate for unresolved life issues and to alleviate inner feelings of distress or desperation. The child is an object, one to be used and then discarded. There is usually no attempt to engage the child in a cooperative and ongoing sexual relationship, nor is there any attempt on the offender's part to reciprocate in any way in exchange for sexual access to the child. Some such offenders confine their sexual assaults to children. In other cases, the offender may intially direct such attacks toward adults but, when these prove unsuccessful, may turn to increasingly younger victims.

Keith is a 30-year-old, white, married male serving time for the rape of a 9-year-old girl. He is the youngest of two children of reasonably affluent parents. During his early years, Keith was fearful of his father and felt alienated from his older brother but was very close to his mother:

> I was very much a "momma's boy," and when I was left with my father and brother I was terrified. I was frightened they were going to kill me, even though, in fact, they left me very much alone.

Keith did well in school, but he was not popular with his classmates and had practically no friends. Then:

> In the 10th grade my world changed. My mother, who alone had the ability to make me feel absolutely wonderful about myself and my existence, developed inoperable cancer. I realized she was going to die, and that's when I realized that I would forever feel alone, unloved, and defenseless. That's when I knew that life would be hopeless. When she died, something in me died too. I was left home alone, lost and lonely. I've been trying to recall those years with my mother, but all that time was spent feeling her existence rather than knowing her.

During his senior year in high school, Keith began dating a girl named Sally with whom he fell deeply in love. His father strongly opposed the relationship because Sally was not of the same religion, and when she became pregnant by Keith, his father arranged for an abortion and sent Keith away to college. During his semester break, Keith returned to see Sally and again impregnated her. Although he resolved to marry her, his father talked him out of it and persuaded Keith to abandon Sally:

> Now when I look back and ask, "At what point did I stop being a decent human being who could live with himself," it was at this point. I felt dirty and immoral. I feel like I've been running ever since. From this point on, I felt out of control of my life. When I got back to college, I was extremely depressed and confused. I couldn't sleep, food didn't taste good, studies weren't interesting, and I went to see a psychiatrist, who told me I needed intensive psychotherapy and advised me to withdraw from school immediately.

Keith did and retured home while he tried to figure out what to do. He took a job in construction for a short time until his foreman

> told me that he thought I acted kind of swishy and perhaps I was really queer.

Keith confided his hurt feelings to a fellow worker who invited him to a bar for a few drinks:

> We ended up at his apartment looking at some porno movies. It wound up with his performing fellatio on me, which I didn't mind a bit. He asked me to reciprocate, but after much trying I realized that this just wasn't my bag, and I couldn't get very excited about making it with another man. I came to this realization with a great deal of relief, but I felt very guilty about this encounter for a long time.

Shortly thereafter Keith enlisted in the Marine Corps:

> Towards the end of the second week before my departure for boot camp, I started feeling very paranoid. I was feeling frightened of everything. It wasn't the first time I felt this way, nor would it be my last, but it certainly was noticeably strong at the time. I remember feeling that way when I was 4 years old and my mother went away for several weeks to visit friends. I was horrified at being left in the care of my father and brother, because I was certain that they meant to kill me. I remember feeling that way every time my parents would leave on their annual vacation. I remember feeling that way when my mother entered the hospital to get treated for her eventually incurable cancer. Anyway, I knew I was on my way into the Marine Corps. I knew I very much wanted to be killed and be relieved of the painful burden of living, to be rid of the horrible loneliness and shame I was enduring because of Sally. And yet I was frightened of dying and frightened of the hard world around me, with little prospect of solace, hope, comfort, or inner peace.

Keith went to Vietnam, where "I twice caught the clap from the village girls." He did well in the service:

> I found myself coming to grips with obstacles of thinking and living that I never could before. By the time I was through, I almost liked myself, but not enough to stop hating myself for running out on Sally.

Keith received an honorable discharge from the service and returned to college to complete his education. There he met the woman
who was to become his wife:

> There was no one I wanted more than Irene. For the first time in a
> long time, I had some reason to live. The first time we made love, I
> was very gentle and tried hard to please her. She told me this was
> only the second time she had had sex and that the first time was a
> painful experience—she had been raped at age 13. After we finished,
> I got up and dressed. As I was leaving the room, I looked back over
> my shoulder and was surprised to see she had already put her
> clothes on and was combing her hair. Then I saw something that
> froze my blood. It was the way she was looking in the mirror and the
> way she was brushing her hair. There was a look of coldness, of ice
> on her face. Not as if she had just made love with a man who loved
> her and tried to make her happy. It was the look I had seen before
> on prostitutes in Vietnam. It was the look of someone to whom love-
> making was no more pleasurable than taking a shit. I felt as if I had
> been betrayed and defeated. I was crushed. At that moment I knew I
> was more than Number 2. I was dealing with someone who was
> every bit as unhappy and as disturbed as I was. Unfortunately, I
> didn't know how to cope with this. Instead, I started using her to
> see how much I could get from her and how far I could go with her.
> From that moment on, our relationship deteriorated to abuse and
> crudeness. We started debasing each other, and liking each other
> died very quickly. We started having intercourse frequently, and I
> tried to cause her as much humiliation as I could, but she stuck
> around, and I was as lonely with her as without her. I felt increas-
> ingly desperate at my futility in understanding or controlling our
> relationship.

This love–hate relationship continued and resulted in Irene's becoming pregnant and her and Keith marrying:

> It was not a good marriage at all. After the baby was born, I wasn't
> wanted or needed. Irene wouldn't sleep with me unless she wanted
> something, and I became extremely angry, upset, frustrated—the
> whole bit. After a year of marriage, I reached the breaking point. I
> felt crushed, humiliated, scorned, and made to look like a fool. It
> was at this time that I entertained my first serious thoughts about
> rape. I purchased a handgun with the excuse that it would be some
> protection against burglars, but I had other reasons on my mind.
> The gun restored to me a sense of power and control I felt I had lost.
> Now I had the ability to manipulate anyone I chose to. Now I had

the ability to control and humiliate anyone I chose to. Now I chose to.

After getting off work that Friday night, I came home. Irene had promised to wait up for me, and I desperately looked forward to some loving. It had been a long time—too long. When I got home, however, she had already gone to sleep. At that instant, I stopped acting and started reacting.

Keith began driving around the college campus:

It was a damp, foggy night, and I saw a young woman walking towards one of the dorms. When I turn my charm on, I can be very effective, and I persuaded her to join me for a drink. She got in the car and I drove off. Then I pulled the gun out, put it up against her cheek, and cocked it. I told her, "Let's make love." She said, "This isn't love, this is rape." "Okay," I said with a smile, "let's make rape." Then I made her start disrobing. While she was undressing, I was driving around looking for a nice, quiet, dark place where I could do what I wanted without interruption. I spotted a pasture and drove in through the gate, but a car pulled in behind me, which turned out to be a police cruiser.

Keith was arrested and charged with attempted rape. His father bailed him out, and Keith admitted himself to a VA hospital for psychiatric treatment. His marriage to Irene ended:

At first I was overcome with a great sadness. Then I felt angry, and finally I wound up feeling relieved.

After his release from the hospital Keith "played the field." In fact, he found that he became intensely preoccupied with sexual desires:

I took a job as a salesclerk, and the store proved to be a place I could make some exciting, fantasy-satisfying pickups. I started making love to as many as three different women a day. The fantasy trip of having all the girls a guy could want lasted about five weeks. I just plain couldn't hack sleeping with different women in different beds at different times, either physically or mentally. There was something unsatisfying—something missing—in such an existence.

Keith began to concentrate all his attention on one woman, Betty, and they began living together. However, he would spend weekends visiting his son and soon entertained hopes of a reconciliation with

Irene. He moved into an apartment of his own, but his hopes of reuniting with his ex-wife soon ended as the result of a bitter argument:

She attacked me, and it was more than I could bear. I had expected to find the loving companion that I had been searching for for too many years and instead found someone who hated me again. I exploded. I went to a couple of nightspots looking for someone to pick up, but time after time I got shot down. I hated being rejected by women, and I began to seriously think of picking up someone at gunpoint to force them to please me sexually. I went to my psychiatrist and told him about these fantasies. He replied that I must remember that my choices are to be straight and stay out of the hospital, or to enter the hospital and quit work and school, or to mess up and go to prison. He told me the choice was mine. I told him I would straighten up and left.

That night I went to Betty's apartment. She was happy to see me again. She had put on a lot of weight. I remember that she offered herself to me to have sex with her, but I found her repulsive and had to leave. After a few hours, I came back and slept with her. The next morning, I woke up and felt horribly filthy and dirty. Betty smelled like me, and I couldn't stand to be with her one more minute. She wanted me to stay in bed so we could make love, but I was strangling with the feeling of how dirty I felt, so I dressed and bolted out of the apartment. I went home, bathed, and changed clothes and then hopped into my car and drove to K-Mart, where I bought a gun. I drove through the streets looking for a pickup. I remember thinking, "Keith, what you're planning on doing is crazy and could land you behind bars." Then I found her. She was pedaling a bicycle. She was prepubescent, and I felt she would be a safe victim. I rolled down my window and stuck my gun out as I called, "Little girl, do you know what this is? If you don't want to get hurt, put your bicycle down and get into my car quickly." She climbed into the car and off I drove to my place with my pistol still trained on her. When we got inside my apartment, I made her take all her clothes off. Then I had her undress me. Then I grabbed her and hugged her, and the feeling I got was overwhelming. I had a hard-on, and I told her to suck it. I told her that when I came in her mouth, she wasn't to spit it out but that she should kiss me and force the semen into my mouth with her tongue. When she did this, I was shocked at how wonderful her kiss was. I couldn't believe it. It really excited me, and I got another erection and masturbated against her. The look on her face was a combination of horror and disgust. I watched her get dressed. She looked incredibly good to me, and I wanted to have intercourse with her, but she was only 9 years old, and I was afraid this would hurt her, so I didn't. As I drove her back to her bicycle she asked if I was going to kill her. I smiled and said, "Of course not," but as I was about to let her go, I told her that she wasn't to tell anyone that I had taken her and threatened that if she did, I would be back to do more of the same to her.

Keith then returned to the apartment, telephoned his therapist, and called the police. He pleaded guilty to a charge of kidnapping and was given a prison sentence of 15 years to life:

> This incarceration made me realize that I was bisexual. I became extremely horny in jail. I had no sexual outlets and felt really attracted to my cellmate. He appealed to me in that he was young, didn't have too much body hair, was slim, and had a beautiful complexion. I gave him a hand job and wanted him to come in my mouth, but he shot his load while I was masturbating him. I can see now the close relationship between the act I forced on my victim and the kinds of activities that I was fearful that I wanted—I can see that my desire for immature children was a way of avoiding my desire for more mature men.

Sadistic Assault

There is a small group of sexual offenders who derive pleasure in actually hurting the child. Sexuality and aggression become components of a single psychological experience: sadism. Such offenders may torture, mutilate, and, in some cases, murder their victims in the context of the sexual assault.

Dean is a 25-year-old, white, single male who pleaded guilty to charges of kidnapping, sodomy, and assault with a dangerous weapon. The charges stemmed from an incident in which he lured a 12-year-old boy into his car, drove to a deserted quarry, stabbed the boy, and then sodomized him after enlarging his anus with another knife wound:

> I tried to kill him and then to fuck him. I had planned something violent and had been cruising around for a couple of weeks without luck. Whether stabbing him was part of the sexual gratification or just to eliminate the witness I wasn't sure at the time—I just felt it was necessary to use the knife.

As he ejaculated, he again plunged the knife into the boy and left him for dead. This assault was a compulsive, ritualistic act that had been rehearsed, and reinforced by masturbation, for approximately a year prior to the event. It was the culmination of an adolescence and adulthood marked by disordered sexuality. Dean did not date and had no sexual relationships with age-mates, but beginning at age 12, he began engaging in sexual activities with animals and established a pattern of torturing the animal during and after the sexual contact. At one point, he killed a pony with a hunting knife:

> At first, it was with muscular-type animals: a pony, a cow, a short-haired dog. I used to fantasize about sticking animals with a knife in their hindquarters without killing them. The animal can't say nothing. When I stabbed the pony I felt myself getting hard, and in order to ejaculate, I rubbed against him until I came off. I wasn't doing this out of anger or animosity—not at all—more a sense of excitement, a turn-on. After I came off, I felt extremely uncomfortable: queasy and scared.
>
> I remember seeing pictures of Roman gladiators—strong, well-built, muscular males with perfect physiques—and in my fantasies, I made a transition from the animals to grown men who were built like that: sticking a knife in the butt of muscular men. I'm not sure when the kids came into it. Little by little, the age went down. There was less trouble getting ahold of kids. Kids were around and they were easy to get to, and there was less risk of getting hurt myself.
>
> I knew this victim casually. I had been to his house once briefly. He was talking with a couple of kids when he saw me and asked me for a ride home. I drove to a secluded spot, and we sat in the car for a few minutes. Then I put my arm around him and pulled him over to my lap. Even then, he wasn't excited or asking what I was doing. I suddenly blurted out, "You know what I'm going to do?" He said, "No." I said, "I'm going to kill you." Then I reached into the glove compartment and took out the knife. He said, "Dean, don't!" and I stabbed him once in the side. He passed out, and I dragged him into the woods and undressed him. I wanted to fuck him, but he tightened up when I stabbed him, and I couldn't get in him, so I used the knife, and then, while I was fucking him, I stabbed him several more times in the side and in the back. The stabbing was originally to immobilize him and then to get rid of the witness. After I had done this, I realized my mouth was dry, my stomach was upset, and I felt like I was in a daze. I returned to the car, connected the exhaust pipe to the rear window, and tried to commit suicide. It was all part of the plan: capture, assault, kill, and then commit suicide. I must have known without knowing that I couldn't get away with it. Then why attempt it? It's a strange thing.

His suicide attempt was aborted by a passing motorist who also saved the life of the victim by rushing him to a hospital, where he remained in intensive care for over a week.

Since rape is a distorted sexual expression of power, victim selection is to a large extent determined by availability and vulnerability. Children are available and children are vulnerable. They are thus a major target group not only for men who rape but also for women who rape and especially for juveniles who rape. They are less threatening than adults.

The age of the child appears to be the major determinant in the selection of a victim—even more important than the sex of the child. There is more sexual victimization of males when they are children than when they are adults. And among men who sexually assault children, there is a greater proportion of offenders who select both male and female victims than there is among men who rape adults. Children are seen as more vulnerable than adults, and women are seen as more vulnerable (physically) than men. In child rape, the age factor predominates since it is equated with vulnerability. Nowhere is this more apparent than in cases where the victim is an infant.

Arthur is a 25-year-old married man who pleaded guilty to the sexual assault of his 3-month-old infant daughter. He denies the charges, but his wife had witnessed him with his penis in the baby's mouth on four occasions. When semen was found in the infant's mouth by a visiting relative, Child Protective Services were notified and the infant was placed in a foster home.

Arthur's own psychosocial history is replete with trauma: "I didn't have that good a life." He has no memories prior to age 6. His natural mother died when he was 3, and his home life was unstable. His developmental years were chaotic. He did not get along well with his stepmother, whom he describes as alcoholic: "She was always drunk, and she'd slap me." His father appears to have been psychologically absent in his life. Arthur functions at the dull-normal level of intelligence, and his schooling terminated when he was expelled from the seventh grade for destructive behavior. From about age 14, "I started running the streets." Although he states that he has never been the victim of a sexual assault, he reports a persistent nightmare in which he is being sexually attacked by a woman. He is very reticent in discussing his sexual experiences, fantasies, or interests, saying that "sex is something that's hard to talk about." He received no formal sexual education and states that he does not remember his initial sexual experiences. However, it appears that with the onset of adolescence, Arthur began exhibiting inappropriate and disorganized sexual behavior. At one point Child Protective Services placed Arthur in a foster home when it was discovered that his stepmother had kept him chained to a bed in order to prevent him from sexually molesting his younger sister. In the foster placement, he sexually assaulted younger girls and boys, masturbated publicly, wore girl's undergarments to bed, and engaged in sexual contacts with animals. As a result, he was placed in a juvenile institution.

Arthur's medical history appears unremarkable, with the exception of his enuresis to age 17 and some alcohol abuse. His vocational history is unstable; he has held a number of unskilled jobs for very short periods of time. He attributes his problems in keeping a job to his "laziness and not wanting to get up in the morning." He would work for a while, collect unemployment insurance, and then go on welfare and public assistance. Arthur has no friends or stable relationships in his life. His application to enlist in the armed services was rejected when he failed the entrance exams. The instant offense constitutes his first conviction for a sexual offense, but he had previously been convicted of stealing from a former employer, for which he was given probation.

At age 20 Arthur married a woman, after impregnating her, who appears to have been mentally disturbed. She initially miscarried but later gave birth to a daughter. Three weeks after her birth, the infant came under the supervision of Child Protective Services because of parental neglect, and it was later discovered that the infant was also being sexually victimized by her father.

A case such as Arthur's is representative of the cases we have seen where the victim of the sexual assault is an infant. We are dealing here with an adult whose sexual offenses are only one indication of multiple and chronic life problems. There appear to be no conflict-free areas of functioning in the offender's life, and he seems to be handicapped by limited intelligence and/or serious psychiatric disturbance. Such offenders appear to be grossly inadequate and immature individuals who are incapable of organizing or managing their lives in an adaptive or responsible fashion and who can function adequately only in a structured, institutional setting.

Victim Impact

Rape is a terrible ordeal for anyone to undergo, but when the victim is a child, there is the further concern as to what impact it will have on the child's psychological development. Children are, by their very nature, extremely vulnerable, and they look to adults for care, guidance, and protection. When they have been raped, there is the very real concern about whether such a violent and distorted exposure and introduction to human sexuality will alter their development in this life area in some irreversible way. Because they are children, they are less likely than adults to have had positive and satisfying prior sexual encounters and experiences to contrast with the negative assault. Further, if the child does not resolve the rape trauma, sexuality may become an area of conflict as she or he matures. The unresolved issue is confronted as she or he progresses toward sexual maturation (adolescence), dating, courtship, marriage, childbirth, and the like.

RAPE OF THE ELDERLY[19]

The act of rape in the minds of many people, both laypersons and professionals alike, is believed to be motivated by sexual arousal and desire on the part of the offender. Consequently, the victim is often regarded as responsible for stimulating her assailant and arousing his impulses. She is frequently stereotyped as a young and attractive woman who dresses and behaves in a sexually provocative fashion. The public does not yet appear to appreciate fully that rape is in fact a distortion of human sexuality and that the victims of some offenders are significantly older than their assailants or that elderly women may be particular target victims for some rapists.

Gebhard and his colleagues[20] report that only 3% of the victims of the convicted rapists that they studied were more than 50 years old. In Amir's[21] study of the incidence of forcible rape in Philadelphia, he found that 3.6% of the reported assaults were directed toward women aged 50 or older, whereas only 1.4% of the offenders fell into this age range. In the Denver study by MacDonald,[22] 7% of the victims were over the age of 50, one of whom was the victim of a gang rape by five men. Fletcher[23]

[19]This section is adapted from A. Nicholas Groth, "The Older Rape Victim and Her Assailant," *Journal of Geriatric Psychiatry* 11, no. 2 (1978): 203–215. Copyright 1978, International Universities Press, Inc. Reprinted by permission.

[20]Paul H. Gebhard, John H. Gagnon, Wardell B. Pomeroy, and Cornelia V. Christenson, *Sex Offenders: An Analysis of Types* (New York: Harper & Row and Paul B. Hoeber, 1965), p. 194.

[21]Menachem Amir, *Patterns in Forcible Rape* (Chicago: University of Chicago Press, 1971), p. 52.

[22]John M. MacDonald, *Rape: Offenders and Their Victims* (Springfield, Ill.: Charles C Thomas, 1971), p. 77.

[23]Patricia Fletcher, "Criminal Victimization of Elderly Women: A Look at Sexual Assault," Rape Crisis Center of Syracuse, Inc., June 22, 1977. An abridged version of this paper appeared in *Response* 1, no. 4 (April/June 1977), p. 4.

cites the incidence of reported rapes against women over 55 in New York City as 2% and in Detroit as averaging to 6.8% over a three-year period. She reports that 5.2% of the victims reporting to the Rape Crisis Center of Syracuse were over 55 years old and notes that the average age of the rape victim is increasing. A study by the Queen's Bench Foundation[24] in San Francisco found that 4.7% of the victims were 40 or older. However, considering the absolute age of the victim may be misleading. For example, in an earlier California study[25] of San Francisco victims that examined the relative age difference between the victim and her offender, it was found that 25% of the victims were 30 or more years older than their assailants.

In the reported literature on rape, the majority of victims fall into the same age bracket as their offenders or are slightly younger. For this reason, perhaps, the older victim has not received much attention in the clinical literature on sexual assault, and the rape of elderly women remains a largely unexplored area.

From 1970 to 1975, we evaluated all sexual offenders sent to a security treatment center for diagnostic evaluation. Of the 170 referred offenders who sexually assaulted adult victims, 30 (18%) selected women who were significantly older than themselves; that is, the victim was at least twice the age of her assailant. Of this study sample, 20 (12%) were offenders who selected victims over the age of 50.

Data pertaining to the offender, his offense, and his victim were retrieved through clinical interviews and examinations of case records so that we could determine the nature of such assaults. The emphasis in this study was placed on descriptive characteristics of the offender and the victim, the offender's social relationship with his victim, the context of his crime, his modus operandi and his precipitating stresses, and the types of acts committed.

Mac is a 19-year-old, single, white male who possesses a formidable physique as a result of his interest in body building. He is a reasonably friendly person who is somewhat embarrassed about his limited schooling—"I sometimes feel dumb"—and who exhibits considerable compensatory behavior to assert his strength and virility: weight lifting, tattoos, heavy drinking "to feel like a big shot," contact sports, fighting, and the like. He dreams of "making a fantastic lift in the Olympics or of

[24]Queen's Bench Foundation, *Rape Prevention and Resistance* (San Francisco: Queen's Bench Foundation, 1976), p. 29.
[25]*California Sexual Deviation Research,* Final Report (Sacramento, Calif.: State Department of Mental Hygiene, 1954).

being in bed with beautiful girls." After leaving school, he applied for
enlistment in the Marine Corps but failed to report for his induction
physical because his "buddy didn't show up and I didn't want to go in
by myself." Mac has had an unstable work history because he would
"take summers off to hang around the beaches." He has had increasing
difficulties in his relationship with his father, a truck driver, who "dis-
approves of my long hair and tight pants." Mac's relationship with his
mother is better, but distant. He describes her as being somewhat inconsistent in her relationship with him, sometimes being very easygoing
and at other times being overly strict. Mac began dating at age 15 and
went steady for a few years with one girl, when at age 18 he met and fell
in love with another girl. He did not engage in sexual activities with
either of these two girls he cared about—"I respected them"—but "was
getting sex off another girl" at the time "who in a way was a whore":

> The construction company I worked for was having a Christmas
> party. It started at nine in the morning and lasted till four in the
> afternoon. All I did was drink. The night before my girl and I had an
> argument and she didn't want to go to the party so I went alone. I
> danced with several girls. One was a married woman who was wear-
> ing a real low-cut dress. She dropped something on the floor and
> took her time bending over to pick it up. I was sitting on a table with
> my legs spread apart, and she came over and put her elbows on my
> knees and asked me to dance. When the party ended, I was standing
> outside waiting to get a ride from my buddy, and I saw two women
> getting into a car. I asked them for a ride.

Although they did not know him, the women, ages 45 and 49, thought
nothing of his request and allowed him to get into the car. He sat in the
front seat between the two women, and as they drove off

> I noticed the woman on my right had her dress high up and I started
> to feel her up. She told me to stop it but I didn't pay any attention to
> her. Instead I took my cock out and asked her for a blow job. She
> refused and I smashed her in the mouth. Then I grabbed her by the
> back of her neck and forced her head down on me. I told her I had a
> gun and if she didn't suck me I'd kill her.

The woman driving the car attempted to pull into a gas station, hoping
to get help, but Mac punched her on the side of her head and stepped on
the accelerator of the car, forcing her to continue driving. Mac then
grabbed her at the back of her neck and told her to drive with one hand,
while he started to undress her. At this point, the driver decided to run

the car off the road across someone's lawn and into a tree. Mac fled on foot:

> I felt scared. My mind was racing. I couldn't think. I came to a house and knocked on the door.

A 76-year-old woman opened the door:

> I said my car had broken down and asked if her husband was home. She told me she wasn't married and I asked to use her telephone. She let me in. I don't know what was in my mind. I ripped the phone off the wall, knocked her down, felt her up, and started taking off her clothes.

Mac struck the woman repeatedly in the face, and when she fell to the floor, he kicked her, ripped off most of her clothing, and attempted to have sexual intercourse with her. However, he was unable to do so because of a corset the victim was wearing, so he instead forced her to perform fellatio on him by holding her mouth open with his hands, after which he left. As a result of this attack, this elderly victim was in the hospital for over two weeks. When Mac was apprehended by the police, he initially denied any memory of his offenses, attributing this to a blackout brought on by his drinking. In subsequent interviews, however, he admitted to the events as described by his victims, but he could not account for his actions.

The Offender

The offenders who assaulted significantly older victims were predominantly young, white, single males. They ranged in age at the time of their first sexual offense from 12 to 38: 3 (10%) were under the age of 16, 8 (27%) were in their middle or late teens, 13 (43%) were in their 20s, and 6 (20%) were in their 30s. The average age for this group of subjects was 23.5. In 24 (80%) of the cases, the offenders were white; 6 (20%) were black. At the time of the offense, 17 (57%) were single (9 of these were 17 years old or younger and therefore too young to be married), 9 (30%) were married, and 4 (13%) were either divorced or separated from their wives. All of these subjects showed difficulty with life adjustment tasks beginning in early adolescence or before: difficulties with schooling, behavioral problems at home, and the like. For half of this group, the conviction constituted their first record of a sexual offense, whereas the other half had a previous record of sexual offenses, the majority of which were assaults; in a few cases, their acts were limited to indecent exposure, peeping, stealing women's undergarments, or making obscene telephone calls. In 12 (40%) cases, these offenders' criminal histories contained sexual and nonsexual offenses, with drunkenness, breaking and entering, and larceny being the most predominant types of nonsexual crimes.

In examining their early development, the quality of family life appears to have been generally poor and the family structure unstable for the majority of these offenders. Only 2 (7%) subjects reported a stable and compatible relationship between their parents. In 4 (13%) other cases, although their parents' marriages were stable, the father appeared to be psychologically absent in the subject's life because of his type of work or his working hours. In another 4 (13%) cases, although the parents remained married, their relationship was characterized by conflict, friction, and/or abuse. In 20 (67%) of the cases, one or both parents were absent during the subject's early years (between ages 1 and 12): 10 (33%) through separation or divorce, 5 (17%) because of death, 4 (13%) because of desertion, and 1 (3%) because of a series of foster home placements. In most cases, the offender reported feeling alienated from both parents. If they were present in his life, the father was frequently described as either something of a nonentity or, more frequently, as a cruel, physically abusive, and alcoholic man who was unfaithful and undependable; the mother was variously described as nervous, "highstrung," and domineering, promiscuous, manipulative, overprotective, or well meaning but ineffective. Love, respect, and admiration were noticeably absent in these offenders' regard for their parents. No one described a genuinely happy home, one characterized by warmth, trust, and a sense of security. Instead, broken homes, family discord, financial hardship, and physical and/or emotional abuse or neglect were frequent sources of trauma in the formative years of the offenders' lives.

The Victim

Since some offenders had assaulted more than one woman, there were 42 victims in all. They ranged in age from 32 to 81: 4 (10%) victims were in their 30s, 7 (17%) were in their 40s, 9 (21%) were in their 50s, 15 (36%) were in their 60s, 6 (14%) were in their 70s, and 1 (2%) was in her 80s. More than half of the victims could be regarded as senior citizens. All the victims were women, 37 (38%) were white, and 5 (12%) were black. (Only one assault was interracial.) With regard to marital status, 5 (12%) of the victims were single, 14 (33%) were married, 8 (19%) were widowed, and 1 (2%) was divorced. The marital status of 4 (10%) other victims was unknown; they were living alone at the time of the offense, and no data were available in regard to the remaining 10 (24%) victims.

The Offense

Location. The majority of victims (32, or 76%) were sexually assaulted either in their own homes (22, or 52%) or in their own automobiles (10, or 24%). The offense took place out of doors for 7 (17%) of the victims (on the street, in a vacant lot, in a quarry, and in a wooded area), and 3 (7%) victims were assaulted in a public building (a laundromat, an elevator, and a public restroom).

Relationship. The majority of the victims (33, or 79%) were complete strangers to their assailants, 3 (7%) were casually acquainted, 3 (7%) were close friends or associates (a landlady, a neighbor, a resident in the same rooming house), and 3 (7%) were relatives (mother, aunt, and foster mother).

Assault. One of the most prominent characteristics of the sexual assaults was the degree of violence exhibited in the offenses. The majority (18, or 60%) of offenders seriously injured their victims: 3 (10%) murdered their victims, 2 (7%) stabbed their victims, and 13 (43%) savagely beat their victims. That far more physical force and aggression was used in the commission of these offenses than would have been necessary had the intent of the offender been simply to overcome his victim's resistance becomes evident from the following case examples.

Harry is a 32-year-old, white, married male who accosted his victim, a 65-year-old woman, in a laundromat and fled. When the police arrived, they found the body of a woman in a pool of blood; she had been beaten to the point where her face was no longer recognizable. An autopsy report showed that she had been sexually abused; a Coca-Cola bottle had also been found in her stomach and had penetrated her liver. She had fractures of 11 ribs and hemorrhages of the head. Harry pleaded guilty to the offense but stated that he had no recollection of it because of an alcoholic blackout.

John, a 17-year-old, white, single male, was doing household chores for a 35-year-old woman. Suddenly, he grabbed the victim around the throat and began choking her; he beat her about the head with his fists until she fell to the floor. He picked up a fireplace poker and struck her repeatedly on the head and punctured her stomach with it. John then undressed her and had sexual intercourse with her. Believing she was dead, he rolled her up in a rug and fled.

The dominating motive is clearly rage rather than sexual desire in these assaults.

Of the remaining 12 (40%) offenders, 4 (13%) bruised their victims and 8 (27%) caused no physical trauma to their victims.

Ralph, a 26-year-old, white, single male, assaulted three female adults ages 56, 60, and 65. He would force his way into the victim's car; drive to a wooded area; strike the woman in the face, and force her to undress and to submit to intercourse.

Stan, a 30-year-old, black, separated male, assaulted a 61-year-old female. As the victim entered an elevator, Stan approached her from behind and put a knife to her throat. He took her to the basement of the building, where he made her perform oral sex on him and then raped her twice. He stole her watch and pocketbook and fled.

Nevertheless, in some of these cases, the assault was interrupted by someone coming upon the scene and thus possibly sparing the victim more severe injury. We also might speculate that a number of homicides involving elderly victims may have sexual components that are not identified for a variety of reasons and, therefore, do not come to our attention in regard to sexual offenses.

The element of overt or underlying violence is also suggested by the use of a weapon (usually a knife) by 17 (63%) of the offenders in the commission of the sexual assault. Since the offenders are young and physically strong men whose victims are not formidable opponents, the emphasis on aggression and the use of a weapon appears highly significant.

Type of Offense. Rape in the form of vaginal intercourse was the most predominant offense committed in the sexual assaults (25, or 60%). In 8 (19%) of these 25 cases, the victim was also robbed, and in 2 (5%) cases, she was also forced to engage in other sexual acts (fellatio and sodomy). Attempted rape was committed against 8 (19%) of the victims: either someone interrupted the assault, or the victim successfully resisted, or the offender desisted for some reason (for example, one offender stopped his assault and fled when his victim's grandchild began to cry). In 6 (14%) of the cases, the victim was forced to perform "unnatural acts" (fellatio) on her assailant; no other sexual acts took place. In the 3 (7%) cases of rape–murder, multiple sexual acts (oral, anal, vaginal, and the insertion of foreign objects into the victim's orifices) were committed, sometimes prior to and sometimes after death.

Intoxication.   The role that alcohol or drugs play in the commission of these offenses is ambiguous. In 18 (60%) of the cases, the offenders reported being under the influence of drugs or alcohol at the time of their offense, and 12 (40%) reported no intoxication at all. For those who allege that they were high on drugs (3, or 10%) or alcohol (11, or 37%) or both (4, or 13%), there is some substantiation from the statements of their victims or others. However, alcohol or drug misuse and/or abuse appears characteristic of the lifestyle of these offenders in general and not specific to their sexual assaults. In other words, although they may have been somewhat intoxicated at the time of their assaults, they had also been intoxicated many other times and had not committed sexual assaults. It seems reasonable, nevertheless, that in a number of cases, the state of intoxication may have contributed to an impairment of judgment and a loss of impulse control when sexual and aggressive impulses had been activated and the offender was under stress.

The victim data suggest that alcohol use was involved in only 3 (7%) cases. In each, the victim was drinking with her assailant just prior to the assault.

Precipitating Stress: Most of the offenders describe being in a state of psychological stress or distress at the time of their offense. The predominant mood state appears to have been one of anger and/or depression, and the offense itself was typically preceded by some upsetting event, usually, though not always, involving some significant woman in the assailant's life. Ten (33%) offenders report a serious dispute with their wife prior to the offense. These arguments revolve around a number of marital issues, such as incompatibility, infidelity, alcohol abuse, and household management. Four (13%) offenders had felt angry at their mothers for imposing restrictions on their activities (like a curfew) or not allowing them to have something they wanted very much (like a car or a motorcycle). Three (10%) offenders cited conflicts with their girlfriends, either being stood up, rejected, taunted, or sexually frustrated. One offender (3%) reported a serious argument with the parents of his girlfriend, who objected to their daughter's seeing him. Another (3%) claimed that his sister and a neighbor lady had been making false accusations about him. A third (3%) offender was "nerved up" because of a barroom fight he was in, and a fourth (3%) was upset by his rejection by the armed services (the Marine Corps). Four (13%) offenders reported being in a "bad mood" but could not identify any reason for this frame of mind. Two (7%) appeared to be in an agitated mental state and feeling "paranoid" at the time of their assault, and no data were available on four (13%) of the subjects.

Intent.   In accounting for their assaults, 10 (33%) of the offenders reported that their aim was to hurt their victim. The sexual assault was an expression of anger. For example, a 28-year-old man who was convicted of the attempted rape of a 61-year-old woman explained that three weeks prior to the offense, he began having an impulse "to go out and hurt somebody." On the day of the offense, the impulse became overwhelming, and he approached his victim with a knife but didn't use it. He insists that he was intent on hurting the woman but is not certain that sex was on his mind.

Five (17%) of the offenders stated that their intent was sexual gratification. The assault was to accomplish sexual intercourse. For example, a 17-year-old who was convicted of the rape of a 60-year-old woman said that he was walking home from a party through a parking lot. He started looking into parked cars, and the victim asked him what he was doing. He got in on the passenger side and told her he wanted "to have a little fun and to get some loving." He struck her several times on the face when she started screaming, and then he raped her.

Seven (23%) of the offenders claimed that they were in a blackout when they committed the offense and therefore could not give an explanation of their intent. Five (17%) offenders denied committing the offense. One (3%) offender (aged 15) said that his intent was to rob his victim (aged 32), but after he hit her, the thought came to him to rape her. "She was good-looking, but I don't know why I raped her." Another (3%) offender said that his intent in approaching the victim was "to have somebody to talk to, but she got all upset and started a commotion and I wound up raping her." And no data were available in this regard on one (3%) subject.

In 15 (50%) of the cases, the assailants described their offense as unplanned and impulsive: "I was hitchhiking and she offered me a ride and I suddenly decided to rape her." In 10 (33%) cases, the offenders reported that their assaults were premeditated. They had thought about them beforehand, had been having rape fantasies, and had planned out their offenses. No data were available on 5 (17%) of the offenders.

Discussion

Age is no defense against rape. Even women of advanced years are vulnerable to sexual assault. Moreover, from our data it appears that when they are sexual victims, they are the targets of particularly brutal assaults. The older woman appears to symbolize an authority figure over whom the offender wants control and/or an actual woman against whom he wants to retaliate or revenge himself. Sexuality becomes the means through which anger and power are expressed and the means by which he can hurt, humiliate, and degrade his victim. The sexual assault of the older victim clearly reveals rape to be a distortion of human sexuality. It is sexual behavior serving nonsexual needs and motives. The majority of victims were assaulted on their own premises by complete strangers. In many cases, their advanced age and the related life situation (for example, living alone) made them particularly vulnerable, and vulnerability and accessibility play a more significant role in determining victim selection than does physical attractiveness or alleged provocativeness. Rape is far more an issue of hostility than of sexual desire.

A number of issues may complicate the recovery from sexual assault when the rape victim is an elderly person. The biopsychosocial impact of rape may be aggravated by the diminished physical, social, and economic resources that often accompany aging. The elderly victim may be more susceptible to physical trauma from the assault. There may be fewer available friends or associates to turn to for support and comfort in this time of stress. The social values of her generation may compound the psychological impact of the offense; for example, she may see it as a shame or a disgrace that she has been sexually victimized and may find it especially embarrassing to relate the sexual details of the assault. She may feel too humiliated to report having had to perform sexual acts that she regards as perverted. The sense of increasing helplessness and mortality may be activated by the experience of the assault. In cases where she is also robbed, she may lose possessions that symbolize important aspects of her life. The theft of money may further jeopardize someone who must manage on a fixed income, and financial considerations may limit her alternatives for coping with her trauma. For example, moving from her living quarters, when this has been the site of her assault, to a new residence may not be feasible. If the victim reports the offense, the effect of aging on her cognitive and perceptual faculties may hinder her assistance with regard to the investigation and the apprehension of a suspect. As one chief of police reported to the newspapers in regard to a suspect who raped and robbed eight elderly women in the course of 10 months, "Apprehension of the suspect was hampered by his method of attack and the ages of his victims. Our Department devoted several hundred man-hours analyzing traces of physical evidence left behind in order to identify the suspect." Finally, if the elderly victim decides to prosecute, she may have particular difficulty in understanding the confusing and frequently frustrating procedures of the criminal justice system.

Rape is underreported in general, and apprehension and conviction are more unlikely than probable. This may be especially so with regard to cases involving elderly victims. The small incidence of such victimization reported in the literature clearly does not accurately reflect the reality and the magnitude of this disturbing social problem, nor the special importance and the particular seriousness of the sexual victimization of this target population.

MARITAL RAPE

Marital rape may be defined as forcible sexual assault on an unwilling spouse. At one time, if the marriage was intact and the partners residing in the same domicile, "it was traditionally ruled that such an unwilling sexual act was not rape."[26] Increasingly, however, the states are repealing the spousal immunity clauses in their statutes and encompassing the sexual assault of one marriage partner by the other in the legal definition of forcible rape.

Although such offenses may be widespread, they are low in visibility for a number of reasons. For example, it has been a traditional view that a wife may not deny her husband sex. He is entitled to sexual relations, and if she does refuse, then he is justified in demanding sex or forcing her to submit. The victim herself may not regard such enforced sexual activity as rape, and if the sexual abuse has occurred in the context of an argument or a fight, she may find it more comfortable to regard it as a battering rather than a rape. This may be less humiliating or embarrassing for her. Or if she does seek relief and redress, the law and the community are not responsive to her request.

In marital rape, the offender is the victim's lawful sexual partner, and the nonconsenting encounters may range from taking advantage of having sexual access to the partner, to forcing the victim to engage in what to her are unacceptable sexual acts or practices, to violent sexual attacks as part of a battering assault. As in child sexual assault, the victim in marital rape may be pressured into unwanted sexual relations in order to achieve some other nonsexual aim or goal, or she may be

[26]E. Sagarin, "Rape of One's Wife," *Medical Aspects of Human Sexuality* 12, no. 2 (February 1978): 153.

forced into undesired sexual activity through threat, intimidation, or physical force.

Although we have observed too few cases of marital rape to offer meaningful statistics in regard to such offenders, we have seen a variety of types of assault. In some cases, the offender takes sexual advantage of his wife when she is intoxicated or asleep.

Andy is a 30-year-old, white male convicted of raping a prostitute. He married a woman whom he had impregnated but found that he was ill equipped for marriage and a family:

> My wife and I were incompatible in regard to sex. We had three kids, and they all were accidents. She was supposed to be on the pill, but she was lazy and would skip a few days and then take them all at once. This is how she got caught with the second and third kid. Sex turned her off after the third kid. She became frigid. We'd go to bed and I'd try to have sex, but she complained that intercourse hurt, so I'd take it out and put it between her breasts to reach a climax. I tried for anal sex. She refused, saying it hurt. She didn't like to give oral sex, and she'd do it for only a short time and wouldn't finish me off. It got to the point that there was no sex relations, and I started going to prostitutes. The only way I could get sex from my wife was to take it. She would go to sleep, and I would be very horny. She was a heavy sleeper. I would roll alongside and pull her legs up and enter her that way, from the back. I would get it into her, and she would wake up and realize what was happening and struggle with me, but I could usually overpower her resistance.

After eight years of marriage Andy's wife divorced him.

In other cases, the husband forces his wife to have sexual relations with other persons. Usually, the motive on the part of this type of offender is not one of financial gain or profit, although in some such cases he may be prostituting his wife.

At the age of 26, Ben married Cindy, a 17-year-old woman whom he had impregnated. It was his second marriage, and he described it as "a big mistake," alleging that his wife was promiscuous and "knew more about sex than I ever will." Ben was physically abusive toward Cindy, and on one occasion, she was hospitalized as the result of a beating she received from him. Other times, he would invite male friends to his home and force Cindy to engage in sexual acts with them while he watched. Finally, at some point, he brought a black man home, and Cindy refused to cooperate. Ben grabbed her by the throat and tore her dress off. He forced her mouth on the other man's penis and then attempted to have intercourse with her. He punched, bit, and kicked her. When the assault was over, Cindy had bruises and bite marks all over her body. Ben had served time in prison just prior to marrying Cindy and claimed that he "encountered all kinds of 'queers' in prison" and that after his release, Cindy became "a release for all I went through in prison." Ben had boasted to his codefendant that he could make his wife do anything he wanted her to do or else he'd beat her up, and his codefendant reported that Cindy "looked and acted like she was scared of her husband." Ben was convicted of rape and given a three- to five-year prison sentence. His codefendant was fined and placed on probation.

In some cases, the husband forces his wife to perform sexual acts, such as fellatio or sodomy, to which she objects, or to engage in objectionable sexual activities, such as those that involve sadomasochistic, coprophilic, or ritualistic elements.

Jed married at age 22 after going with Kathy for approximately one year, during which time she became pregnant. Although he didn't love his wife, Jed felt that marriage was "the right thing to do." He states that Kathy was completely faithful to him, and four children resulted from their union. Jed believes that Kathy became frightened of sex because of the number of pregnancies she had experienced and began to make up a variety of excuses to avoid sexual relations with him. He felt that he and his wife drew apart from each other, and both felt frustrated and rejected. They argued much of the time, and Jed began having sexual crime fantasies, which frightened and disturbed him. He began an extramarital affair as a way of offsetting the problems he was experiencing at home, and although his girlfriend wanted him to run off with her, he finally ended their relationship. Jed found himself increasingly preoccupied with fantasies of sodomy and bondage of women. He began reading pornographic novels with titles such as *The Dominant Male, Punishment and Discipline of the Female,* and *Whipping and Spanking,* and prior to his sexual offense, he attempted to live out his fantasies with his wife.

Kathy noted that

> Jed seemed possessed with sex. He demanded relations at least once a day and frequently more often, and he spent most of his spare time around the house reading dirty books on sex! He kept this material

in a bureau drawer, and in another drawer, he collected all kinds of ropes—some were even jump ropes that he said he used in practicing to keep fit. Since he was athletically inclined, I believed him.

Kathy described Jed as having a bad temper and resenting ever being questioned or criticized. On more than one occasion, when in a bad mood, he had struck both her and the children.

When Jed demanded that Kathy submit to sodomy, she refused and became quite angry with him and accused him of raping her before their marriage. Jed then took some rope and bound her hands behind her back. Although Kathy fought and struggled, he succeeded in inserting his penis into her rectum. Kathy told him it hurt and cried because it was so painful, but Jed paid no attention to her cries and continued performing the act. He tried to justify this assault by telling Kathy she had "brought it on herself." Jed claimed that he did not have any interest in inflicting physical pain on his wife but wanted, instead, to dominate and degrade her. Their marriage continued to deteriorate. Jed's feelings of guilt and anger increased toward Kathy, and he made a conscious decision to go out and commit a rape. He attacked a 50-year-old woman, found he was not able to maintain an erection, became furious with her, saying she was just like his wife, beat her up, and made her perform oral sex on him.

In still other cases, the husband is a wife beater, and as part of the battering, she is also sexually assaulted or abused.

When Sam was 18 years old he married his girlfriend, Carol, who had become pregnant as a result of having been raped by him. One day, while they were walking along the seashore, Sam suddenly knocked Carol to the ground, held her down, tore off her underpants, and raped her. Carol continued to be a target of Sam's physical and sexual violence for the two years that their marriage lasted. He would take offense at such things as the baby's crying or his food not being prepared to his liking and react by attacking his wife. He would kick and beat Carol and sexually abuse her. On one occasion, he forced his fist into her vagina; on another occasion, he strangled her until she passed out and then sodomized her. Any refusal of sexual relations by Carol was certain to bring violent reprisals from Sam, not only against her but also against their infant daughter.

Interestingly, in the cases of marital rape that have come to our attention, we have observed that the refusal of sex is not, in and of itself, the reason for such assaults: rather it is how such denial is experienced by the offender in the context of the marital relationship:

1. *Sex may be equated with power.* As Morton Hunt observes:

> The typical marital rapist is a man who still believes that husbands are supposed to "rule" their wives. This extends, he feels, to sexual matters: When he wants her, she should be glad, or at least willing; if she isn't, he has the right to force her. But in forcing her he gains far more than a few minutes of sexual pleasure; he humbles her and reasserts, in the most emotionally powerful way possible, that he is the ruler and she the subject.[27]

Such offenders do expect their wives to engage in sex on demand, and when their wives refuse, the refusal confronts them with an underlying and pervasive feeling of not being in control of their lives or able to manage marital and other life demands effectively. Marital rape becomes an assertion of power and strength and a denial of feelings of weakness, helplessness, and vulnerability. Sexual domination is their desperate attempt to establish control in the face of overwhelming powerlessness.

2. *Sex may be equated with love and affection.* Not having developed ways to experience and express closeness and affection in nonsexual ways, such offenders equate getting sex with being loved. When their wives refuse them sex, they interpret this as not being loved. They find the withholding of sex intolerable since it confronts them with underlying fears of not being cared for or valued: "If you loved me you would give me sex." The person who is closest to them, who knows them best, finds them unlovable. This is their deepest fear, that they are of no value, that they don't deserve love or respect. For men who are insecure in regard to their feelings about their personal worth, such rejection is devastating. Sex, even if it is forced, is an affirmation of their worth, a defense against such rejection, and proof that their fears about their wives' not loving them are groundless.

3. *Sex is equated with virility.* Such men feel that in getting sex from their wives their manhood is reaffirmed. To be denied sex is to be emasculated. For men who are insecure about their masculinity or have few other avenues of personal expression, physical strength and sexual activity become their means of self-assertion. Marital rape, then, becomes a way of proving their potency and assuaging their doubts about their manhood.

4. *Sex is equated with debasement.* Just as sex may be seen as a reward or an expression of approval, when their wives withhold sex the offend-

---

[27]M. Hunt, "Legal Rape," *Family Circle* (January 9, 1979): 38.

ers experience this refusal as an expression of disfavor and an intended punishment. In the context of marital disputes, such offenders use sex to punish their wives. The wife is degraded by being forced to do something she does not want to. By sexually assaulting her, the offender "teaches her a lesson." He retaliates in this fashion for his displeasure with her. Marital rape becomes an expression of anger and contempt. Sex becomes an expression of his hostility and rage.

5. *Sex is seen as a panacea.* In a very simplistic way, such offenders regard sex as a measure of the success of their marriage relationship. If the sex is OK, then everything else is OK. Sex is also seen as the solution to any marital problem. It is through sexual intercourse that these men seek reconciliation following marital disputes. Sex is the solution to all of life's problems: "This will prove that despite everything, I really am a man, I'm in control, and everything is really all right."

Marital rape may be the most predominant type of sexual assault committed, yet, because of prevailing social attitudes and legal codes, it goes largely undetected. Like other family problems, it is kept within the family, and both mental health and criminal justice agencies have traditionally been cautious in "interfering" in family matters. Intrafamily sexual abuse, however, whether it be marital rape or incestuous child assault, is becoming an increasingly visible concern in our society. Human service providers will be encountering increasing demands for services to help address this problem.

Unlike the situation in which a victim is sexually assaulted by a nonfamily member, in marital rape the victim is living with her assailant. She is under his scrutiny and surveillance, and he has continual access to her. The person to whom she looks for protection and caring is her victimizer. She is at risk in her own home from the man she is wed to. Yet, she may have mixed feelings toward him. Although she may at times fear and hate him, she may also love and care about him. She may be dependent on him, emotionally or financially or otherwise, and feel that she has few options except to tolerate his sexual abuse. She may see termination of the marriage as a personal failure or disgrace or be concerned as to the impact of such an action on their children. She may feel pressured to keep her victimization a secret from others. Social or religious values may preclude divorce.

As an alternative or as an adjunct to legal action, social service or mental health programs providing individual and marital counseling, family support services, and shelters for victims may be a more effective intervention and disposition in those cases in which sexual assault appears to be confined to the marital relationship and is, in part, a product of family dysfunction than when it is exhibited by the offender both within and outside of the marriage. Probably, the majority of men who rape their wives do not rape other persons. It would be interesting to know how many of the married men who rape other persons also raped their own wives.

THE ADOLESCENT SEXUAL OFFENDER[28]

Although currently a great deal of attention is being focused on the serious problem of forcible rape, the major emphasis has been on the adult offender. Relatively little attention is being paid to the adolescent male who commits sexual assault. In fact, there appears to be a reluctance on the part of the courts and other agencies to view juvenile sexual offenses as significant or serious. Sometimes, the concern is voiced that such a youngster will be stigmatized and that a conviction will jeopardize his plans for enlistment in the armed services. But more often, it appears that such an offense is regarded as merely sexual experimentation, situational in nature, or as an expression of the normal aggressiveness of a sexually maturing male.

In some states—Massachusetts, for example—by law no male under the age of 14 can be convicted of rape since, when the statute was written (over 100 years ago), it was believed that a male younger than 14 was incapable of achieving sexual penetration. Even apart from such technical loopholes, it is at the discretion of the court whether a male between the ages of 14 and 17 who is charged with a sexual assault shall be tried as a juvenile or as an adult. Yet, about 20% of the adult offenders we worked with had had a juvenile criminal history of juvenile sexual assault, and an even larger number admitted to having committed a sexual assault in their early teenage years for which they were never apprehended.

Juvenile sexual offenders can be subdivided into three groups on the basis of the age of the victim relative to the age of the offender.

1. *Those who assault significantly younger victims* (that is, a preadolescent child at least five years younger than the assailant).

[28]This section is adapted from A. Nicholas Groth, "The Adolescent Sexual Offender and His Prey," *International Journal of Offender Therapy and Comparative Criminology* 21, no. 3 (1977): 249–254. Copyright 1977, Association for the Psychiatric Treatment of Offenders. Reprinted by permission.

Kenny is a 9-year-old boy who forced a 3-year-old girl to perform oral sex on him. He explained that it was "just a trick" and that he promised the girl some candy if she would do it. He then had the little girl remove her underpants and laid down on her and simulated intercourse. This assault was discovered as the result of an investigation prompted by the discovery that the victim had gonorrhea of the throat. Kenny admitted the sexual contact and said he received the idea of oral sex from pornographic pictures that he found under the mattress in his parents' bedroom. VD tests on him were negative, and he denied ever being the victim of a sexual assault. The court continued his case for one year without a finding, with the requirement of individual and family counseling.

2. *Those who assault peer-age victims.*

When Gordon was 13 years old, he was charged with two counts of indecent assault and battery on a child under 14. The charges were filed. Two months later, he was charged with two more counts of indecent assault. He was adjudicated delinquent and committed to a detention center. Six months later, he was paroled from that institution and was receiving outpatient psychiatric treatment when he grabbed an 11-year-old girl around the throat and dragged her into the woods. He wrestled her to the ground, got on top of her, and punched her a number of times in the face. Then he pulled down her pants and was going to put his penis into her when he discharged on her, between her legs. Gordon explained the assault as due to his "hatred for young girls."

3. *Those who assault significantly older victims* (that is, an adult victim at least ten years older than the offender).

Jack was only 12 years old when he committed his first sexual assault:

> I was walking home from school, and I decided to pull a B & E. I came to the last house on the street and checked it out. I knocked and a woman came to the door. She was white, around 50 years old, and a complete stranger. I became sexually aroused—her being home by herself—and I was big for my age. I pushed her on the floor, tied her up, and had intercourse with her. Then I took some money and a radio and left. This wasn't my first sexual experience, but it was my first offense. I got caught and sent to a state school for boys for two years.

Jack has committed two subsequent rapes (see below).

Descriptively, the composite profile that emerges of the adolescent offender we worked with reveals the boy to be 15 years old, white, and of average intelligence. He carries out his assault alone, and his victim is a white female about a year younger than he. It is equally as likely that the offender and the victim know each other, at least casually, and the offense is twice as likely to happen indoors as outside—in fact, the single most frequent place of assault was the victim's own home. The use of a weapon played a part in about one-third of the offenses, but the use of alcohol or drugs appeared insignificant. What does seem especially significant, however, is that in almost three-quarters of the cases, the offender was likely to have committed a previous sexual assault. These earlier offenses, for the most part, were disposed of without any type of referral or commitment.

In differentiating adolescent sexual offenders who assaulted peers or older victims from those who assaulted younger children, we found that the former tended to be relatively more aggressive or violent in their assaults. They were more likely to use a weapon in their offenses, to target female strangers as their victims, and to achieve sexual penetration in their acts. In comparison, the juvenile offenders who assaulted preadolescent children were a somewhat younger group than those that selected victims the same age or older than themselves. Their assaults were directed at a larger proportion of male victims, and they were more likely to be at least casually acquainted with their victims. They had the highest percentage of friends and relatives as victims among these three offender groups. In the majority of their offenses, they did not attempt sexual penetration but confined their activities to touching, fondling, sucking, masturbating against their victims, and the like.

In comparison with those offenders who assaulted peer-age victims, the adolescent offenders who raped significantly older persons chose females exclusively as their victims, and their assaults were more likely to occur indoors, in the victim's own home, and were physically more violent. Greater use was made of weapons, and practically all the assaults involved actual or attempted intercourse. There was more evidence that alcohol or drug use played a part in the commission of the offense. In contrast, peer-age assaults showed a higher incidence of gang rape, of familiarity between offender and victim, and an out-of-doors locale of the assault.

In only a few cases did his sexual assault appear to be the first interpersonal sexual experience in the offender's life. The majority of these boys had had previous sexual experiences—an observation that discredits the popular assumption that adolescent sexual assaults constitute merely sexual exploration or experimentation.

One of the observable characteristics of the offenders studied has been their consistency over time in regard to their assaults. With adult offenders who had committed juvenile sexual assaults, there was a very close, essentially identical, correspondence between their juvenile sexual offenses and the ones they committed as adults that brought them to our attention. They selected similar victims in regard to their relative ages, sex, and social relationship. They committed similar acts with the same degree of aggression or violence, and the offenses took place in characteristic locales, with the exception that the offender's car played more of a role in his later offenses as he became old enough to qualify for a driver's license.

For example, compare the following assault by Jack at age 21 with his first assault at age 12, reported above (p. 181):

> I got out of prison last year and got a job recycling wood, but the money wasn't enough, and there was a lot of things I needed, so I decided to do a B & E. I went up to a house and knocked on the front door. I could see inside and thought I saw a woman. I went to the back door and it was unlocked. A woman came out of the bedroom, and I got a tremendous urge to fuck her. She was white and in her late 50s. I grabbed her and held onto her, and she pleaded with me. The more she pleaded, the more excited I got sexually. I pulled her onto the bed, tied her hands, and gagged her. Then I pulled off her underpants, spread her legs, and took myself out. I didn't have a full hard-on, but I got my penis in her. After that I took a small TV and her pocketbook and left.

Likewise, the previous offenses of the juvenile offenders whom we examined were identical to their current offenses in regard to victim choice and modus operandi.

Another observation was that frequently there were more incidents of antisocial sexual behavior that were known to the parents, neighbors, police, or other authorities than appeared on the offender's criminal record. Again, these incidents were typically dismissed as unimportant, especially when the victim involved was a sibling of the offender or the child of friends or neighbors.

The dynamics of forcible sexual assault by adolescent offenders were the same as those exhibited by adult offenders: a sexual expression of anger and/or power. The adolescent *rapists* also exhibited psychosocial characteristics similar to those of adult offenders. They tended to be "loners" who had little skill in establishing close or meaningful peer relationships. They were "underachievers" who found few outlets for personal expression or a sense of identity. Their predominant mood state appeared to be one of emptiness and dull depression. They were impulsive, and, because of low frustration tolerance, they quickly became irritable and were unable to persist in long-range, goal-oriented activities, most noticeably in regard to their problems with schooling. They found the ordinary demands of life overwhelming and tended to act out under stress. These same qualities appeared in the *aggressive* adolescent *child molester,* but there is a category of adolescent child-offenders who appeared to identify with their victims and who used psychological or social pressures more than physical force to engage the child in a sexual act. These offenders were characteristically more passive in their orientation to life and appeared to be immature and dependent persons who were more comfortable with children than with peers. Characteristically, they tended to associate with children much younger than themselves.

The incident of forcible sexual assault may be viewed as symptomatic of a crisis in both the offender and the victim. Clinical work with aggressive sexual offenders indicates that the act of rape may represent a symptom of a developmental defect: a failure to achieve an adequate sense of self-identity, the consequences of which become especially acute in adolescence. These defects in regard to the male's identity or sense of self-esteem are exhibited in the frustrations he experiences in his efforts to achieve an adequate masculine image, the stereotyped image he has of what it means to be a man, and the conflicts and pressures he cannot tolerate in his desire to gain mastery over his life in an active and assertive way. Forcible sexual assault, in this context, represents an internal or developmental crisis in the offender.

In conclusion, adolescent sexual offenses, especially those involving assault, need to be regarded as equivalent to the more traditional symptoms of emotional disturbance and thus warrant careful psychological assessment by the courts and other related agencies. The all-too-frequent "diagnosis" of "adolescent adjustment reaction" often means that the defects and needs of the offender go unrecognized and that the jeopardy he constitutes to the community is perpetuated. His offense may signal the adolescent offender's own sexual victimization and constitute an attempt to cope with such trauma by becoming the powerful aggressor rather than the helpless victim.

Rather than dismissing the sexual misbehavior of the juvenile offender as adolescent mischief, the boy should be carefully and competently evaluated. Is his behavior in fact age-appropriate sexual play and experimentation? Or is it the use of sex to control and/or punish others? Is it a consenting encounter? Or is it coerced? Are there any unusual, ritualistic, or bizarre qualities in the sexual activity (such as bondage or humiliation)? How did this activity become disclosed? These and other questions need to be answered in order to determine the significance and the seriousness of the adolescent's behavior.

When one is dealing with the problem of rape, the juvenile offender needs special consideration. The possibility of effective intervention and rehabilitation appears more hopeful when one is dealing with a youngster who is still in the process of psychological growth and change than when one is dealing with an adult whose criminal sexual behavior has been established for an extended period of time. Attending to the adolescent offender also has an advantage in regard to researching and learning about the etiology of rape. What are those factors, those salient life experiences, in what interrelationships, at what critical times, and with what intensities, that combine to create a predisposition to rape? The study of juvenile sexual offenders may offer better insights into what produces men who rape. What factors before and during adolescent development contribute to this sexual psychopathy? Studying the adolescent sexual offender and his family at the time of his sexual maturation may prove more fruitful in obtaining answers to these questions than hoping that the offender can accurately recollect and retrieve such information in his adulthood.

Clinical services need to be provided for this target population, and security treatment facilities as well as community-based programs should be made available if the courts are to make meaningful dispositions in such cases.

THE FEMALE OFFENDER

Very little attention has been paid to women who commit sexual assaults. Occasionally, an item appears in the news about a female rapist or child molester, but such incidents seem to be quite rare. Sexual assault appears to be perpetrated predominantly by males. There are a number of reasons that women are underrepresented in regard to this type of offense. For a man, rape is a sexual expression of anger and contempt. He retaliates against a woman by doing something to her that he sees as degrading. A woman, on the other hand, is more likely to withhold or deny sex to a man as an indication of her disfavor or anger. Refusal of sex is one way in which she punishes or retaliates against him. It would not be regarded as degrading for a man to be subjected to sexual relations. Rape is also the sexual expression of power. A man equates manhood with being in control and thus may use sex to assert or maintain control: "to teach the woman who's boss," "to keep her in line," etc. Again, a woman may use the granting or withholding of sexual favors to control or manipulate a man. Sex is his reward for fulfilling the woman's expectations and demands.

We have noted that rape typically reflects deep-seated feelings of inadequacy, and men may, on the whole, feel more inadequate as persons than women do. It may be that in the psychosocial development of the male, it is more difficult to achieve a secure sense of identity than it is for the female, for a variety of psychological and sociological reasons. The primary parent for both male and female children is the mother. Although the girl has a concrete and visible model with whom to identify, the boy must nevertheless relinquish his mother as an identification model and substitute his father as his model—someone who is less visible to him. The result is that the male is never as secure of his sense of identity in terms of being a man as the female is in terms of being a woman. The role definitions for the male are more artificial. Aggression and sexuality are tolerated or encouraged, but emotional and affectional expression is inhibited. For example, when a male is hurt or upset, it is not as socially acceptable for him to complain, or cry, or act hurt. Instead, his distress is transformed into anger. Qualities such as warmth, tenderness, and affection toward other males go undeveloped, and competitive interaction is encouraged. It appears psychologically that there is a greater gap between what it is to be a "man" in our culture and what it is to be a human being than between what it is to be a "woman" in our culture and what it is to be a human being. For this reason, males exhibit more maladaptive behavior than females: more males drop out of school than females, prisons and mental hospitals house many more men than women, among transsexuals far more men want to be women than women want to be men, and distortions of human sexuality, such as rape, child molestation, exhibitionism, voyeurism, and the like are predominantly male behaviors.

If women are perceived by men as psychologically superior, they are regarded as physically more vulnerable. Rape is an interpersonal assault, and in such confrontations, women and men are not equally matched. Women are therefore not as physically aggressive toward men as men are toward women. Since rape is an act of aggression, women are much less likely to commit rape than men are.

Technically, a woman may be charged with rape if she aids or abets a man in committing such an assault; in other words, if she lures, restrains, or subdues a victim whom the man then rapes. For example, on some pretense, a woman who was a member of a motorcyle gang invited another woman to her apartment, where male members of the club were waiting and gang-raped the victim. In some cases, the woman may participate in the sexual assault of the victim along with the man. In Massachusetts, for example, where the statute defining rape does not differentiate in regard to the sex of the offender or the victim, two women were recently sentenced to life imprisonment for the rape of an 18-year-old woman.[29] The victim was picked up by the defendants and three men in a bar in Boston, driven around the city, and forced to participate in various sexual acts with all five offenders. She was then taken to a cemetery, where she was stabbed and beaten and her throat was cut. Although left to die, she managed to crawl to a nearby home for help. Women may sexually assault other women independent of men, as, for example, in prison settings, where one female inmate sexually assaults another.

Cases in which men are raped by women usually involve a single victim and two or more offenders. In Dallas, Texas, two women kidnapped a 37-year-old man at gunpoint and forced him to have sex with both of them on the pavement of a parking lot.[30] In Los Angeles, a man met a woman at a singles bar and went to the apartment of two of her women friends. A game of strip poker developed, during which the man was ultimately tricked into being handcuffed, following which he was sexually abused, urinated on, and injured.[31]

Some cases of homicide are sex-related. For example, one woman drugged her lover, who was going to leave her, and, when he became unconscious, castrated him.

Men who have been sexually assaulted by women are understandably reluctant to report such victimization. Not only will they be regarded with skepticism, but, since rape is confused with sex, will be

---

[29]Tom Sullivan, "Two Women Sent to Prison for Life in Rape," *Boston Herald American* (April 19, 1978).
[30]"Female Rapists Sought in Dallas," *Crime Control Digest* (March 28, 1977).
[31]Lois Norbeck, personal communication, 1977.

thought of as fools to complain about such an encounter. Since it is commonly believed that men are ever-ready and indiscriminate in regard to sex, it may be difficult to convince a judge or a jury that a man had to be forced to perform a sexual act with a woman. In one case, in which two women were picking up male hitchhikers and, at knifepoint, robbing them and forcing them to perform oral sex, the defendants were charged only with armed robbery and assault. They were not charged with a sexual offense. Therefore, although the incidence of adult men being raped by female offenders appears negligible, it can and does happen.

Children, however, are more likely to be targets of sexual assaults by female offenders than are adults, since children are more vulnerable. Again, for a variety of reasons, such victimization is not highly visible, but the dynamics in the female offender appear to be identical to those operating in the male offender.

In some cases, the sexual abuse is part of child battering. One offender whose injuries as a child were medically documented reported:

> When I was 8 years old my mother burned my feet with hot water. She used to kick me in the testicles, and once she took my penis in her mouth. My father wasn't around. She would grab my penis and pull and yank, pull and yank, and she would squeeze my testicles. She would hit me and jab me with broom handles. She was weird. When I was 11, I ran away from home.

In other cases, the child was tricked or pressured into the sexual activity:

> When I was around 6 or 7, my aunt would make me perform oral sex on her. All us kids would play a game. We would have to find each other and then kiss who we found. My aunt would arrange it that I would only find her, and then I would have to kiss her between the legs, and she would tell me to use my tongue. This went on for two years.

Or the offender may use physical force in the assault:

> I was about 13 and she was 18 or 19. She was baby-sitting for my mother. I came into the kitchen, and she dragged me into the bedroom. I didn't know what was happening. She pulled down my pants and masturbated me. Then she laid down on the bed and put me on top of her. It was painful. Her pubic hair was sharp, and it felt like spikes were cutting and sticking me. I was shaking and tremb-

ling. It scared the hell out of me. I didn't tell anybody about it, but after that, I told my mother I didn't want a baby-sitter anymore, and I stayed by myself.

In our professional work to date, we have encountered only three adult women—as compared to over 250 men—who have committed sexual assaults against children. Two admitted to their assaults and one denied it. In two cases, the victim was female; in one case, male. As in cases where the offender is a male, in these cases sexual gratification did not seem to be the motivational issue.

Kay is a 20-year-old, white, single woman who was convicted of sexually assaulting her 3-year-old niece:

> I don't remember how it happened at all. I just remember I did it. I don't know what for. It involved Suzy and took place in our house. I was giving Suzy a bath. She lives with us. I told my mother I would clean her up because she came in from playing outside and was dirty. I took her into the bathroom, got the water ready, and put her into the tub. And I started messing around with her. She yelled, "Don't!" but I put my finger into her vagina part, and she started to cry. My mother came into the bathroom and caught me. I don't know why I did this. I wasn't feeling anything—I didn't get any sexual feelings, nothing.

Kay herself was an abused and neglected child. In addition, she was handicapped by limited intelligence and an unstable family life. Although she assaulted a female child, Kay was heterosexual and sexually active with men.

The use of sex to express nonsexual issues is even more evident in the case of Agnes.

Agnes is a 34-year-old, white, widowed female. When she was 5 years old, her father pressured her into an incestuous relationship that extended into her young adulthood and included intercourse, up to age 19. In addition, she became sexually active with other men while in her teens but found that "no one really wanted me when I got pregnant." Agnes married a man a few years older than herself and had three children: two boys and a girl. The marriage, however, was an unhappy one, and Agnes became involved in a number of extramarital affairs with other men:

> I can get any man I want to into my pants. They're a stupid bunch of pricks. It's a test. I've been hating and using men all my life. All they

want is sex, and then they cool off fast—slam, bam, thank you, ma'm, and it's over. The relationship with my husband got to the point where I couldn't stand to touch him, I hated him so much.

Agnes engaged in sexual relations with her two sons for a number of years, starting when they were about 10 years old:

> I would chase them around the house and grab them between the legs. They were scared of me. I would blow them and fuck them. Afterwards I'd feel guilty, but then I'd do it again.

Eventually, Agnes became seriously involved with a man named Mike:

> I was looking for a man who's not jock-happy. Mike treated me rough and slapped my ass around. I couldn't manipulate him.

Agnes found her marriage intolerable and contemplated suicide:

> Thinking about killing yourself is just an escape, or a warning. I told my husband, "Look, Fred, I almost did it once before. Don't make me try it again." So it came down to I couldn't do it to myself, so I'll do it to Fred. I got smart. I don't think I could have ever done it by myself though. I don't think my mind could have adjusted to it. I'm afraid I would have snapped. I was always afraid of that. So many times I thought I was going crazy. I couldn't remember things. I couldn't find things. It used to scare me. I felt so inadequate. How could I run my life, let alone my kids' lives?

Agnes conspired with Mike to murder her husband and make it look like suicide:

> I had to pretend grief and loss at Fred's funeral, but underneath I was rejoicing. I think some people knew it was no accident but overlooked it.

Ultimately, however, the truth was discovered.

During her extramarital involvements, Agnes also had become sexually attracted to a woman friend, Donna:

> She is one of my other hang-ups. I've been in love with her for almost two years now. She's the only woman right now that turns me on physically. I guess that's because I want to turn her on, but she's too smart for that, and I respect her for it. I think she knows if

we had a physical relationship, I wouldn't like her anymore. I'd lose respect for her. As it is now, I'm testing her, and she's stronger than I am.

Agnes's psychological evaluation revealed a woman torn between two opposing needs: dependency versus self-sufficiency. On one hand, strong needs for affection, approval, caring, and attention operate to motivate her to reach out for others in a passive–submissive fashion. On the other hand, fear of vulnerability, of being hurt and exploited by others (possibly because of her sexual victimization by her father at age 5), leads her to withdraw from such need gratification and to counter-react in an aggressive, assertive, independent fashion. The consequence, however, is a sense of loneliness and isolation from others, which then intensifies her need for interpersonal affection and warmth. Sex becomes the arena in which these conflicts are acted out. Agnes describes being sexually preoccupied—even obsessed—and her relationships involve a struggle for power and control in which sex becomes the test or mode of relating. This conflict between passivity and aggressiveness, between dependency and autonomy, between weakness and strength, becomes manifest in her relationships with both women and men. Women are seen either as competitors (strong), whom she struggles against for the attention of men, or as gentle, loving (and therefore vulnerable) persons, to whom she relates in a kind of child-to-mother fashion. Men are cast into one of two categories: saviors or destroyers. The former are strong, independent males whom she cannot manipulate, who set limits (controls) for her, and, at the same time, are gentle and caring—they give her a sense of worth and make her want to live. The latter are weak, passive, dependent males whom she can control and manipulate—something for which she despises them. The test in all relationships is sexuality: if she achieves seduction, she feels strong and in control, but she despises her partner for such weakness and feels, at some level, not loved for herself but wanted only for sexual gratification. The result is that she loses respect for both her partner and herself. If she is sexually unsuccessful, she feels rejected, worthless, and lonely. The result is that Agnes is caught between feeling used or feeling rejected. Her fears of being unloved, or of being loved only in a sexual way, together with her intense need to be loved for herself and her doubts that she is worth loving, undermine her life.

Another feature of this dilemma is Agnes's emotional experience of being caught between depression and rage. Depression is the automatic

reaction to her feelings of vulnerability, helplessness, and worthlessness, and rage is her attempt to deny her helplessness, to ward off the
depression, and to retaliate against her persecutor. Under extreme pressure and stress, as she becomes increasingly depressed, she experiences
her alternatives as destroying (rage) or being destroyed (depression).
Suicidal thoughts and actions are prompted by desperation and self-
hatred and appear to be a defense against turning her rage against
others. Her indiscriminate sexual activity may, in part, serve to alleviate
the underlying feelings of depression, to reaffirm her worth, to provide
a sense of power and control, and to retaliate against and humiliate her
husband. Her sexual involvement with her sons may constitute a re-
capitulation of her own incestuous victimization and, insofar as the boys
symbolize her husband, an effort to degrade and punish him through
them. Agnes is an emotionally unhealthy and sexually immature person,
but she is intellectually bright, and, in spite of the severe tensions operating within her, there is no evidence of any psychotic distortions in this
woman.

Although the sexual victimization of children by women is not as
common as the sexual victimization of children by men, it may be not as
infrequent an event as might be supposed from the small number of
identified cases. For one thing, the woman may mask sexually inappropriate contact with a child through the guise of bathing or dressing the
victim—child-caring activities permit a certain amount of intimate contact. Also, from what few victims and offenders we have had an opportunity to observe, the female offender's offenses are more incestuous in
nature, and the children are more reluctant to report such contact when
the offender is a parent and someone they are dependent upon. It also
may be that male children are more commonly the targets of female
offenders than are female children, and, as we have learned from the
work of the Oakland County Homicide Task Force (see "Sexual Abuse of
Children," p. 149), boys are less likely to report or disclose sexual
victimization than are girls. The female offender, however, remains an
incompletely studied and insufficiently understood subject.

5

Guidelines for Assessment and Treatment

What can be done to prevent an identified offender from repeating his sexual assaults? Incarceration is, in and of itself, insufficient to alter those personality defects that have led to his committing such an offense. Therefore, in addition to security safeguards, we must also turn to the medical and behavioral sciences for help in remedying those psychological handicaps in the offender that lead him, under certain stressful situations, to jeopardize the safety of others. Any efforts at rehabilitation must take into consideration four basic issues: (1) the client—whom are you going to treat? (2) the setting—where are you going to treat him? (3) the modality—how are you going to treat him? and (4) the outcome—how are you going to measure response to treatment and determine when the offender is rehabilitated?

CLINICAL EVALUATION OF THE OFFENDER

The first basic step in any process of rehabilitation is assessment. *Assessment* refers to the procedure of clinically evaluating the offender in order to identify the factors that are related to the commission of his offense—the characterological features or traits of the offender, the emotional or psychological issues lived out or expressed in the offense, and the situational events or conditions that activated or supported such acts—as well as the degree to which these same factors continue to operate both in the offender and in the environment in which he functions. Through such evaluation, the offender–client's need for, interest in, amenability to, and potential performance in treatment can be assessed. The diagnostic procedure itself involves an extended period of study; a number of participants; diverse clinical, behavioral, and social data; and a variety of assessment techniques.

Although diagnostic evaluation is a precondition for treatment, it is a process that involves considerable time and effort. Also, since typically the offender is not self-referred but has been pressured by his family or mandated by the court to submit to such examination, he may regard the clinician as an adversary. The referral questions typically address issues of motivation, repetition, dangerousness, and disposition. Why did he commit the sexual offense? Is he likely to repeat the assault? Is he likely to harm someone? What should be done to rehabilitate him? Often the clinician is given a limited period of time in which to provide the answers to these questions and must do the best she or he can with the limited resources at hand and the incomplete data that are immediately available. It is important, therefore, to regard the results of the initial evaluation as a preliminary judgment and to regard the process of assessment as continuing from the point of referral, through all successive stages of involvement (intake, treatment, discharge, and aftercare), to the time of termination. Initial impressions should be refined and revised with increasing study, additional information, and more extensive contact.

The use of a clinical team not only serves to expedite the evaluation process but also provides a multidisciplinary orientation and approach to this task and helps to ensure greater thoroughness in the accumulation and processing of the data. The task of clinical assessment is customarily assigned to mental health professionals trained and experienced in conducting such examinations, but it is important to recognize that other persons, both professional and nonprofessional, can make valuable contributions as advisers and consultants to the team. Criminal justice personnel, volunteer staff, victim advocates, and even other offenders can contribute significantly to the assessment process.

The evaluation itself consists of as full and complete a psychological investigation as is realistically possible. Detailed information is retrieved pertaining to the offender's background and development, his psychological makeup, the nature of his sexual offenses, and his current level of functioning. The areas encompassed in this assessment include the offender's family background and early home life, his medical and psychiatric history, his social, sexual, and educational development, his military history, his vocational development and work history, his marital history, his recreational interests and habits, and his criminal history and institutional adjustment.

Clinical Assessment Guide

Identifying Information

Record the offender's name, address, date of birth, age, race, religion, marital status, and physical characteristics (height, weight, body build, etc.).

In addition to identifying the offender, such information may have clinical significance. What type of reaction or impression does his physical appearance create? If, for example, he is powerfully built, he may be physically intimidating to others; if he is handsome, his appearance may have overemphasized the role that sexuality plays in his interpersonal relationships; if he is short, his stature may have affected his self-image or his sense of manhood, etc. The clinician would then need to further pursue the issue raised in order to determine whether or not the clinical implications of such impressions are supported by other information.

Family Background

Obtain a description of the offender's family history, his parents and siblings, his birth order; the nature and quality of the intrafamily relationships; the intactness of his parental home; the stability and quality of his early family life; the economic stability of his family; the nature of his upbringing and religious background.

Clinical Significance. How the offender has been brought up and the type of role models he has had have major significance in the formation of his personality and the development of his attitudes, values, and behavior patterns. Family crisis, disruption, trauma, and hardship should be carefully explored to determine what impact they have had on the offender. Have they served to jeopardize his feelings of security, self-worth, or competency? What shortcomings or limitations in his personality makeup or what maladaptive attitudes, values, and behaviors have resulted from his early development that interfere with his ability to negotiate life demands successfully and adequately manage the activities of daily living? What unresolved maturational issues continue to undermine his current level of functioning?

Target Areas. Determine if there is disruption in family unity (abandonment, death, divorce, separation, illness, foster placement, institutionalization of parents, etc.); poor or ineffective parenting (child abuse or neglect, inadequate role models, family violence, alcoholism, mental illness, criminal behavior; inappropriate sexual behavior, etc.); behavior problems (running away, chronic rebelliousness, intense sibling rivalry, temper tantrums, etc.).

Medical History

Obtain an account of the offender's previous and current physical and mental health problems; his prenatal, delivery, and neonatal development; any illnesses, handicaps, injuries, operations, hospitalizations, and the like sustained during childhood, adolescence, and adulthood.

Clinical Significance. Here the clinician is concerned not only with actual physical traumas, which may temporarily or permanently handicap the offender in managing certain life demands, but also with what effect they have had on his self-image in terms of feelings of vulnerability and his perception of the world as a dangerous place. What anxieties have been created in regard to being in a passive–dependent position? For example, not only might a condition of epilepsy create real obstacles in terms of job opportunities and social relationships, but it may also impact on how this individual sees himself. Does it frighten him to have periods in which he is not in control of himself? Does he see himself as defective or inadequate in certain ways? Does he overcompensate in an effort to come to grips with this issue? The offender's medical and psychiatric history may provide important clues in regard to his self-image, his impulse management and control, his feelings of adequacy and self-worth, and the like. His history of alcohol or drug use not only may be symptomatic of emotional problems but also has implications for the way he deals with stress; that is, it may reveal to what extent he relies on impersonal, nonhuman sources for tension relief in dealing with life problems, as well as indicating problems in regard to impulse control, feelings of anger or depression, and the like.

Target Areas. Look for major illnesses or accidents; serious injuries, disabilities, impairments, or handicaps; hyperactivity, encopresis/ enuresis, accident-proneness, addiction, venereal disease, brushes with death, organic insult, persistent nightmares, blackouts, psychosomatic complaints, suicide gestures/attempts, mental illnesses.

Educational Development

Examine the offender's school adjustment and academic performance; his level of intellectual functioning and cognitive skills, his scholastic interests, aptitudes, abilities, and achievements; the number of grades completed and his marks; his classroom behavior, study habits, and attitudes toward education; his relationships to teachers, administrators, and classmates.

Clinical Significance. An examination of the offender's academic development and performance may reveal an early indication of his ability to persist with reality-oriented, long-range goals and activities. It may signal that early psychological concerns and tensions entered and interfered with developing self-discipline, handling responsibilities, and mastering life tasks. His school adjustment may offer some information about the development of peer relationships and his ability to relate to authority figures in a productive manner. In his relationships to his classmates, was he cooperative, antagonistic, or withdrawn? If he repeated grades, what was the reason: situational (such as moving from one school system to another), intellectual (inability to master the work), psychological (immaturity), or some combination of these factors? What impact did repeating a grade have on his self-image? What effect did it have on the formation, development, and maintenance of his peer relationships? Schooling is one of the first major life experiences that places demands on the child to handle responsibilities, and his performance here may be a prototype of his later success or difficulty in fulfilling life demands.

Target Areas. Determine if there are school phobias; learning problems or disabilities (special classes, illiteracy); changes in IQ scores or dramatic shifts in grades; behavior or discipline problems (truancy, fighting, suspensions); repeated grades; dropping out of school.

Military History

Examine the nature and quality of the offender's military service record; the branch of the armed services selected; his military adjustment and performance; his type of discharge; his attitudes toward military service and his combat experiences.

Clinical Significance Military history allows the clinician to explore the offender's self-image, his male peer relationships, his ability to take instruction and follow orders, his relationship to authority figures, and the like. The branch of the service chosen and his reason for this selection may reflect his aspirations in regard to self-image and definition of manhood. His military performance and type of discharge may indicate how he responds to an organized and structured environment. What did he like or dislike about the service? How well did he do? Again, such data may have implications in regard to feelings of self-worth, competency, responsibility, and the like.

Target Areas.   Was application for enlistment rejected? Was offender unable to adjust to military life? Look for infractions (AWOL), disciplinary action (reprimands, court-martial), less than honorable discharge; service-connected disability; traumas experienced during military service (violence, risk of injury or death).

Interpersonal Development

Obtain an account of the offender's social, sexual, and marital history.

Social.   Examine the nature and quality of his interpersonal relationships; the type of friendships and relationships he forms with persons older than himself, with age-mates, with others younger than himself, with males, and with females; the basis for his friendships and the kind of persons he selects as friends or associates; the relationships that are important to him; the number of friends he has; his social interests, activities, and memberships.

CLINICAL SIGNIFICANCE.   To a large extent, personality is both the product of and defined by the sum total of one's interpersonal relationships. Therefore, an examination of the character and quality of the offender's social reactions is perhaps the key issue in his clinical assessment. It should be kept in mind that his sexual assault is an interpersonal act. To what extent does he regard others as objects to be used or obstacles to be overcome in the pursuit of his own interests? What value do people have for him, and how successful is he in negotiating interpersonal relationships? How much of a loner is he? Defects in his regard for others, problems in making or keeping friends, relationships based on power and control, stereotyped perceptions of men and women, and a lack of warmth, trust, tenderness, and affection in his relationships all reflect serious defects in his personality development. A careful study and analysis of his relationships to others will reveal his affiliation needs; his social and empathic skills; his mode of relating; the depth, range, and stability of his relationships; his ability to differentiate among others; his perceptions of men and women; what importance he places on such relationships; and his interpersonal effectiveness. The type of person he tends to associate with offers some insight into his self-image and value system.

TARGET AREAS.   Look for instances of social isolation (few or no friends); superficial or unstable relationships; poor associates; tendency to relate mostly to others much younger/older than himself rather than to peers; excessively controlling or competitive; very susceptible to the influence of others; self-centered; uses others (relates through intimidation, exploitation, manipulation); keeps others at a distance.

Sexual. Examine the nature and quality of the offender's sexual development, his experiences, habits, and interests; his sexual education; the age at which he had his first sexual experience; types of sexual encounters; partners; fantasies; sexual attitudes, values, and orientations; sexual performance and subjective reactions; frequency of sexual activity; influence of alcohol and drugs; premarital, marital, and extramarital relationships; sexual offenses.

CLINICAL SIGNIFICANCE. The way an individual conducts his sexual life may be a prototype of the way he deals with the world in general. How does he achieve sexual relationships: through negotiation and consent, pressure and exploitation, force and assault? How conservative are his sexual attitudes and values? What correspondence is there between his stated values and his actual behaviors? How comfortable is he with his sexuality? What nonsexual motivations underlie his sexual activity? The offender's sexual behavior and fantasies will reflect his self-image, his regard for others, quality of his impulse management, his mode of relating, and his comfort or discomfort with interpersonal intimacy. It is important to ascertain what meaning human sexuality has for the offender and its relationship to positive (affectional) or negative (hostile) needs and feelings. How organized or disorganized is his sexuality, and what role does it play in his life? Why has his sexuality become the symptom of his psychological dysfunction?

TARGET AREAS. Look for sexual trauma or victimization; pathological sexuality within the family; sexual dysfunction, sexual offenses; unconventional sexual interests and behaviors (sadomasochism, obscene telephone calls, etc.); sexual violence.

Marital. Obtain an account of the offender's marital history; the reason for his marriage; the quality of his relationship with his wife; the number of times he has married; the sexual compatibility and fidelity of husband and wife; the number of offspring and his relationship with his children; his attitudes and expectations regarding marriage; his success in the role of husband and father.

CLINICAL SIGNIFICANCE. The character of the offender's marriage has implications in regard to his impulse control, his psychological needs, the quality of his interpersonal relationships, his success in handling adult responsibilities, and his ability to communicate. Data in regard to his marriage may reflect underlying dependency needs, needs to assert his power and control, or other unresolved psychological issues. The reason his marriages fail may point to the deficiencies he has in forming relationships. His interest in his children—how much time he spends with them and in what ways—reflects both his capabilities and his needs. Repeated failures at marriage may indicate an inability to self-correct or the living-out of some unresolved need. To marry is to take on the responsibilities of adulthood, and this area of the offender's life becomes a test of his ability to handle the demands of adulthood in a mature and responsible fashion.

TARGET AREAS.   Determine if there was a forced marriage, or marital discord; spouse abuse; infidelity; dissolution of the marriage (divorce, separation, abandonment); child abuse or neglect; psychological problems on the part of the wife (mental illness, addiction, criminal activity, etc.) and/or on the part of the children (school problems, behavior problems, emotional problems, alcohol or drug abuse, delinquency, etc.).

Occupational History

Obtain a description of the offender's work history and job performance; stability of his employment; his vocational skills and the types of jobs held; job satisfaction; relationships to co-workers and those above and below him; advancements and achievements; his ability to support himself and his family.

Clinical Significance.   An offender's vocational history may give some indication of the value he places on work and his sense of pride in doing a good job, and consequently, it has implications in regard to his self-image; his ability to tolerate frustration and persist in long-range, goal-oriented activity; his sense of competency; and the like. Here, too, some impression can be gained in regard to his ability to relate to others in a cooperative fashion and how much he experiences his work as an avenue of personal expression and validation. What are his attitudes toward working? How does he deal with authority and handle responsibility? How dependable is he? What sense of recognization does he get from what he does?

Target Areas.   Determine if there is a history of unstable employment (dismissal, quitting, suspension); unemployment compensation or welfare assistance, work-related disabilities; economic hardship.

Recreational Interests

Obtain a description of the offender's leisure-time interests and activities; sports activities, hobbies, clubs; his investment in and regard for possessions.

Clinical Significance. The variety of interests and activities enjoyed by the offender may indicate what amuses him and to what extent he finds life enjoyable. Is his life empty and boring? Does it offer him few pleasures and rewards? Is he unable to relax and enjoy himself? Again, his recreational interests may reflect his self-image, his impulse control, his social skills, and the like.

Target Areas. Look for solitary, high-risk activities: drinking; gambling; speeding; obsession with weapons; overinvolvement in feats of strength (weight lifting) or physical violence; a habit of overspending.

Criminal History

Obtain an account of the offender's antisocial behavior and his problems with the law; his arrest record; his age at the time of his first offense; the types of crimes committed; disposition; institutional adjustment; probation or parole record.

Clinical Significance. The criminal history of the offender will help to differentiate the sexual offender whose offenses are one of many expressions of a criminal personality from the offender whose sexual crimes constitute a departure from an otherwise law-abiding life. Criminal behavior can be viewed as symptomatic of personality defects. How long-standing are these problems? How far back does his antisocial behavior go? What do his criminal habits reflect about his social skills, his self-image, his motives, and the like? The offender's criminal record has important implications in regard to his dangerousness and his failures in leading a responsible and adaptive life.

Target Areas. Look for preadolescent delinquent behavior (stealing, property damage to parental home, fire setting, cruelty to animals/ children); felonies; crimes against the person; crimes of violence (arson, murder, sexual assault); prostitution; pornography; recidivism.

In examining all these areas of the offender's life, it is important to retrieve both objective data (facts, events) and subjective data (the prominent attitudes and feelings that accompany the factual data) as well. The task of assessment then involves taking the data accumulated from various sources in regard to the offender's developmental history and processing it to arrive at a clinical impression of his personality characteristics: his self-image and sense of personal worth, his social skills and interpersonal relations; his cognitive functions and defense mechanisms; his predominant emotional reactions and mood states; his impulse control and tolerance of frustration; his attitudes and values; his overriding concerns and fantasy life. A clinical judgment or opinion is then reached as to what components of his personality are maladaptive or developmentally insufficient to cope with ordinary life demands and what the risk is to others of his personality dysfunction when he is faced with these life demands.

In addition to this factual material, it is necessary to assess the personality characteristics of the offender: his physical and behavioral traits; his needs, attitudes, and values; his perception and judgment; his social skills; his predominant mood states; his ability to cope with stress and manage his life; his ability to communicate effectively and to establish and maintain positive relationships with others; his emotional expressiveness; and his sense of humor. Of major importance is a detailed study of his sexual offense: his frame of mind at the time of the crime, the precipitating stresses, his motivational intent, his perception and selection of the victim, his style of attack and the type of acts performed, his physiological response, and his subjective reaction to the offense. Finally, the impact of his crime and his apprehension must be examined, together with an assessment of his current level of functioning: his impulse control, his tolerance for frustration, his emotional stability, his contact with reality, his self-image and sense of personal worth, his interpersonal relations, his system of defenses, and his adaptive strengths. The clinician must next view the offense against the background of the offender's developmental history, the social-environmental context of this development, the environmental-situational context of the crime, the current psychological and emotional life of the offender, and the social-environmental features of the life situation that the offender would reenter if released. The clinician must then attempt to answer three key questions: How probable is it that this offender will behave in a way that will jeopardize the physical safety of another person? Under what environmental conditions is such behavior most likely to occur? What is the likelihood that these environmental conditions will prevail? To reach an answer to these questions, an assessment of both external factors (early family experiences and social development, current life stresses) and internal factors (motivation, attitudes, values) is crucial.

DATA SOURCES

There are a number of sources from which information can be retrieved through a variety of techniques (observation, interviewing, testing) to provide a data base for the clinical evaluation of the offender.

Behavioral Observation

Information about the offender can be acquired through interaction and involvement with him over an extended period of time. The systematic observations of mental health and correctional–security staff members, fellow inmates–patients, consultants, volunteers, and the like can provide direct, firsthand impressions in regard to the way the offender conducts himself, relates to others, deals with authority, handles frustrations, etc., and impressions can be gained about his social skills, values, attitudes, and interests. Such observations should be recorded and the observer's impressions documented. The development of an observation schedule or rating scale will serve to expedite and facilitate this task as well as to provide uniformity and ensure completeness among observers.

Clinical Interview

The clinical interview is a standard procedure for accumulating information in regard to the offender's background and current status. Not only are life history data retrieved through interviewing the offender, but impressions are also gained in regard to his attitudes, values, feelings, and thought processes. The clinician is able to note the behavior of the offender during the interview, his relationship (rapport) with the examiner, his engagement in the task, his emotional tone and its intensity, his manner of dealing with the questions posed, the quality of his verbalization, and the like, as well as any physical reactions such as trembling, stuttering, retarded speech, etc. The interview itself should be structured sufficiently to ensure that all relevant issues and areas are explored and may be supplemented by self-administered questionnaires or problem checklists to expedite or facilitate the retrieval of information from the person being interviewed.

Field Investigation

In addition to the interview of the offender himself, field investigations may reveal additional information about the client from independent sources. It may be important and profitable to conduct a home assessment and to contact members of the offender's family: his parents, siblings, wife, and children. The police, his victim, the prosecuting attorney, his lawyer, and his probation or parole officers are also major sources of information about the offender, as are his employer, clergyman, doctor, counselor, and the like.

Medical Examination

A comprehensive medical examination is an important component in the assessment process that will help to identify the offender's previous, current, and incipient health problems and to determine whether there may be any connection between his physical condition and his criminal sexual activity. A thorough physical and neurological examination serves to confirm or rule out any medical issue uncovered in the history of the offender that is suspected of being a contributing factor in the etiology of his sexual offense, such as organicity, alcoholism, and the like.

Documents

Important information about the offender can be retrieved from the records and files of other educational, military, vocational, mental health, social service, and criminal justice agencies with which he has had previous contact. Such prior evaluations will offer a base for comparison to his current status as well as provide a longitudinal view of his performance in dealing with specific life tasks. For example, work reports from former employers can document the quality and stability of his job performance and his vocational history. Of vital significance are the documents pertaining to the instant offense, especially his victim's account of the offense, as well as his prior arrest record, trial transcripts, presentence investigations, parole–probation records, and the like. Not only will such documents contain essential information about the offender that may otherwise no longer be available, but in many cases, they will serve to expedite the assessment process by reducing the time that would be needed to collect such data from the start.

An examination of the correspondence between the offender's and the victim's versions of the sexual assault has important implications for the diagnostic assessment and treatment of the offender. It is impossible to evaluate the offender without knowledge of the victim's perception of the offense. If the offender is interviewed without the evaluator's knowing the victim's version of the offense, a number of significant details may not be retrieved because of distortions in the offender's perception or because of deliberate falsification. With both versions, the clinician can then determine what the offender can acknowledge, what he minimizes or distorts, and what he evades or denies. The closer the correspondence between the victim's and the offender's versions, the fewer the questions raised as to distortion, evasion, or projection of responsibility on the part of the assailant. Qualifications may have implications regarding areas of conflict; for example, an offender may be comfortable with aggression but not with sexuality. The nature and the quality of his defenses likewise have important diagnostic implications. For example, denial is fairly primitive, whereas repression suggests a higher-level conflict over impulse behavior. Prognostic issues are also raised: to what extent can the offender explore his feelings and observe his behavior, or to what extent must he avoid this approach and externalize the responsibility for his actions? How much does he experience himself as a victim, as being helpless and adrift in a hostile world? How much does he have access to his feelings? And what is the nature and the quality of his self-image and his empathic perceptions of others, both men and women?

The obtaining of information in regard to the offender's and the victim's versions of the offense is only one of the sources of data necessary for an assessment of the offender's dangerousness and the prediction of repetition, but it is indispensable and perhaps the single most important factor in our clinical evaluation.

Psychometric Examination

The administration of standard psychological tests and other psychometric instruments, such as questionnaires, self-report inventories, rating scales, and problem checklists, is another procedure that may prove helpful in the assessment of the offender and may provide useful information in regard to his psychological status and functioning. Such instruments may be used as screening devices to uncover current emotional difficulties and to identify potential problem areas; for example, the results of a self-administered personality inventory may reveal a deep-seated feeling of inadequacy operating in the offender that makes it difficult for him to deal with authority figures. Or tests may be used to further evaluate—confirm, clarify, contradict—impressions gained from other sources in regard to the offender; for example, a suspicion of intellectual retardation can be resolved through the administration of a dependable IQ test.

A wide variety of standard psychometric instruments exists to assess various components of an offender's personality, such as his self-esteem, intelligence, contact with reality, sexual attitudes and values, maturity and moral development, impulse control, and the like, which can be used by the clinician to analyze the psychological factors operating in the offender that contribute to his offense, to assess his potential for recidivism, and to estimate the risk or danger he constitutes to others. There is no test or battery of psychometric instruments that alone will suffice to evaluate the offender, but they do offer an additional systematic technique for observing and examining the offender.

Physiological Measurement

The use of instruments such as a polygraph, a voice-stress evaluator, or a penile plethysmograph, to record physiological reactions of the offender can provide additional useful data. The lie detector or stress indicator may serve to confirm or negate the truthfulness of the offender's allegations when these are inconsistent with information acquired from other sources and to differentiate intentional deception on his part from genuine misperception. Phallometric instruments may identify deviant sexual arousal patterns or interests in an offender as well as assessing their intensity. Likewise, deficiencies in appropriate and adaptive sexual responses can also be determined with the use of this instrument.

As is the case with psychological testing, techniques of physiological measurement are not infallible but do offer another approach that may contribute important information to the diagnostic process.

Referrals

The task of assessment is one that encompasses all dimensions of the offender's life management. We are not dealing with clients who have a single factor or a set of factors that can be isolated as the determinants of their sexual offenses. The person we are dealing with is a multiple-defect individual. Therefore, although the clinical team is ultimately responsible for the diagnostic assessment of this subject, a thorough and extensive examination may extend into areas that exceed the knowledge and training of the individual members of the team. In such cases, the offender can be referred to appropriate agencies or services for specific evaluation of that particular aspect of his behavior. For example, a question of alcohol or drug abuse may arise, and the client could be referred to an agency specializing in alcohol or drug dependency evaluations. Likewise, education specialists could be used to assess the client's academic performance and to identify any learning disabilities. Ideally, the use of specialists for each area of the offender's life functioning (medical, educational, vocational, etc.) would ensure extensive, detailed, and expert evaluation, but this may not be feasible. The process of evaluation, however, should be continuous, and, over time, target areas can be pursued more completely.

Since it is a sexual offense that brings this client to the attention of the clinician, the major emphasis in this chapter is on the assessment of the offender's sexual development, experiences, and functioning; the types of questions to be asked; the kinds of information to be retrieved; and the areas of experience to be explored. It is this dimension of the offender's experience that many clinicians often feel unequipped to handle in an interview.

PROTOCOL FOR THE CLINICAL ASSESSMENT OF THE OFFENDER'S SEXUAL BEHAVIOR

Obtain the offender's account of the sexual offense that brought him to your attention as well as any and every previous sexual offense committed by him, and explore the following aspects of each:

1. *Premeditation:* To what extent did the offender plan out the offense beforehand?
   a. *Intentional:* Did the offender set out in search of a victim with the deliberate intent to commit a sexual assault?

b. *Opportunistic:* Or did the idea suddenly come to mind when an opportunity presented itself that gave him access to a victim and did he act on impulse?

c. *Spontaneous:* Or did the offender not ever anticipate committing a sexual assault until it erupted unexpectedly?

2. *Victim selection:* What were the descriptive characteristics of the victim, and what part, if any, did each play in the offender's selection of his victim?

a. *Age:* Was the victim the same age as the offender, significantly older, or significantly younger? Have his victims been adults, adolescents, children, or of various ages?

b. *Race:* Was the victim of the same race as the offender, or was the assault interracial?

c. *Sex:* Does the offender sexually assault only females, only males, or both?

d. *Social relationship:* What was the social relationship between the offender and his victim—that is, were they complete strangers, casual acquaintances, close friends or associates, family members, relatives, or marriage partners?

e. *Situation:* What was the victim doing just prior to the offense? Did her or his activity, location, status, or occupation serve to make her or him accessible or significant to the offender?

f. *Physical characteristics:* Was there anything about the victim's physical appearance (such as size, shape, or attractiveness) or about her or his condition (such as a physical handicap or state of intoxication) that prompted the offender to target her or him as his victim?

   Can the offender describe his victim? Does he know what she or he looked like? Did any of the characteristics of his victim have symbolic importance to him?

3. *Style of attack:* How did the offender achieve control over his victim and carry out his offense? Did he use deception and entrapment, threat or intimidation, physical force or violence, or some combination of these techniques? How did the offender gain sexual access to his victim?

a. *Exploitation:* Did he use a position of authority to manipulate and pressure the victim into the sexual activity?

b. *Threat:* Did he use verbal threats?

c. *Intimidation:* Did he intimidate the victim with a weapon? If so, what type?

    d. *Incapacitation:* Did he render his victim helpless or incapacitated through intoxication or the use of some type of restraint?

    e. *Physical force:* Did he resort to physical force to overpower his victim?

    f. *Violence:* Was he violent—that is, did he physically injure his victim?

4. *Accompanying fantasies:* If the offender's assault was preceded and accompanied by sexual and/or aggressive fantasies, the nature of these thoughts and wishes needs to be carefully examined.

    a. *Content:* What was the content of his fantasies? How did he imagine the assault's occurring and his victim's reacting? Was the victim in his fantasies identifiable? Were the fantasies pleasurable, or disturbing, or both? Were they accompanied by masturbation? Did he exhibit an interest in pornography or other material pertaining to sexual violence or aggression as an expression of his fantasy interests? What types of pornography did he find stimulating? Did he eroticize nonerotic materials or aspects of his environment?

    b. *Development:* When did these fantasies first begin? Did they have reference to any actual experiences or events in the offender's life? Did the content change or did the fantasies increase in frequency or intensity over time? Did they become obsessional? Does the offender currently continue to experience such thoughts or fantasies? What triggers them? Are they immediately activated simply by the presence of a child or an adolescent, or an adult?

5. *Role of aggression:* If the offender resorted to physical force in the commission of his offense, to what purpose was the aggression directed, and how seriously was the victim injured?

    a. *Establishing control:* Did the offender initiate his assault by grabbing or striking his victim, not with the intent to hurt her or him but more as a display of force to show he "meant business"?

    b. *Reactive aggression:* Did the offender resort to physical force only when his victim resisted him in order to counter her or his indocility?

    c. *Discharging anger:* Did the offender use much more force than was necessary simply to overcome his victim's resistance and overpower her/him? Was his intent to hurt or injure his victim?

    d. *Erotic aggression:* Did the offender experience erotic excitement in the expression of physical aggression. Was his victim sexually abused or tortured in a deliberate and ritualistic fashion? Did he find pleasure in hurting and degrading his victim?

6. *Conversation:* What type of sexual dialogue did the offender direct toward or demand from the victim during the assault?
   a. *Hostile:* Did he make degrading remarks or swear and curse his victim and use obscenities?
   b. *Instructional:* Did he give his victim orders and commands or sexual instructions and demands?
   c. *Inquisitive:* Did he inquire as to his victim's sexual interests, responses, and reactions to him?

7. *Sexual behavior:* What was the nature of the offender's sexual activity, behavior, and experience during the offense?
   a. *Sexual contact:* What type of sexual acts did the offender demand from and/or perform on his victim (kissing, fondling, masturbating, breast sucking, digital penetration, vaginal intercourse, oral intercourse, anal intercourse, oral-anal contact, etc.)? If this victim was a male, did he force his victim to ejaculate? If his victim was a female, did he make her simulate orgasm? Were there any ritualistic qualities to the sexual activity (e.g. shaving the victim)? Did he take pictures of the victim? Were there any sadomasochistic elements (bondage, penetration with some type of object or instrument, etc.)? Did he subject the victim to other degrading acts, such as ejaculating or urinating on her or him?
   b. *Duration:* How long did the assault last? Over what period of time did he keep control of his victim? What made him terminate the assualt?
   c. *Sexual dysfunction:* How did the offender function sexually during the assualt? Was there any evidence of sexual dysfunction? Did he have any difficulty achieving or maintaining an erection during the offense (impotency)? If so, what did he do to achieve erection? Did he have any difficulties with ejaculation—that is, did he find he ejaculated very quickly during the offense (premature ejaculation) or prior to insertion (spontaneous ejaculation) or had difficulty in achieving ejaculation (retarded ejaculation)? Was such dysfunction specific to his offense, or does he experience the same type of sexual dysfunction in his consenting relationships?
   d. *Sexual response:* What type of subjective sexual response did the offender experience in regard to the assault? Did he ex-

perience the offense as sexually pleasurable or satisfying, as disappointing, or frustrating, or as disgusting and repulsive? Did he find that he ejaculated without reaching an orgasm, or did he reach an orgasm without ejaculating? Did he both ejaculate and reach orgasm, or neither?

8. *Mood state:*What was the offenders predominant mood state at the time of the assault?

   a. *Feelings:* How was the offender feeling at the time of his offense? Were his emotions those of anger, fear, depression, frustration, sexual arousal, excitement, etc.?

   b. *Change:* Was there any change in his mood state or feelings before, during, and after the sexual assault?

   c. *Subjective reaction:* Did the offense provide any type of satisfaction, relief, or gratification for the offender? If so, what type? Did he experience any feelings of guilt and remorse?

9. *Contributing factors:* What factors played a role in activating the offense?

   a. *Precipitating stresses:* Can the offender identify any sources of frustration, aggravation, or anxiety that triggered the offense? Did some event occur to which he reacted by sexually assaulting his victim? What were the interpersonal, vocational, economic, physical, or situational pressures that, alone or in combination, prompted the offense? What life events or situations (marital discord, social isolation, interpersonal conflicts) did the offender experience as threats to his sense of adequacy, competency, or virility that activated the sexual assualt?

   b. *Compounding conditions:* To what extent is the issue of sexual assault compounded by the physical and/or mental condition of the offender? Is there any evidence that severe psychiatric problems (psychosis), mental deficiency (retardation), organicity (brain dysfunction), or addiction to alcohol or drugs may have served to diminish the offender's self-control and judgment at the time of his offense?

   c. *Release mechanisms:* What situational factors or events may have served to disinhibit the offender and release his sexual aggression? What part did factors such as a codefendant, an automobile, access to a weapon, drug or alcohol consumption, fatigue, and the like play in the commission of the assault? How did they contribute to the activation of the offense?

10. *Responsibility:* Does the offender acknowledge his responsibility

for his offense or does he maintain that he is a victim of circumstances?

   a. *Full admission:* Does the offender's version of his offense correspond in all major aspects to the victim's account and the crime with which he has been charged or convicted?

   b. *Qualified admission:* Does the offender essentially admit to the offense but either claim he cannot remember the incident, minimize what he is accused of doing or its seriousness, or externalize his responsibility for the offense, for example, by attributing his conduct to a state of intoxication? In some cases, the offender may justify his behavior by stating that the victim "asked for it."

   c. *Denial:* Does the offender disclaim his culpability, alleging false accusation, mistaken identity, victim consent, or the like?

11. *Recidivism:* How long has the offender been sexually assaultive? How often has he repeated his sexual offense?

   a. *Onset:* How old was the offender at the time of his first sexual offense, regardless of whether or not he was apprehended?

   b. *Frequency:* How many sexual offenses has he committed over what space of time? How many offenses has he committed for which he was never apprehended, or for which he was acquitted, or for which he plea-bargained to a nonsexual offense? How many other sex-related crimes (e.g., arson, breaking and entering, homicide) did he commit that may not have been identified as sexual offenses?

   c. *Intervention:* What type of disposition was made in regard to the previous sexual offenses of which the offender was convicted or accused? What effect did such intervention have?

   d. *Progression:* What changes have occurred over time, if any, in regard to the nature of the offender's sexual assaults? Have they become more frequent? Has there been any increase in the amount of aggression exhibited in the commission of the offenses? Have there been any changes in the types of sexual acts demanded or the types of sexual crimes exhibited over time? Have there been any changes in regard to the type of victim selected (for example, are his victims getting younger or older)?

12. *Deterrence:* Has the offender ever been deterred from committing an intended offense or from completing an attempted assault? If

so, what deterred him (e.g., victim behavior, external intervention)? If not, is there anything an intended victim might say or do that would serve to deter him? What type of strategy (conversation, actions, etc.) would help to discourage him from committing an offense?

13. *Sexual development:* What have been the nature and quality of the offender's sexual development and experiences apart from his offenses?

   a. *Sex education:* How did the offender learn about human sexuality? Did he receive any formal sex instruction at home or at school? What was the tone of his parents' attitudes toward sex? What was his religious teaching in this regard? How sexually knowledgeable or uninformed is he and in what areas?

   b. *Conventional sexual behavior:* What experiences has the offender had during childhood, adolescence, and adulthood in regard to masturbation, sexual activity with other males, and sexual encounters with females? What were the age of onset; the circumstances surrounding the activity; the age, sex, and social relationship of his partner(s); and his reactions? Who initiated the activity?

   c. *Unconventional sexual experiences:* Has the offender been involved in any sexual experiences he regards as unusual or unconventional, such as exposing himself, spying on the intimate activities of others, incestuous relationships, sexual activity with animals, cross-dressing, or finding himself sexually attracted to articles of clothing, such as women's undergarments? Has he ever engaged in prostitution or in the manufacture of pornography? Does he like to participate in sadomasochistic practices?

   d. *Marital relations:* If the offender is or has been married or involved in a common-law relationship, what has been the quality of the sexual relations? Are his and his wife's sexual interests compatible? Have there been any extramarital involvements? Does he have any complaints or dissatisfactions about his sexual relationship with his wife? Has he ever sexually assaulted his wife or forced her to participate in unconventional sexual activities, such as making her have sex with others while he watches?

   e. *Sexual lifestyle:* What is the offender's sexual orientation:

heterosexual, homosexual, bisexual, asexual, pedophilic, etc.? What are his customary sexual outlets? How sexually active is he (i.e., his frequency)? What type of sexual encounters does he initiate? Is he reasonably comfortable and satisfied with his sexual lifestyle? What is his gender identity?

f. *Sexual fantasies:* What are the nature and quality of his sexual fantasies? What does he fantasize about when he is engaged in sexual activity (masturbation or intercourse)? What types of sexually oriented material (photography, films, books, etc.) does he read or own or subscribe to? Does he ever fantasize about being a woman or wish he were a woman? What are his sexual interests? What does he see as ideal?

g. *Sexual concerns:* What concerns, if any, does the offender have in regard to his sexual competency, adequacy, and attractiveness? Does he have any concerns about his virility, his genitalia, his sexual performance? Is he handicapped by any type of sexual dysfunction (impotency, premature or retarded ejaculation)? Is he conflicted over some of his sexual urges? Does he have any sexual fears, phobias, or aversions?

h. *Sexual tramas:* Has the offender had any sexual experiences that he found upsetting, confusing, or frightening? Has he witnessed any disturbing sexual activity on the part of others, expecially family members? Was the offender himself ever the victim of a sexual assault at any time in his life? Was he ever pressured or forced into sexual activity against his will? If so, assess the details of the incident and its impact on him. What bio-psycho-social reaction did he have to the incident? What did he find disturbing about it? Did he report it to anyone? If so, to whom, and what was their response? Has the offender suffered any injury to his genitalia? Has he ever contracted venereal disease? Is he sterile?

TREATMENT APPROACHES

From the initial assessment, the psychological defects of the offender are identified, together with an estimation of their seriousness, which leads then to the development of an individualized plan of treatment or management of the client.

The diagnostic task is to determine what is wrong with the offender, what has led him to commit his sexual offense, and what can be done to remedy this situation. Since rape is the sexual expression of power and anger, each facet of the offender's life, each area of his development and functioning should be explored to determine how traumatic or how conflict-free it has been. Two key questions to keep in mind are: (1) How competent is he in managing this life task (the power issue), and (2) how frustrated or dissatisfied is he with this aspect of his life (the anger issue). The greater and more extensive the impairment of the offender in regard to his life management functions the greater is the risk of repetition of his sexual offenses, which are symptomatic of his dysfunction. In contrast, the more adaptive strengths and resources he possesses, the more avenues he has for obtaining personal satisfaction in a responsible and appropriate fashion, and the better is his prognosis.

Since rape is an aggressive act, careful assessment should be made in regard to the role aggression plays in his functioning. Is he a violence-prone individual? What risk of injury does he constitute to others? Is he likely to harm someone because his ability to appreciate the consequences of his behavior is deficient or impaired? Or because his controls are inadequate? Or because he lacks empathic identification with others, so although he may realize the impact of his behavior and has the ability to control his actions, he just does not care and is concerned only with himself? Or because under the impact of stress his cognitive–perceptual functioning is impaired and he misinterprets what is happening and consequently responds inappropriately? Or because he is a person who intends harm because he finds such an experience intrinsically exciting and gratifying?

The Modality

Rape is not a symptom of mental illness but of personality dysfunction. It is the result of defects in human development. Diagnostic assessment identifies the nature and the severity of these defects, which, in turn, determine the offender's prognosis or treatability. The clinical assessment leads to the development of a treatment plan designed to address and remedy the identified defects. *Treatment* may be defined as any type of intervention designed to reduce, inhibit, or eliminate the sexual assaultiveness of the offender. It would be misleading, however, to suggest that we have reached a state of clinical knowledge that ensures the successful rehabilitation of men who rape. As yet, no single method of treatment or type of therapeutic intervention has proved to be a totally effective remedy. And given the wide range of individual differences found among men who rape, it is unlikely that any single treatment approach will ever prove suitable for all such offenders.

Instead, treatment has to be tailored to the specific needs and abilities of the individual offender. There are a number of basic techniques or treatment modalities that can be drawn upon to approach the task of helping the offender to change his assaultive sexual behavior:

Chemotherapy. One technique for combating sexual assaultiveness is the administration of an antiandrogen hormone that temporarily reduces the offender's interest in sexual activity. Depo-Provera (medroxyprogesterone acetate) is administered by intramuscular injection on a weekly basis and lowers the offender's level of serum testosterone and thereby diminishes his sexual arousal or responsiveness. The offender experiences a release from his compulsive urges to commit sexual assault.

There are major advantages to such endocrine therapy. Relatively speaking, it takes immediate effect and reduces the risk of sexual assault on the part of the offender. Its administration is simple and can be easily and closely monitored. Not only is it applicable to offenders who are poor candidates for other modes of therapy, but it can also serve to facilitate and expedite response to other treatment approaches by allowing the offender a respite from intensive impulses. It is a reversible procedure, and, finally, it is a relatively inexpensive form of treatment.

Although this pharmacological approach appears to represent a major breakthrough in the treatment of sexually assaultive males, it is still in the investigational stages of development. Depo-Provera itself has not yet been approved by the U.S. Food and Drug Administration, and any potentially adverse effects on males as a result of extended maintenance on this drug are not known because of the relatively recent development of this approach and the small number of offenders treated. To date, there are only two programs in the United States specializing in this type of hormonal treatment: the Phipps Clinic program founded by John Money, Ph.D., at The Johns Hopkins Hospital in Baltimore, Maryland, and the Gender Clinic program under Paul A. Walker, Ph.D., at the University of Texas Medical Branch in Galveston.

Psychotherapy. The most common technique currently employed in the treatment of sexual offenders is psychotherapy, which views sexual assaultiveness as the result of internal emotional conflicts and which aims to relieve such problems by helping the offender to become more aware of and to better understand these underlying issues. Through such introspection, the offender is expected to arrive at better controls over his undesirable behavior. The term *psychotherapy* encompasses a broad variety of styles and techniques, ranging from individual counseling to milieu therapy and including group therapy, family and marital counseling, psychodrama, self-help groups, and the like. Whatever its particular format, psychotherapy generally involves a verbal interaction that focuses on the offender's life experiences and concerns in order to help him to achieve increased insight into the way that past events have undermined his current functioning and to appreciate in what ways he needs to change his behavior in order to cope with life issues in a more appropriate and adaptive fashion. Psychotherapy is also an interpersonal interaction and therefore seems particularly relevant in treating a problem, sexual assaultiveness, that by its very nature is interpersonal.

This mode of rehabilitation has major limitations. The most serious is that there is no real evidence that such a technique is effective. Furthermore, prognosis appears to be a function of the offender's intelligence and his capacity for abstract thinking and self-observation, a subjective sense of distress and motivation for change, and an ability to form a working relationship with a therapist and to persist in an enterprise that may extend over a very long period of time and that may involve considerable emotional discomfort and frustration. None of these qualities is prominent among the majority of men who rape. In addition, extremes of age, retardation, or organic pathology counterindicate the use of a psychotherapeutic approach. It is also a relatively expensive and time-consuming procedure.

Courses in Human Development.   Another approach to the rehabilitation of the aggressive sexual offender is to educate and train him in regard to the life management skills in which he is deficient. Much as a person who has no work skills would be given job training as part of his vocational rehabilitation, the offender is given education and training to remedy the defects in his human development as part of his psychosocial rehabilitation. Some of the major components in such a psychoeducational program would be the following:

a. *Sex education:* Since aggressive sexual offenders are often sexually uninformed persons, a basic program in human sexuality would be of benefit to help improve both the offender's understanding of and his attitudes toward the various dimensions of human sexuality. More advanced programs may include sexual counseling and, where indicated, sexual therapy involving a wife, a partner, a friend, or a surrogate to address specific sexual concerns or performance problems.

b. *Empathic skills:* Sensitivity training, consciousness-raising groups and encounters, and the like may assist the offender to become more in touch with other people. He can be taught how to better identify, recognize, differentiate, understand, and respond to the needs and feelings of others.

c. *Social skills:* Another common problem among offenders is difficulty in negotiating interpersonal relationships. Social-skills training may improve the offender's ability to interact and communicate effectively with others. It may strengthen his ability to form close and stable relationships.

d. *Emotional expression:* Anxiety, frustration, and anger are feelings most offenders have problems dealing with. Relaxation exercises and biofeedback techniques can teach the offender ways to cope with anxiety and frustration. Assertiveness training can help the offender strengthen his sense of self-control and teach him how to be less aggressive. Strategies for modulating anger and expressing it in a more constructive and adaptive fashion as well as learning how to express more positive, caring, and tender feelings comfortably are key aspects in his development of emotional expressiveness.

Other components could include parent effectiveness training, religious or spiritual counseling, morals development, and the like, as well as programs addressing identified life-management problems, such as alcohol- or drug-dependency treatment, vocational and educational rehabilitation, physical therapy, and recreational therapy.

This psychoeducational approach has some attractive features in that it identifies the goal to be achieved and approaches that goal in a structured and organized fashion. It aims to develop the resources the offender needs in order to cope with his life and thus offers him alternatives to his maladaptive and harmful ways of behaving. Each component is time-limited, which is particularly suitable for men who tend to seek instant gratification and who need to see some visible results and receive some immediate feedback in regard to a sense of accomplishment or achievement. The effectiveness of this approach is also largely untested, however and many of the prognostic criteria required for psychotherapy also apply to this approach, limiting who is a good candidate for this mode of treatment.

Behavior Modification. Another approach in treating aggressive sexual offenders is behavior modification, which specifically addresses the offender's symptom, the inappropriate sexual response (i.e., the offense), and attempts to eliminate it through a variety of behavior tech-

niques and by instilling more appropriate sexual responses and behaviors. In aversive conditioning, the offender's inappropriate sexual
response (such as erection to themes of violence) is repeatedly paired
with a noxious event (such as an electrical shock or an obnoxious odor)
until it is eliminated. In covert sensitization, the offender imagines a
fantasy of his offense and then immediately counters it with a fantasy of
a frightening, upsetting, or disgusting nature. In some cases, hyp-
notherapy may be used to implant a posthypnotic suggestion inhibiting
the inappropriate sexual behavior. More appropriate responses are instilled through fading (where the offender masturbates to the fantasy
that typically arouses him, and, as he is about to reach climax, he
switches to the more acceptable images) and through systematic desen-
sitization (in which the offender makes successively increasing approx-
imations to what is expected sociosexual behavior).

This modality has the advantages of directly confronting the problem behavior of the offender and objectively measuring the treatment
results (usually with some type of phallometric instrument). However,
its application to assaultive sexual offenders is fairly recent, and the
long-term effect (its dependability) is largely unknown. The course of
treatment, however, is relatively short, typically under a year, and not
as expensive as psychotherapy. Unfortunately, it is not a readily available program. The most ambitious program to date is that directed by
Gene G. Abel, M.D., and his colleagues at the Psychiatric Institute in
New York City.

Incapacitation. A final effort to prevent the offender from repeating
his offenses is to incapacitate him physically. Although psychosurgery
and surgical castration have been practiced to a limited extent, their
results are indecisive, and such procedures have the disadvantage of
being irreversible, thus raising a number of legal, moral, and ethical
questions. The most common type of incapacitation practiced today is
that of imprisonment or institutionalization, where the offender is confined and prevented access to the targets of his sexual abuse. Although
there is the risk of sexual assault within the institutional setting, the risk
of danger to the community is reduced while the offender is incarcerated. Although this is in most cases not a permanent solution, neither
are any of the above alternatives. It can be noted that most men who
rape are relatively young. It is rare to find such an offender past the age
of 45—the sadist or lust murderer being an exception. Like most aggressive criminals, the rapist tends to "mellow" or "burn out," that is, become less aggressive with age. This phenomenon would argue for a

sentence of sufficient length to ensure his incapacitation during his violence-prone years. However, given the difficulty in convicting such offenders and the major use of plea-bargaining in the criminal justice system, as well as the reluctance to incarcerate juveniles, effective detention seems unlikely.

These, then, are the major types of intervention that are available to deal with men who rape. In fact, all are necessary and each one alone is insufficient. An ideal program of rehabilitation should incorporate elements of each modality. However, from a practical standpoint, the choices are limited, not only by what is available but also by the setting in which the offender is being treated.

The Setting

In general, the sexual offender in need of services may come to the attention of human service providers through the criminal justice or mental health systems. He may be a voluntary admission or legally mandated to receive treatment. He may be incarcerated in a prison, committed to a mental hospital, or involved with a private or community agency on his own volition or as a condition of parole or probation. There need to be treatment services, developed to address the needs of the sexual offender, available in community-based agencies, such as outpatient mental health clinics, crisis intervention centers, self-help groups and organizations, halfway houses, and the like. Likewise, treatment programs need to be developed for sexual offenders within mental hospitals to which offenders who require such hospitalization can be referred or committed. In a similar fashion, mental health services within correctional institutions need to address the needs of the inmates sentenced there for sex-related crimes (not just those identified as sexual offenders). Some states have developed special security treatment centers to which sex offenders who are regarded as dangerous (i.e., likely to repeat their offense and, in so doing, to jeopardize the physical safety of their potential victims) can be indefinitely civilly committed in addition to or instead of receiving a fixed criminal sentence.

The place in which the offender is being treated will serve to facilitate or handicap various aspects of the therapeutic intervention. What is feasible in one setting is prohibited in another. Whether the offender is seen in an institutional setting or in the community, and whether his treatment is mandated or voluntary, must also be taken into consideration. Obviously, there are modalities of therapeutic intervention (such as conjugal visits) that can operate more comfortably out in the community than within an institutional structure. Other programs (such as chemical castration or aversive conditioning) would raise civil rights issues of coercion within a prison setting, which would not be the case in non-mandated, voluntary programs. There is a need, then, for a comprehensive, statewide, interrelated plan of treatment services that will address the wide variety of men who rape.

Aftercare

Whatever the primary treatment plan, there also need to be follow-up and aftercare services. None of the modes of therapeutic intervention currently available have proved to be cures for sexual assaultiveness. Although each may offer some help to the offender in controlling such urges, his potential for committing sexual assaults must be regarded as a chronic one, something that will need to be addressed for an extended period of time. Since a relapse will jeopardize the safety of another individual, persistent contact and supervision are required to support and continually assess his adjustment. Backup services need to be readily available in case of an emergency or a setback.

Treatment Evaluation

One of the difficulties in assessing the effectiveness of treatment and the rehabilitation of the offender is determining how to measure change or success, especially in an institutional setting. In comparing the pretreatment and the posttreatment behavior of the offender, clear improvements may be apparent. For example, he may show freer emotional expression, have an improved attitude toward social and community responsibilities, withstand frustrations and disappointments better, demonstrate increased sensitivity toward others, and have more self-confidence and self-respect. The question becomes: How much of this is due to genuine psychological maturation and how much is simply a temporary change, the product of being in a structured environment? Although prisons are not intrinsically pleasant environments, they do remove many responsibilities from the inmate's shoulders. He no longer has to get up mornings to go to work and earn a living and support a family or bring up children. Liquor and weapons are not easily available. Intimate relationships with women are not available. Entertainment, recreation, and treatment are provided him. And his every activity is closely supervised by security staff. Major life responsibilities, sources of difficulty and strain on the outside, are nonexistent in the prison setting, which masks the sexual offender's difficulty in organizing and structuring his life. Much of his improvement, then, may be due to the fact that his environment does not stress him as life outside of prison did, and, therefore, it is important that his release and reentry into the community be a gradual one with continuing support and treatment.

The success of any treatment program is also difficult to measure since success is usually measured by the recidivism rate of those offenders who have been through the program. Recidivism is usually operationally defined as conviction for a subsequent sexual assault. This is not a reliable estimate of rehabilitation for a number of reasons. First, the majority of rape victims do not report their assaults to the police. The National Center for the Prevention and Control of Rape estimates that the incidence of unreported rape is between 2 and 10 times as high as the incidence of reported rape.[1] It may be, then, that for every reported sexual assault as many as nine such offenses go unreported and, therefore, the offender has 9 chances out of 10 of not even being identified as having committed an assault simply because his crime is not reported.[2] Second, even when the offense is reported, no suspect is apprehended in a majority of cases. In a two-year study, conducted by the Battelle Law and Justice Center,[3] it was found that only 26% of the rape complaints resulted in an arrest, and only 27% of those suspects arrested were charged with rape or attempted rape. Then, only 19% of those charged ever went to trial, and only 6% of those that went to trial were convicted. Of 635 rape complaints filed in Seattle, Washington and Kansas City, Missouri only 10 offenders—less than 2%—were convicted. Holmstrom and Burgess[4] saw all sexually assaulted persons who were admitted to the emergency room of Boston City Hospital during 1974, a total of 109 victims, all of whom reported the assault to the police. At the time of this writing, almost six years later, no suspects have been apprehended in 41 (38%) of the cases. Of the remaining 68 cases, 44 (40%) never reached trial for a variety of reasons, and of the

[1]Elizabeth S. Kutzke, Chief, National Center for the Prevention and Control of Rape, United States Department of Health, Education, and Welfare, National Institute of Mental Health, Washington, D.C., personal communication, April 27, 1979.

[2]National Organization of Women, Rape Prevention Committee, *Myth and Fact: What you Should Know About Rape*, New York, brochure (undated).

[3]*Cleveland RAPE CRISIS Newsletter* (Cleveland, Ohio, September–October 1978, pp. 1–2).

[4]Lynda Lytle Holmstrom and Ann Wolbert Burgess, *The Victim of Rape: Institutional Reactions* (New York: John Wiley & Sons, 1978), pp. 150, 151, 238, 239.

24 that did, 10 cases resulted in acquittal, 7 were plea-bargained, 3 resulted in convictions for lesser charges, and 4 resulted in rape convictions, for a total of only 14 (13%) convictions in all. Since 43 (39%) of the victims in these cases were gang-raped by multiple assailants, the actual conviction rate is even lower than the above figures indicate. Finally, it has been our observation that when apprehended, a sizable number of offenders successfully plea-bargain their charges down to a nonsexual offense. Since the actual recidivism, then, is much higher than the reported recidivism, what confidence can anyone have that a low recidivism rate is an indication of the success of a treatment program?

That we do not have a cure does not mean, however, that we should abandon the idea of rehabilitating offenders. Some offenders are undoubtedly helped by such services. Even more important, such efforts offer the opportunity to increase our knowledge about the sexual offender and his offenses. This knowledge not only may be of benefit in helping victims but also may contribute to preventing the development of future offenders.

Clinical work with men who rape can make some contribution to the serious problem of sexual assault in our society, but a solution to this problem will require making basic changes in our society. Rape is more than a clinical issue, it is a social, economic, legal, cultural, and political issue that requires multidisciplinary and interagency cooperation. There is no room for professional conceit or territorial possessiveness if we expect to combat sexual assault successfully.

Index